THE YALE CHILD STUDY CENTER
MONOGRAPH SERIES
ON CHILD PSYCHIATRY, CHILD DEVELOPMENT,
AND SOCIAL POLICY

The Yale Child Study Center monograph series on Child Psychiatry, Child Development, and Social Policy is published in association with Yale University Press. The series is a forum for the discussion of major scientific, clinical, and policy issues relating to children and families.

Children in Jeopardy

CAN WE BREAK THE CYCLE OF POVERTY?

Irving B. Harris

THE YALE CHILD STUDY CENTER

NEW HAVEN

DISTRIBUTED BY YALE UNIVERSITY PRESS

The excerpt "It Begins at Birth" in chapter 7 is copyrighted by the *Chicago Tribune,* all rights reserved, and is used with permission.

The excerpt from *Unfair Shares* in chapter 7 is reprinted by permission of Richard G. Wilkinson, Trafford Centre for Medical Research, University of Sussex, and the Centre for Health and Society, University College London.

The excerpt in chapter 7 from Keith Bradsher's article, "Low Ranking for Poor American Children," and figure 7-3, "The Gap between Rich and Poor Children," originally appeared in the *New York Times* on 14 August 1995 and 1 September 1995, respectively, and are reprinted with permission by The New York Times Company, copyright © 1995.

Library of Congress Cataloging-in-Publication Data
Harris, Irving B. (Irving Brooks), 1910–
Children in jeopardy : can we break the cycle of poverty? / Irving B. Harris.
    p. cm. — (The Yale Child Study Center monograph series on child psychiatry, child development, and social policy : vol 1)
    Includes bibliographical references and index.
    ISBN 0-300-06892-1 (cloth : acid-free paper)
    1. Child welfare—United States.   2. Socially handicapped children—Services for—United States.   3. Poor children—Services for—United States.   4. Teenage pregnancy—United States—Prevention.   I. Title.   II. Series.
HV741.H338   1996
362.7′0973—dc20   96-10329
                                                                                            CIP

Designed by Thos. Whitridge
Set in Monotype Bembo by Ink, Inc. of New York City
Printed in the United States of America

A catalogue record for this book is available from the British Library.

The paper in this book meets the guidelines for permanence and durability of the Committee on Production Guidelines for Book Longevity of the Council on Library Resources.

ISBN 0-300-06892-1 CI   *OCLC# 3428 3281*

10 9 8 7 6 5 4 3 2 1

First, to my wife, Joan Harris, and to my children—Roxanne Frank, Virginia Polsky, William Harris, and his wife, Robie Harris—who along with Maria Piers have taught me about the enormous importance of very early childhood development.

Second, to our progeny in the hope that their world will be more civilized and more livable than it is today or promises to become.

Third, to the many federal, state, county, and city legislators and other elected officials I have known: decent, intelligent men and women who really try to help make our world a better place in which to live and raise our children with opportunities for them to grow, learn, and continue to grow.

No American—white or black—can escape the consequences of the continuing social and economic decay of our major cities. Only a commitment to national action on an unprecedented scale can shape a future compatible with the historic ideals of American society.

—Kerner Commission report, 1968

CONTENTS

A Fence or an Ambulance

'Twas a dangerous cliff, as they freely confessed,
Though to walk near its crest was so pleasant;
But over its terrible edge there had slipped
A duke and full many a peasant.
So the people said something would have to be done,
But their projects did not at all tally;
Some said, "Put a fence around the edge of the cliff,"
Some, "An ambulance down in the valley."

But the cry for the ambulance carried the day,
For it spread through the neighboring city;
A fence may be useful or not, it is true,
But each heart became brimful of pity
For those who slipped over that dangerous cliff;
And the dwellers in highway and alley
Gave pounds or gave pence, not to put up a fence,
But an ambulance down in the valley.

"For the cliff is all right, if you're careful," they said,
"And, if folks even slip and are dropping,
It isn't the slipping that hurts them so much,
As the shock down below when they're stopping."
So day after day, as these mishaps occurred,
Quick forth would these rescuers sally
To pick up the victims who fell off the cliff,
With their ambulance down in the valley.

Then an old sage remarked: "It's a marvel to me
That people give far more attention
To repairing results than to stopping the cause,
When they'd much better aim at prevention.

Let us stop at its source all this mischief," cried he,
"Come, neighbors and friends, let us rally;
If the cliff we will fence we might almost dispense
With the ambulance down in the valley."

"Oh, he's a fanatic," the others rejoined,
"Dispense with the ambulance? Never!
He'd dispense with all charities, too, if he could;
No! No! We'll support them forever.
Aren't we picking up folks just as fast as they fall?
And shall this man dictate to us? Shall he?
Why should people of sense stop to put up a fence,
While the ambulance works in the valley?"

But a sensible few, who are practical too,
Will not bear with such nonsense much longer;
They believe that prevention is better than cure,
And their party will soon be the stronger.
Encourage them then, with your purse, voice, and pen,
And while other philanthropists dally,
They will scorn all pretense and put up a stout fence
On the cliff that hangs over the valley.

Better guide well the young than reclaim them when old,
For the voice of true wisdom is calling,
"To rescue the fallen is good, but 'tis best
To prevent other people from falling."
Better close up the source of temptation and crime
Than deliver from dungeon or galley;
Better put a strong fence round the top of the cliff
Than an ambulance down in the valley.

—Joseph Malins

FOREWORD

TOO MANY of America's children are not thriving. We may differ about the causes and cures, but not about the terrible problems faced by infants and young children. There is broad agreement among professionals and citizens and across the political spectrum that our nation suffers from poor public schools, where students do not learn as they should; from murder rates that are higher than in any other nation in the world; from an underclass plagued by premature births, infant mortality, functional illiteracy, and a sense of hopelessness; from violent inner cities, where children are exposed both as witnesses and victims; from massive drug problems; from high welfare and health costs—though hundreds of thousands of children and families still have poor health care; and from children vulnerable to drugs during gestation and throughout childhood. There is a lack of consensus about what can be done to effect change, and there is a general feeling of helplessness.

Irving Harris has been studying America's children and young families for more than forty years from a distinctive vantage point. As a businessman, he is pragmatic about what will benefit American children and improve the economic and social functioning of American society. As an advocate and philanthropist, he has used his personal resources and position to educate politicians and voters, to influence public policy, to promote research and training in early childhood development, and to fund innovative approaches to serving young children and their parents. He has not had the usual restraints that burden politicians and academics; he calls things as he sees them, even though his observations and recommendations are sometimes painful.

In the 1950s Harris focused on the high drop-out rate of high-school students as the primary cause of a range of social problems, including unemployment and family dysfunction. He recognized that if children are to stay in school and develop the skills necessary to become productive workers, they must be helped long before they enter high school. He learned that the proper time to begin helping children to graduate is *before* they enter the school system.

Unless children are given proper attention from conception to age three, cognitive, emotional, physical, and social delays will limit their development. Of fundamental concern are prevention and very early intervention to reduce (1) school failure, (2) low vocational and academic achievement, (3) the need for subsequent intervention, and (4) the probability of delinquency or early parenting. Irving Harris knows that as a nation we do not have the funds to continue business as usual, where programs are too limited or start too late. We cannot afford, he argues, not to intervene early and effectively.

Once Irving Harris became convinced that primary prevention was the key to breaking the cycle of poverty, he focused his attention on two groups: teenage girls and boys who are likely to bring unwanted children into the world; and children aged zero to three who have already been conceived or born into poverty. His views are thoughtful and well reasoned, and his interest is deep and compassionate. By initiating and funding programs geared to children and families, he has sought to break the cycle that begins when a child is born to a poor, single mother, lacks suitable stimulation, goes to school developmentally unprepared, feels unable to succeed and so tunes out, suffers the trauma and anxiety of inner-city life, drops out of school, and enters the world of early parenthood—perpetuating the cycles of danger and despair. Irving Harris is sensitive to the multigenerational nature of the many problems facing the most disadvantaged in our society; he is aware that multiple factors conspire early in the lives of millions of children to channel them into developmental pathways that lead to unfairly limited academic, economic, and social achievement.

Irving Harris has centered on the role of adequate, early caregiving and the dangers of teenage pregnancy. He has championed the value of good parenting and sex education in the schools, easy access to reproductive health measures for adolescents, school-based clinics, and family planning. In his concern for the role of the family in the lives of children, he is clearly pro-choice. For him, access to counseling and abortion services is consistent with ensuring that children will be born to couples who are ready and eager to be good parents.

He has encouraged research in child development and has created programs that inspire young scholars to pursue work in early childhood development. He believes that if the United States does not invest in the infants and children who are most at risk before their problems become severe, not only will they suffer, but the nation will suffer as well.

The position Irving Harris takes in *Children in Jeopardy* is critically important to the future of this nation and deserves passionate discussion and debate, informed by both science and morality. If this book helps to advance the discussion by defining problems and offering solutions, it will have succeeded in making the lives of young children of vital concern for everyone.

Donald J. Cohen, M.D.
Director, Yale Child Study Center
New Haven, Connecticut

IHAVE BEEN LUCKY IN LIFE, in many ways. I consider myself lucky to have been born with a lifelong curiosity. As one of millions of Americans who recognize the importance of education, my curiosity has caused me to wonder about ways to encourage students to stay in school and to keep learning.

Most ideas about how to improve public education have not worked; I have seen a good many failed experiments. The more I have learned, the more I believe that very early motivation is the key to positive change. I believe that God's gift of brain potential in Homo sapiens is not discriminatory; our brain potential is more than adequate for a college education for all races.

Yet the motivation of different human beings and different groups varies greatly. For every individual the pattern of motivation is developed very early in life. Self-esteem and the expectation to succeed are implanted early by our environment. If parents look at their children with high expectations and value and admire them, they set the stage, and they encourage them to try. Our self-image automatically mirrors the radiant admiration of our parents. If they tell us we can, we can; we learn to believe that we can do almost anything.

If, however, as infants and later as toddlers, we are treated as though we were without value, our self-image will be affected. That uncaring, hostile environment cannot help but cause us to sink into apathy, hopelessness, and low self-esteem. As they grow older, children who feel this way will often seek refuge in alcohol, drugs, continual excitement, and violence. If people think of themselves as no good, they are likely to be angry with everyone. When they learn that they can cause pain like the pain they feel, they think: why not inflict on others what life has inflicted on them.

This is not a happy way to live. It does not lead to the effort needed to be successful in life and to participate positively in a civilized society. People who grow up knowing they will fail live with a self-fulfilling prophecy. Such people are alienated. As children they learn to hate their teachers and to hate school; they refuse to learn; and they tend to become friends with other children who feel the same way they do. Many days they skip school and hang out and drop out. Such a life trajectory hurts the individual first, then the community, the city, the state, and every citizen.

I was lucky as a very young child to mirror my parents' conviction that almost anything is possible if you try. That environment produced in me a curiosity about what lies ahead and what more there is to life. My experiences in the past decades have been fascinating for me. I have learned from my associations with the Erikson Institute, Family Focus, the Yale Child Study Center, the University of Minnesota, the Bush Foundation, the University of Chicago, the National Center for Clinical Infant Programs, and the Ounce of Prevention Fund. I have learned a good deal about state government bureaucracies and their potential for cooperation, about state legislatures, federal bureaucracies, and Congress. They all have in common many interesting, humane people, including many competent individuals who at one time or another are parts of the puzzle along with the people who are trapped in poverty. I have often found that they really want to work together. It is not impossible, just difficult, to work out a system that can succeed.

Can we motivate children born into poor environments to look at life and school with an expectation of success? The task is a difficult one, but we can learn how to ensure good self-esteem in all our children and encourage them to begin life motivated to succeed and with a belief that they can succeed. We already know how to create an environment that will lead to positive motivation in individual cases. We must expand the scale of our efforts to match the scale of our knowledge.

The word *infant* comes from Latin, meaning 'incapable of speech.' Perhaps this lack of speech causes many to believe that children cannot learn at the very early stages of life. In fact, children begin learning from the day they are born, and they learn at a fast pace. Kindergarten is much too late for us to worry about whether a child is ready for school. Long before infants can talk at the age of six months to fourteen months they know a great deal: they can follow instructions, and they usually understand what is being said to them.

We must begin in the first days and weeks and months of life to get children ready to learn. Our hopes for our society's future depend on our being able to bring about improvements in education.

ACKNOWLEDGMENTS

I HAVE LEARNED most meaningfully from personal contact. The following individuals have given me new insights related to the jigsaw puzzle I have been putting together in my mind for more than forty years. Collectively they have stimulated me to think constantly, and sometimes obsessively, about the problems of poverty, school drop-out, and early childhood learning we face in the United States.

ELECTED OFFICIALS

Governor Elmer Anderson of Minnesota, an outstanding human being, political leader, and businessman.

Senator Christopher "Kit" Bond of Missouri.

Jimmy Carter, who as governor of Georgia clearly recognized the importance of healthy early childhood development.

Michael Castle, who as governor of Delaware some years ago told me about an eighteen-year-old sentenced to life in prison for murder. When he looked into this boy's history, Castle found that at age three he was dyslexic, "headed for prison before he could even learn to read."

Governor Lawton Chiles, who as a senator for Florida was a strong supporter of the Beethoven Project.

Governor Bill Clinton of Arkansas.

Governor James Edgar of Illinois and his wife, Brenda Edgar, who are both strong advocates of early childhood programs and have a keen understanding of the importance of early childhood development.

Governor Thomas Kean of New Jersey.

Senators Edward Kennedy, Jay Rockefeller, and Christopher Dodd, who have been enormously important in sponsoring programs related to healthy early childhood development. Senator Kennedy, an especially effective legislator, took the lead in Congress to fund thirty-eight replications of the Beethoven Project.

Governor Richard Lamm of Colorado. He and his wife, Dottie Lamm, became interested in ensuring healthy early childhood development as a cost-effective means of preventing later school failure and lives of crime.

Michael Madigan, as Democratic speaker of the Illinois House of Representatives, and Lee Daniels, as Republican speaker, both able, dedicated men.

Representative George Miller, who has long been a leading voice for children in the House of Representatives.

Ambassador Walter Mondale, an old Minnesota friend, who as a senator recognized the importance of early childhood development.

Senator Daniel Moynihan, an early and continuing student of the breakdown of American families.

Richard Phelan, who as president of the Illinois Cook County board of trustees courageously reinstated abortion at Cook County Hospital. He is a superior public servant.

Colorado Governor Roy Romer and Bea Romer. One day at breakfast Roy told Bea that he was going "to a meeting to talk about building more prisons." She told him she was going to a meeting about helping very young children learn. She added, "If you would spend more time as I do, you would be able to spend less time doing what you are planning to do today."

Governor James Thompson of Illinois, an especially competent and intelligent politician of the highest qualifications.

PUBLIC SERVANTS

Philip Bradley, director of Public Aid for the state of Illinois, and Teresa Stroika, his able deputy, for their keen interest in school-based medical clinics.

Gregory Coler, who as director of the Department of Children and Family Services in 1982 brought the state of Illinois into a public-private partnership with the Pittway Corporation to create the Ounce of Prevention Fund. Later, in Florida, he created another successful public-private partnership, the Florida Ounce of Prevention Fund.

Joycelyn Elders, former U.S. Surgeon General. Through her work in Arkansas, I knew her as an effective advocate of school-based medical clinics to prevent teen pregnancy.

David Ellwood of the Harvard Kennedy School and Ann Ellwood, his mother, who developed the Minnesota Early Learning Design. I learned from them both.

Dorcas Hardy, President Ronald Reagan's assistant secretary of Health and Human Services, and her capable deputy, Richard Shute. Both saw the wisdom of the government becoming a partner in what would become the Beethoven Project.

Wade Horn of Head Start, whom I met while serving on the National Commission for Children.

Jess McDonald and Gordon Johnson, two distinguished directors of the Department of Children and Family Services for the state of Illinois.

Nicholas Pastore, New Haven, Connecticut's police chief, for his recognition of the importance of posttraumatic stress disorder in children. As he witnessed crime he saw the need for the police to bring these children into psychiatric therapy as soon as possible.

Howard Peters, an administrative assistant to Governor James Edgar in charge of all early Illinois childhood development programs. As a child Howard had to repeat the first grade. Two teachers fought against the privilege of having him in their class a second time. He was able to change schools, and his new teacher, after three days of class, kept him after school, saying, "Don't try to convince me you can't learn to read. I know you can, and now you will." He did. He graduated and began a most successful life.

Julius Richmond, longtime researcher and a powerful advocate for early childhood development. Later he was a preeminent U.S. Surgeon General.

Theodore Sanders, superintendent of education for Illinois and later deputy secretary of the U.S. Department of Education.

Donna Shalala, first as the president of Hunter College in New York, and then as secretary of Health and Human Services, a longtime advocate of the Career Beginnings program.

Sargent Shriver, for his early work with Head Start and for his encouragement to begin the Erikson Institute.

Susan Suter, as director of the Illinois Rehabilitation Department. Early on she saw the advantage of the Beethoven Project.

Reed Tuckson, as director of Public Health for the city of Washington, D.C.

SCHOLARS AND SCIENTISTS

Mary Ainsworth, who early on moved to London to work with John Bowlby and developed an important test of parent-child attachment.

Heidelise Als of Harvard University, who has discovered much about preemies and taught me about brain development and the general capacities of infants weighing only two pounds at birth.

Kathryn Barnard, as dean of the School of Nursing at the University of Washington, has done wonderful research on infant-parent interactions.

Henry Betts, director of the Rehabilitation Institute in Chicago, who ardently believes in the prevention of mental illness.

Justice Harry Blackmun, who taught me the justice of providing abortion services, particularly for poor women.

Benjamin Bloom of the University of Chicago, a creative thinker who convinced me early on that "general intelligence appears to develop as much from conception to age four as it does from age four to eighteen. The capacity to learn grows at a decelerating rate."

John Bowlby of the Tavistock Institute, for his original concepts about attachment and bonding.

Barbara Bowman, inspiring leader and president of the Erikson Institute.

T. Berry Brazelton of Harvard University, an inspiring advocate of the importance of very early childhood development.

Urie Bronfenbrenner, Cornell University developmental psychologist and a founder of the national Head Start program, who pioneered the concept that the whole environment, including parents, shapes young children. His program at Cornell has been a shining beacon for more than thirty years.

Dante Cicchetti, University of Rochester, and Felton Earls, Harvard School of Public Health, child psychiatrist and professor of human behavior and development, Harvard Medical School, who have both taught me about the impact of violence.

Donald Cohen, wise and energetic director of the Yale Child Study Center.

James Comer, a pioneer in turning mental health concepts into practice at public schools.

Ezra Davidson of the American College for Obstetrics and Gynecology, a person greatly interested in preventing infant mortality.

Bernardine Dohrn and her husband, William Ayres, of the University of Illinois Department of Education.

Robert Emde of the University of Denver, a leader in infancy and child studies.

Erik Erikson, a pioneer and giant in the field of early childhood development.

Robert Fogel of the University of Chicago, Nobel Laureate, who taught me about the increase in life expectancy in the United States.

Selma Fraiberg, originally of the University of Michigan and later the University of California, whom I had the opportunity to know well in Lisbon fifteen years ago. The concepts she expressed in "Ghosts in the Nursery" (1975) are extraordinary contributions to the study of healthy and unhealthy early childhood development.

Anna Freud.

James Garbarino, former president of the Erikson Institute, who has done excellent work in the study of violence.

Linda Gilkerson, director of the eleven-year-old Infant Studies Program at the Erikson Institute.

Jane Goodall, who studied chimpanzees and how they bring up their children.

Stanley Greenspan, who worked with Reginald Lourie at the National Institute of Mental Health. He has done pioneering work in providing effective therapy for children who get off to a bad start in life.

Ruth Gross of Stanford University, who headed a study of the Robert Wood Johnson Foundation in conjunction with the medical schools of eight universities to learn what would happen if a group of low-birthweight babies were to receive the special help of a year of home visiting followed by two years of nursery schooling, with a ratio of one teacher for every four children. The answer was: a lot.

David Hamburg, an eminent thinker and psychiatrist and president of the Carnegie Corporation, who among other things taught me a great deal about early childhood development in humans and chimpanzees.

Asa Hilliard of Georgia State University.

Peter Huttenlocher, brain researcher at the University of Chicago.

Sheila Kammerman, professor of social services at Columbia University and a student of American and European cultures.

John Kennell and Marshall Klaus for their work with *doulas* (Greek, a *doula* is a woman caregiver, or experienced labor companion)[1] and their concept of the bonding of infants to parents.

Heinz Kohut, a seminal thinker and a Chicago psychoanalyst.

J. Ronald Lally, first at Syracuse University and then at the Far West Laboratory, who for many years ran the program conceived by Julius Richmond and Bettye Caldwell at Syracuse to learn how children might benefit from good nurturing at a nursery school from age six months to five years.

Leon Lederman, Nobel Laureate and the moving spirit who saw the need for the Illinois Math and Science Academy that appealed so much to Governor James Thompson that he made it happen.

Bennett Leventhal, child psychiatrist at the University of Chicago and a great clinician.

Reginald Lourie of the National Institute of Mental Health, the first president of the National Center for Clinical Infant Programs.

Gillian McNamee and Joan McLane of the Erikson Institute, who have researched how very young children learn to read.

Mary Main, who worked on infant attachment and the intergenerational phenomenon of attachment.

Steve Marans, an extraordinary clinician at Yale University, for his work with children who have witnessed violence.

Joseph Markus of the University of Chicago, a psychiatrist who first taught me that a keen observer can be trained to identify anomalies in infants that can be treated and corrected.

Stephanie Marshall, the splendid president of the Illinois Math and Science Academy.

Linda Mayes of Yale University, for her research on infants, their span of attention, and the impact of drugs on infants.

Samuel Meisels of the University of Michigan, an expert in student testing.

Karl Menninger and Will Menninger, who taught me much over many years about mental health and mental illness.

Robert Michael, the excellent dean of the Harris School of Public Policy Studies at the University of Chicago, who has studied the economics of people living in poverty. He has also studied sexual behavior in America.

Arden Miller of the University of North Carolina, a student of prevention in the United States and the world.

Naomi Morris, for initiating the training of public health personnel at the University of Illinois.

Norval Morris, dean of the University of Chicago Law School and a national authority on crime, punishment, and prisons.

Judith Musick, first director of the Ounce of Prevention Fund and author of an important book on why some teenagers choose to become mothers at a very early age.

Dolores Norton, a professor at the School of Social Service Administration at the University of Chicago.

Joy Osofsky, whom I met first at the Menninger Clinic. For the past several years Joy has directed a major program at Louisiana State University Medical Center in New Orleans.

Jeree Pawl and Alicia Lieberman, protégés and extraordinary successors to Selma Fraiberg at the University of California at San Francisco. They do impressive research, therapy, and teaching involving infants and toddlers.

Helen Perlman, professor of social work at the University of Chicago, a valuable and much-esteemed adviser and friend who is also my cousin.

Bruce Perry of Baylor University and formerly of the University of Chicago, an original thinker on the brain in posttraumatic stress disorder.

Jean Piaget, who lectured at the Erikson Institute and received an honorary degree from Loyola University.

Maria Piers, who conceived of the need for the Erikson Institute, and her husband, Gerhardt Piers, psychoanalyst and esteemed director of the Institute for Psychoanalysis in Chicago. Thirty years ago they interested me in helping to start the Erikson Institute for the Advanced Study of Child Development.

Norman Polansky, whose insight into the concept of damaged parents was most important in my thinking.

Sally Provence, an outstanding clinician and researcher, who worked closely for many years with Albert Solnit of Yale University.

Kyle Pruett of Yale University for his research on the importance of fathers in the lives of infants and young children.

James Robertson and Joyce Robertson for their early studies in London about the problems caused when children are separated from their parents. They came to the Erikson Institute to teach students about separation based entirely on their clinical observations. Twenty-five years later their theories were confirmed by physiological and neurological findings that came from new techniques of brain imaging.

Jeannie Rosoff, president of the Alan Guttmacher Institute, which has done pioneering work in the study of family planning.

Arnold Sameroff for his discovery of the impact of multiple-risk factors on children's failure in school.

Milton Senn, the second of four great administrators of the Yale Child Study Center.

Albert Shanker, the well-known president of the American Federation of Teachers.

Rebecca Shamoon Shanok, a sensitive therapist and teacher of how to treat problematic children in school settings.

Jack Shonkoff, researcher on the use of services by handicapped children, now dean of the Florence Heller Graduate School at Brandeis University.

Marilyn Siegel of Fort Lauderdale, Florida, who started and runs wonderful programs for handicapped children.

Albert Solnit, creative innovator, conceiver of the Comer schools in New Haven, Connecticut, and the third in succession of great leaders of the Yale Child Study Center.

Renee Spitz, Maria Piers's friend from Austria, who early recognized the unpopular fact that good food and adequate shelter alone will not keep infants alive. They need love and affection and human contact.

L. Alan Sroufe and Byron Egeland of the University of Minnesota for their extraordinary longitudinal study of infants born in poverty.

Harold Stevenson of the University of Michigan, who compared the education of children at ages five and nine in China, Japan, Taiwan, Chicago, and Minneapolis.

Frances Stott, current dean of the Erikson Institute.

Thomas Trabasso, former chair of the Department of Psychology at the University of Chicago, and his able researcher-wife, Nancy Stein.

Lorraine Wallach, who with Maria Piers and Barbara Bowman started the Erikson Institute.

David Weickart, developer of the Perry Preschool Project, which was the forerunner of Head Start.

Roger Weissberg, who heads a novel training program on the prevention of dysfunctionality at the University of Illinois.

Sheldon White of Harvard University, who pointed out to Congress that although compassion originally motivated Congress to invest in orphaned children in 1910, economics and cost-effectiveness cogently dictate the country's investment in children today in order to help prevent poor education and later failure and possibly prison.

Rosemary White-Traut of the University of Illinois School of Nursing for her original work in recognizing that fragile premature babies can be helped by tender, loving, and sensitive care.

G. Gordon Williamson, an expert in occupational therapy and a rich resource who teaches on the relation between early childhood development and occupational therapy.

William Julius Wilson of the Harris School at the University of Chicago, whose insights about poverty have been invaluable, including the concept of an index of marriageable males based on employed and unemployed young men.

Edward Zigler of Yale University, one of the original driving forces of the Head Start program in Washington.

Barry Zuckerman of Boston, chief of pediatrics at Boston University Medical School and a pioneer in studies of drug-using mothers whose children need help as the mothers are being treated.

OTHERS

G. Carl Ball, a successful businessman and a student of educational research.

Owen Brad Butler, chief executive officer of Procter and Gamble, later chair of the Committee for Economic Development, and the man who really pushed the concept in the business community that the health and education of a child start prenatally and that the early days and months of a child's life are critically important.

Judy Carter, second director of the Ounce of Prevention Fund, who is wise and politically savvy.

Maria Chavez, a skillful advocate and the director of a superlative family support program in Albuquerque, New Mexico.

Hillary Clinton, as chair of the Children's Defense Fund some years before her becoming First Lady.

Dorothy Coleman and Patricia Brady, first-class clinicians in the Ounce's Beethoven Project. They recognized that it often takes years of just being there before some mothers will begin to trust them.

Charles Daly, a supportive ally, former president of the Joyce Foundation.

Richard Day and Peter Hart for their public-opinion research into attitudes toward spending money on education for very young children.

Marian Wright Edelman, president and organizer of the Children's Defense Fund.

Emily Fenichel, for many years the associate director of the National Center for Clinical Infant Programs, an original thinker with an encyclopedic mind.

Rae Grad, director of the National Commission to Prevent Infant Mortality.

Sol Hurwitz, president of the Committee for Economic Development, who brought me into contact with the subcommittee to study education.

Terrance Keenan of the Robert Wood Johnson Foundation, who encouraged me with funding, understanding, and many good research projects, including school-based medical clinics.

Margaret Mahoney, notable leader for many years of the Commonwealth Fund.

Harriet Meyer, third director of the Ounce of Prevention Fund and an inspiring colleague.

Gwill Newman, a great leader in encouraging research in brain development.

James Renier, former chair of Honeywell, who early on developed a program that evolved into the "Success by Six" program in Minneapolis.

Ruth Rothstein, director of Mount Sinai Hospital and later Cook County Hospital, who not only knew how to run a good hospital, but also had a great interest in helping poor people.

Lisabeth Schorr, well-known author.

Bernice Weissbourd and her husband, Bernard Weissbourd, who were the moving spirits behind Family Focus, created for the purpose of supporting families and mobilizing their strengths to help raise their children.

Doris Williams, an educator in the Chicago schools who convinced me that day after day, week after week, we shortchange all the children in our public schools.

My personal staff, who have helped me enormously: Ruth Belzer, for many years the thoughtful and able director of the Harris Foundation; Nancy Hughes, my secretary, ever patient and always helpful; and Jo Sawyer, my personal assistant, whose initiative was invaluable. I thank Alison Siegler, who devoted an entire summer to wading through the many speeches I had written over the years and all their supporting documents. She helped organize the disparate pieces into a cohesive structure from which this book was developed. I am grateful for the diligence of my research assistant, Delane Sanders, throughout the preparation of the manuscript. Her skill as an information and network specialist has made this book a reliable resource.

ORGANIZATIONS

I wish to acknowledge the following organizations, which were especially helpful in providing information for this book: Advocates for Youth (formerly the Center for Population Options); the Alan Guttmacher Institute; Child Trends, Inc.; the Illinois Department of Children and Family Services; the Illinois Criminal Justice Authority; the Michigan Department of Public Health; and the Population Reference Bureau.

A special debt of gratitude is owed to my editor, Lorraine Alexson. It is customary for authors to acknowledge the trials they inflict on their editors, and I feel compelled to confess my own. Lorraine worked diligently throughout numerous revisions and a constant flow of additional information. Her attention to detail never wavered. She was unfailingly professional and at all stages cheered me on.

ABBREVIATIONS

ACT	American College Testing program
AFDC	Aid to Families with Dependent Children
AGI	Alan Guttmacher Institute
CDC	Centers for Disease Control
CDF	Children's Defense Fund
CED	Committee for Economic Development
CER	Coalition for Educational Rights (Illinois)
CFAT	Carnegie Foundation for the Advancement of Teaching
CNS	central nervous system
CPP	Children's Policy Project (University of Chicago)
CSCD	Center for Successful Child Development (the Beethoven Project)
CSSP	Center for the Study of Social Policy (the Annie E. Casey Foundation)
DCFS	Department of Children and Family Services
EMR	educable mentally retarded
GAO	U.S. Government Accounting Office
GED	general equivalency diploma
HHS	U.S. Department of Health and Human Services
HIV	human immunodeficiency virus
IIT	Illinois Institute of Technology
MDPH	Michigan Department of Public Health
MDSS	Michigan Department of Social Services
MPFSY	Multiproblem Family Syndrome
MRI	magnetic resonance imaging

NAEP	National Assessment of Education Programs
NARAL	National Abortion Rights Action League
NCC	National Commission on Children
NCCIP	National Center for Clinical Infant Programs
NCHS	National Center for Health Statistics
NCPCAN	National Committee to Prevent Child Abuse and Neglect
NIMH	National Institute of Mental Health
OECD	Organization for Economic Co-operation and Development
PET	positron emission tomography
PRAMS	Pregnancy Risk Assessment Monitoring Systems (MDPH)
USDE	United States Department of Education
WPPSI	Wechsler Preschool and Primary School Scale of Intelligence

AN ODYSSEY OF LEARNING

B Y ONE CHINESE VIEW a human being's position in time is that of a person sitting beside a river, always facing downstream while watching the water flow past. The future is behind you, above you, and below you, where you cannot examine it. My own odyssey of learning and reflecting on the cycle of poverty began more than forty years ago. Many of the landmarks on that journey consist of highly personal experiences, such as a book or an article I happened to read or a chance encounter. Other landmarks are more familiar, like the launching of the War on Poverty and the success of the Head Start program.

The ramifications of poverty are alarming, and it would be foolhardy to ignore the cycle of poverty, which affects the lives of a great many children in our nation. If doing nothing about poverty can be called a strategy, then that is our national strategy against poverty, what I think of as a let's-not-rock-the-boat policy. It is a policy that is letting us sink quietly.

There is a huge economic cost to poverty. The U.S. Department of Justice has told us that of the cohort of Americans who have reached the age of twelve, five out of six will become victims of violent crime. We all pay for poverty in the form of taxes, which buy such band-aids as welfare programs, prisons, and homes for the retarded.

In 1993 in Illinois the child abuse and neglect hot line brought in almost one hundred sixteen thousand reports that required investigation. Each of more than two hundred investigations a day required on average thirteen hours of a trained worker's time. Seventy-six children died in 1994 in Illinois alone (tel. comm., NCPCAN, 1995) as victims of either abuse or neglect, and there were hundreds of cases of broken bones and thousands of kids beaten into submission or psychologically battered. In Chicago in 1985 there were forty-seven thousand arrests for juvenile delinquency, or an average of more than one hundred arrests each day.

There are at least three kinds of poverty. First, there is temporary poverty, which results from the temporary loss of a job or temporary illness. Second, there is poverty that results from a permanent inability to work— the result of a long-term illness or other incapacity. Third, there is what is frequently called underclass poverty, when a temporary or permanent inability to get a job or hold a job results in abject poverty unless relatives, friends, or organized welfare step in to help.

What society complains about is being asked to support the millions of people it views as physically able to work but who are lazy, incompetent, or unwilling to work. Society resents this third kind of poverty and tends to think of its victims as guilty of causing their own failures.

When most employed individuals think about people on welfare, they tend to "blame the victim." Obviously this approach has not solved the problem; poverty has not lessened. It has grown worse. In the United States today we have a virtually permanent underclass that is disproportionately black, Hispanic, Native American, and very young. The number of poor is growing faster than the population as a whole. The cycle of poverty is closely associated with school failure, school drop-out, and births to uneducated mothers, who are usually not married, unstable emotionally, poor, and too immature to nurture their infants. Their pregnancies are generally unintended.

In 1951, I went to Yale University for my twentieth reunion. Five years later I returned for my twenty-fifth reunion. It was hard for me to believe how much had occurred in my life and changed in my way of thinking in those five years. In 1951, I was still with the Toni Company, interested in advertising, and concerned about television ratings and how to sell Toni home permanent wave kits. By 1956, I had left Toni and become part of an educational publishing company that was particularly concerned with providing materials of instruction for school counselors. One of the problems that began to interest me was high school drop-out and how to prevent it.

Several years later I read *Crisis in Black and White* (1964) by Charles

Silberman, a book that made a great impression on me. Many people were swept up in the excitement of preparing all children for school by starting much earlier than age five or six: starting at age three or four. The purpose was to give poor kids the head start they needed so that when they entered kindergarten two years later, they would be as well prepared as their middle-class contemporaries were. The evidence seemed clear that if a child was one year or more behind as she entered kindergarten, she would be two or three years behind before she completed elementary school.

Along with thousands of others, I was sold on the logic of getting to the child early and therefore was prepared to help start a graduate school to train preschool teachers, an idea presented to me in the fall of 1965 by Maria Piers and Gerhardt Piers, who were brought up in Vienna. As youngsters, both had been exposed to Freud's teachings and later to Anna Freud's ideas regarding child development.

The Pierses were concerned about the need to train specialists in early childhood development. They recognized that this nation was beginning to focus attention on early childhood education, and, with the rush into Head Start, that there would be a great demand for preschool teachers.

Head Start administrators developed a model for training teachers based on crash training programs developed during World War II. Maria Piers and I made a pilgrimage to Washington in 1965, and we were strongly encouraged by the Office of Economic Opportunity to proceed immediately with our plans for training teachers of teachers. Our graduate program would be anything but a six-week crash course. Nevertheless, the Office of Economic Opportunity said that it was eager to fund it. We sent our proposal in before the 15 January 1966 deadline, and then we started to wait, and we waited and waited. As the weeks turned into months, we reached a point of no return in April of 1966. Maria Piers, along with Barbara Bowman and Lorraine Wallach—all graduates of a program developed by the Institute for Psychoanalysis for social workers who wanted to deepen their knowledge of child therapy—had to notify their employers that they would not be back in the fall. They were willing to cast their lots to start a new school. We decided to go ahead even if the promised federal support proved illusory.

We began to recruit a class for September 1966 and to select the additional faculty members needed. As it turned out, the federal government left us hanging out to dry for more than two years. Not until 1968 did we get some support from Washington, and when that support arrived, it was meager and lasted for only two or three years.

In 1968 the Erikson Institute opened. Its first faculty included people well qualified in cultural anthropology, pediatrics, perceptual psychology, preschool education, psychoanalytic psychology, and social work. Maria Piers aimed to train educators who would understand the problems of the whole child and of different cultures. From that day to this, the Erikson Institute has provided an interdisciplinary approach to training its graduates to look at the world from the perspective of children. Today we have more than six hundred such graduates.

The great excitement about early childhood education in 1965 and 1966 had more or less disappeared by 1970. That fire is now being rekindled. Senator Daniel Patrick Moynihan has used the term *syzygy* as a metaphor to describe the concurrence of events that are once more focusing attention on the cycle of poverty and the importance of trying to break it. Perhaps this time around the increasing interest results in part from the recognition that it is not only the poor who are in trouble. We are all in trouble.

Many people understand, for example, that our Social Security system is no longer safe. The system is currently based on a ratio of three beneficiaries of old-age assistance to ten workers. By the year 2020 that will have changed: there will be five beneficiaries for every ten workers. We had better be sure by then that all ten of those in the right age brackets to be working are working, are able to hold a good job by doing a good job, and are able to pay their Social Security taxes; otherwise the entire system of old age benefits will collapse.

Social changes occur slowly. The institution of public school education in the United States originally started with the premise that a family will bring a child to kindergarten ready to learn. Today, the institution of education still starts with children at age five and "educates" them from that point forward. As a nation, we spend $500 billion annually on that educational system beginning from age five. We spend not much more than $5 billion for the important years preceding kindergarten, when the most essential part of a child's development occurs.

It is ironic that now, with the increasing nationwide attention paid to preschool, we have advanced to the point reached by Silberman and Head Start thirty years ago. With all the new recognition given Head Start's cost-effectiveness, Head Start continues on a starvation diet. It has never had enough funds. Currently its programs reach only 34 percent of three- and four-year-olds and only 3 percent of eligible children aged zero, one, and two.

I became a trustee of the Bush Foundation of St. Paul in 1970, at the time one of eight new trustees. All fifteen trustees were queried about their preferences regarding the direction that the Bush Foundation's grant giving should take. I favored funding programs in early childhood development and public television. The trustees were sent a ballot listing the areas suggested for grants and inviting each trustee to indicate which ideas he or she favored. The final ballot revealed only one vote for early childhood development and one vote for public television—mine.

Partly because of my persuading, the Bush Foundation over a period of time did move in the direction of meaningful grant making for early childhood education, and in about 1972 it brought to St. Paul a panel of outstanding child advocates: Urie Bronfenbrenner, Julius Richmond, Sheldon White, and Edward Zigler. After a long day spent discussing their perceptions of the status of early childhood education in the United States, White said, "You know, we four have been asked to visit Washington time and again to testify. We are all getting older and a little tired. We are wearing out. What is really needed is a new generation of advocates. Why don't you [the Bush Foundation] fund a program to develop child advocates?" That idea resulted in a series of grants for the Bush Center at Yale as well as Bush Centers at the Universities of California at Los Angeles, Michigan, and North Carolina. Many of the predoctoral and postdoctoral graduates funded by the Bush Centers have now moved into key positions in many states and in the federal establishment.

In 1975 in Chicago, Bernice Weissbourd started talking to me about her idea for organizing a family support system. In 1965 and 1966, Weissbourd, with Joan Costello, had operated a Head Start program in a housing project in the inner city of Chicago. She said the children they worked with could be divided into three groups. The top group, about one third of the children, seemed to have had good nurturing at home and would probably make it in life even without a Head Start program. She thought the second third needed and had really benefited from Head Start, but they had demanded extremely good teaching. The final third of the children were so badly damaged by the time they arrived in Head Start that the program could never reach them. She realized that the only way to address that problem was to work with the mothers of those children from the time the babies were born and even prenatally, going back to six to nine months before birth.

After a solid year of planning, Weissbourd started Family Focus in Evanston in 1976. Family Focus is a nonprofit social service organization that works with families with children under age three and that helps parents to improve their knowledge of healthy child development and to enhance their parenting skills. Bernice's husband, Bernard Weissbourd, and I shared the principal part of the cost. We were able to mobilize some foundation support, but it was difficult to obtain and was almost certain to stop after three years. There seems to be some law ordained in heaven requiring most foundation trustees to favor innovative projects that they can fund for one to three years. After that, the program by their definition is no longer innovative and is presumably old enough to have been replicated or abandoned as a bad idea. Most new social programs with which I have been associated are lucky if, in their third year, they begin to operate more or less as they were originally planned. It takes at least another three years for such programs to stabilize. Only then can they be intelligently evaluated.

Evanston is a mixed community of about one hundred thousand people who range from affluent to poor; about 77 percent are white and 23 percent are black. Weissbourd expected about fifty families to use the center in the first year. We were all surprised that, all told, 250 mothers came with their children.

Weissbourd had hoped to attract a cross section of Evanston mothers, including black and teenage mothers especially—but the center failed to attract either. Four years later we solved the problem when we started a second center, adjacent to Evanston High School, that did attract high school youth (principally blacks), who named the center Our Place. We attracted not only teenagers from the high school who were pregnant or parenting, but also many who were not. The center was highly success-ful: the health of the young mothers clearly improved, and the number of low-birthweight babies diminished. The Public Health Department of Evanston provided a public health officer who visited the center two or three days a week. This officer was one of an extremely talented group of workers who staffed the program.

In 1977, I commissioned David Harman, an Israeli scholar who lived for several months a year in the United States, to write a brief study of the history of federal legislation related to children. He found that since the White House Conference of 1909 and with the establishment of the Children's Bureau in 1912, all early federal support was based on humanitarian considerations. It had seemed logical to members of Congress that if a mother had lost her husband and had to bring up young children on her own, society ought to help her, as a matter of decency. This humane approach characterized federal grants for chil-dren for many years. It was not until Sheldon White, in a report to Congress in 1973, specifically alerted legislators that in addition to humanitarian concerns, society should realize that there is an economic cost in failing to socialize and educate our children.

The history of Family Focus, fully examined in chapter 2, showed that the cost of intervention would not be cheap. Yet the cost of prevention would have to be justified by humane considerations or by cost-effective-ness. Estimating these costs is difficult. Not until 1985 was a study done in Illinois to calculate the costs attributable to the 24,364 births to teenagers in 1983. The total estimated annual cost of only the first five years of those children's lives was $853 million, or about $35,000 per birth.

In 1981, even after five successful years, Family Focus continued to find it difficult to get funding. It is still difficult. At one point, I thought we might be able to interest corporations. We thought that if we could place a center near a factory site, a corporation's self-interest would warrant a substantial investment. This might create a replicable model. One obvious corporation to participate in the experiment was the Pittway Corporation, of which I was chair. (In Aurora, Illinois, Pittway then manufactured First Alert® smoke detectors.) Aurora has a large poor pocket of Hispanic families, and many Pittway employees were Hispanic. Pittway was willing and eager to help this community, as well as its own interests, by supplying a substantial part of the funds needed to finance a Family Focus drop-in center in Aurora. The plan was for a three-year experiment, with the idea of trying to interest other Aurora employers in becoming financial supporters.

As our plans progressed, Bernice Weissbourd suggested that we ask the Department of Children and Family Services (DCFS) for $25,000 a year toward our estimated $100,000 budget. We pointed out that the Aurora center would be a model primary prevention program and should therefore be of interest to the state as a means of cutting down on child abuse and neglect. Gregory Coler, then director of DCFS, reacted by saying that it was high time his agency provided significant funding for programs that would broadly test the concept of primary prevention. Rather than invest $25,000 in Aurora, he volunteered to commit $400,000 if Pittway would match it. His goal was to establish six experimental sites that would really test the concept of prevention. The Pittway Board agreed to match the grant. Coler invited me to think up a name for our public-private partnership, and that is how the Ounce of Prevention Fund was created.

In 1982 President Reagan's Commission on Excellence in Education determined that of all the seventeen-year-olds in this country, 44 percent of the blacks and 56 percent of the Hispanics were functionally illiterate. The employment rate of minority youth in this country is below 50 percent. About this time in my own process of learning, I read *Damaged Parents* (1981), Norman Polansky's book. He wrote convincingly about the intergenerational problem: the poor nurturing of a child produces a teenager who, already damaged as a child, would, upon becoming a parent, damage her child.

In 1984, the *New York Times* reported that the superintendent of education in Minneapolis had decided that in order to improve school results he would institute matriculation examinations for students so that they could not pass into the tenth grade without having passed the ninth grade; and to enter the eighth grade they had to pass the seventh grade; and so on for the fifth grade down to kindergarten. The purpose was to ensure that students would not be allowed to enter the next grade unless they were ready to do the level of work of that grade. Much to everyone's surprise, of 3,010 kindergartners tested, 291 (or roughly 10 percent) were classified as not ready to enter the first grade.

The reaction of a counselor in the Chicago public school system to the Minneapolis study interested me. Doris Williams had taught kindergarten in both the inner city and in an affluent Chicago suburb. She said that she knew from experience what "not ready" meant. She explained that aside from cognitive test results (such as those used in Minneapolis) not being ready could mean a low span of attention, hyperactivity, a child prone to violence, speech and hearing difficulties, or any one of many other learning disabilities or developmental delays. Williams said that when you had a child in your class who was not ready, you knew it. "As an experienced teacher, I can handle one such child without shortchanging the rest of the class, but when I have two or three children like that, there is no way I can avoid shortchanging the whole class."

In their first years of operation, the Ounce of Prevention Fund and Family Focus were not really achieving primary prevention but secondary prevention, or intervention. They worked with adolescents who were already pregnant or who had had a baby. At best, the programs were trying to help these mothers bring up their babies well and to encourage them not to have a second or third baby while still in school or of school age.

It dawned on me about that time that *primary* prevention would have us try to prevent the first birth to an unmarried adolescent. I became curious about whether anything was being done successfully anywhere in our nation to prevent first births to adolescents. The Harris Foundation hired an educator named William Young to investigate the comprehensive school-based medical clinic approach. His research indicated that a St. Paul, Minnesota, clinic program claimed to have cut births to teenagers in a high-risk high school by 59 percent.

When I learned that the St. Paul clinic program worked, I talked again to Coler, who had become director of Public Aid. He quickly agreed to fund half of the cost of two such medical clinics if I could find private funding for the other half. These clinics, to be modeled on the St. Paul program, would offer comprehensive medical care and family planning services. To match the state's funding, we would have to raise $2 million: $1 million for each clinic to be spent over eight years. The Pittway Corporation Charitable Foundation agreed to give $75,000 a year for several years, and the Joyce Foundation gave $50,000 for each clinic as starter money. Ruth Belzer, the executive director of the Harris Foundation, had the inspiration to go to New York and talk with the heads of several large foundations. She was able to get two grants of $50,000 each from the Commonwealth Fund for each of the two clinics and a grant of approximately $1 million for two clinics over a period of eight years from the Robert Wood Johnson Foundation. Since then, ten more Chicago foundations have agreed to join the funding consortium, including the Chicago Community Trust, with a grant of $250,000.

With a great deal of intelligent effort supplied by Belzer and Young, we succeeded in April 1985 in getting the administration and the board of education of Chicago to agree to permit the establishment of medical clinics at two high schools. The vote of the board was ten to one. Their action was reported appropriately in both the *Chicago Sun-Times* and the *Chicago Tribune;* both also noted that contraceptives would be dispensed to the students and that, in order to use the services of the clinic, students would need written permission from their parents.

The DuSable High School clinic opened in June. All went well. No news was good news. Then, three months later, a black minister named Hiram Crawford, head of the Moral Majority movement in Illinois, wrote a letter complaining to the governor about the clinic, sending copies to fifty well-placed individuals, including the editor of the *Chicago Sun-Times.* The *Sun-Times,* then under the ownership of Rupert Murdoch, decided to help the Reverend Mr. Crawford. The paper ran a banner headline on the front page of the Sunday edition: "The Pill Goes to School." The fact that 85 percent of the visits were for medical problems and only 15 percent for family planning was not newsworthy. Only sex is news.

The next day, right-to-lifers came out to picket DuSable High School, attracting local television cameras. The following day, the cameras were from the networks. Interestingly, all the excitement generated by the newspaper and the television cameras was of zero concern to the families of students at DuSable High School, where the clinic was operating. Neither the principal of the school nor the superintendent of education received a single call from a parent on either Sunday, Monday, Tuesday, or Wednesday following news coverage. The parents, the students, the principal, and the faculty wanted the clinic there.

Before opening the second clinic at Orr High School, we were required to survey the community and the students. When we surveyed the students, faculty, and parents at Orr we found that each group favored, by a vote of 85 to 15, the establishment of a clinic that would dispense contraceptives. A survey of the larger Orr High School community again resulted in an 85-to-15 vote in favor of the clinic. Throughout this highly publicized confrontation, the governor of Illinois, James Thompson, stood tall, as had Coler; neither flinched in the face of the opposition, which was not so numerous but highly vocal. Since 1985 the state of Illinois has appropriated funds for two more high school clinics operated by the Ounce, in addition to one other high school and three elementary-school clinics.

I continued to think about inner-city students being shortchanged because too many arrive in kindergarten not ready. Rather than depend solely on one person's assessment, I arranged to meet separately with each of four other kindergarten teachers. I asked the same basic questions I had asked before: Were some kindergartners arriving in school at the beginning of the school year not ready? They all said yes, indeed.

Even then I thought to myself that they must be exaggerating. Then I began to put two and two together. First, the Westinghouse study (see chapter 1) had shown Head Start gains that disappeared in the first and second grades after Head Start kids were mixed into elementary school classes in a ratio of one to five. Second, a major study of the Chicago public schools by Designs for Change, of Chicago, an independent, not-for-profit research group, had reported in 1984 that in the twelve poorest of the fifty-eight city high schools they studied only 4–8 percent of graduating seniors could read at the twelfth-grade level. That meant that more than 900 youngsters out of 1,000 who had entered as freshmen were at age eighteen reading at levels below the twelfth grade, and in most cases below the eighth-grade level. Third, in 1986 the *Chicago Tribune* reported on a Chicago board of education finding that more than 50 percent of students failed two or more courses each year.

The kindergarten teachers I had interviewed had not been exaggerating. Westinghouse was not wrong. Silberman, it turned out, was on the right track in 1964 when he identified the roots of educational failure being in the cradle and in the lack of early stimulation. Silberman had assumed that this lack of stimulation very early on in life could be cured by preschool programs starting at age three or four. Apparently, for some children it can be cured, but not for others.

The full scope of the problem of the schools struck me in the fall of 1984. Just about then I was invited by Dorcas Hardy, then a deputy secretary of the Department of Health and Human Services (HHS), to attend a conference at Princeton to answer the question, What will the needs of HHS be in the year 2000? Obviously, on average, the population will be older, and more people will draw old-age assistance. There will probably be more illness in an older population.

Yet many of the problems that HHS will face in the year 2000 are not related to old age. It will still face infant mortality, infant morbidity, child abuse and neglect, the need for special education, the failure of inner-city schools, functional illiteracy, teenage pregnancy, delinquency, adolescent homicide, adolescent suicide, alcohol abuse, drug abuse, unemployment, unemployability, crime, and prisons.

In the groups of ten and then of twenty at our conference and then in plenary session, I made my little speech about it costing $300,000 over a lifetime when we fail to prevent a child from failing. Much to my astonishment, as the hours of the two-and-a-half-day conference went by, this idea seemed to become increasingly acceptable. As a consequence, when the final HHS report about the year 2000 was published, it contained a full page spelling out the costs of a policy of doing nothing, of being unwilling to invest in children who are at a high risk of failure. The group had agreed that if prevention could be achieved at a cost of up to $10,000 for each child, then it made economic sense to do so, and that we ought to develop experimental programs to prevent these failures in our social system.

Richard Shute, a Hardy deputy, had a key role in this conference and in moving ahead with its findings. He saw the importance of prevention and also recognized the potential for an important experiment, to be made possible by public-private partnerships.

The consequence of the Princeton meeting was a request for proposals, which came out in the *Federal Register* of September 1985. The Department of Health and Human Services offered to fund three experimental programs such as those we had discussed. Each would require fifty-fifty matching funds from a local foundation. We responded in Illinois, the Heinz Foundation responded in Pittsburgh, and the Kamehameha Schools/Bishop Estate Foundation responded in Hawaii. Three programs were funded. Our program has become known as the Beethoven Project because the elementary school district that we chose to focus on was the Beethoven Elementary School.

The federal government agreed to fund the project with $600,000 over three years, and the Harris Foundation matched it. That gave us our start. We have excellent relations with the Illinois Department of Children and Family Services, which is keenly interested in prevention. They were already funding many infant and toddler day care slots in the catchment areas. They were confident they would see a drop in reports of child abuse and neglect, which were unconscionably high in that area.

The Harris Foundation invited the Chicago Urban League to join the Ounce of Prevention Fund in applying for the grant. As director of the project, the Ounce hired an experienced Head Start supervisor, Gina Barclay-McLaughlin. The president of the Urban League in Chicago, James Compton, was enthusiastic in his support. Barclay-McLaughlin did an excellent job of involving community leaders. We started with strong support from the residents of the community. They realized what a great opportunity it was for them and their children.

Late in November 1986 Kathleen Teltsch of the *New York Times* learned about the Beethoven Project. She came to Chicago on a four-day visit to find out more about it and then wrote a fine piece on Beethoven. That story made the front page of the Sunday *New York Times* on 28 December. The publicity that attended the project since has far exceeded anything we ever imagined.

Another strand of the story began with Congress in the fall of 1986. Lowell Weicker, then a senator from Connecticut, has been a powerful advocate for handicapped children. In developing Public Law 99-457, he included $50 million in his legislative program to be spent nationally for handicapped children from birth through age two. One predictor of hand-icapping conditions is low socioeconomic status. Congress wisely decided to allow those funds to be spent on high-risk children, irrespective of whether the handicapping condition was yet evident, because the earlier the intervention, the more likely it is that the handicap can be prevented.

When I was alerted by the National Center for Clinical Infant Programs (NCCIP) of the passage of this law, I immediately took it upon myself to see whether some of the money could be used by Illinois for programs like the Beethoven project. In December 1986, I approached Governor Thompson with a proposal to use the money to replicate the Beethoven Project in two or three new sites. I said it would probably take $2.5 million in state funds, in addition to $2.5 million in federal funds. I also said that $7.5 million would likely be required in the second year.

For many reasons, including a strong commitment to reducing infant mortality in Illinois, the governor, his transition team, his staff, and the directors of various agencies in human services all liked the idea of doing more to work prenatally with high-risk children. They really believed that prevention is the name of the game and for education to work, we have to start with children when they are very young. As a consequence, we now have limited additional state funds for programs like Beethoven. Prevention is not only wise, it is good politics.

I wish I could say that with money and publicity the problem has been licked. That has not happened. It is no easy task to change the medical, social, cultural, and parenting habits of a large group of people. In addition, I am well aware that the pockets of poverty are not necessarily similar to one another. The inner city is not uniform. Hispanic underclass children do not present exactly the same problems as poor blacks, poor Native Americans, or poor Appalachian whites; all pockets of poverty are not the same.

There was a great deal that we did not know when we started, but one thing was clear: we had an excellent opportunity to learn. In bringing together able staff to recruit and train community people who were eager to go to work to improve their lot, we knew we would have a fair chance of being successful.

Illinois has an extremely good group of early childhood experts. We have people who fully understand the importance of the prevention of delinquency and recognize that as a society we must move in this direction and move vigorously. I have learned from these people. It is our hypothesis that to prevent delinquency it is important to improve very early childhood development so that infants and toddlers learn to trust, to believe in themselves, and to feel they can shape their environment.

All over the country today there is a growing interest in doing something about children. The *Chicago Tribune* and the *New York Times* continue to be genuinely interested in preventing poverty and helping children. The enormous impact of these newspapers seems to have brought increased interest from many directions.

I have asked you to look backward with me on what has been for me a voyage of discovery. I have learned enough about the cycle of poverty to realize that its causes are complex and interwoven. If we are to address these causes, we will have to attack them all concurrently. We will have to reduce dramatically the unintended births to poorly educated adolescents who have dropped out of school or are about to drop out. We will have to work hard in the school classes from sixth grade on to motivate students to take charge of their lives and to choose not to drift into early parenthood. This means we will have to offer the hope of jobs, particularly summer jobs, to these young people. We will have to offer training for real jobs that will be there so that young people can conceive of a future where they can respect themselves and be respected for their ability to earn their own livings and, in turn, hold out hope to their children. We must make the necessary investment in children not only from the time they are born but in the prenatal months as well.

Theoretically, we know how to organize our public services and to coordinate our branches of government. We know how to train adolescents and adults who are living in poverty so they can help themselves, their children, and their neighbors escape the dreadful trap of poverty. We know how to do all these things in small pilot programs. We must learn to put it all together and work in larger communities, such as whole school districts. The challenge is something like a giant jigsaw puzzle with thousands of parts that *can* be put together with patience, skill, dedication, and courage.

Twenty-eight years ago the Kerner Commission report (1968), inspired by the Watts race riots, described the difficulties facing our society and warned that unless we did something to prevent racial divisions, the problems were going to get worse. They have become worse. From time to time Republicans and Democrats in their respective orbits happen to be temporarily aligned in wanting to address welfare reform and think about ways to prevent welfare. At other times their main interest is to quarrel. We should all join in and ask why so many poor blacks, poor Hispanics, and poor whites have to live lives of despair, only to end up in hospitals, welfare lines, prisons, and morgues.

My voyage of discovery leads to a clear starting point: children at risk, those children in danger of not growing up healthy and not developing well because they are unwanted or born to mothers who are young, poor, alone, and uncounseled. The focus, then, must be on teenage girls and early childhood development, from conception to age three.

Working together, we can use our education and God-given intelligence and human insights to begin to understand the causes of social failure and weed out those causes. Human motivation and social organization should not be insoluble mysteries, nor should it be beyond the talent of human beings to organize society to eradicate the malignancy of a permanent underclass. Poverty is not preordained in heaven. It is a problem created by human beings; if we really want to, we can solve it.

RAISED IN JEOPARDY

WHEN CHILDREN are born unplanned for and unwanted, they start life at a disadvantage. They are raised in jeopardy of poor outcomes in their level of socialization and education. Without proper nurturing, poorly cared for, they are raised in jeopardy of living their lives out of control, their destinies determined by the interacting risks and consequences of poor health, poverty, child abuse and neglect, out-of-home placement, violence, drug use, sexual victimization, and adolescent pregnancy.

In the course of a long life I have come to appreciate the force of George Bernard Shaw's observation that the mark of a truly educated man is to be moved deeply by statistics. Although many people feel overwhelmed by numbers, the truth is that numbers are essential to understanding the magnitude of the problem of children born at risk. What is significant is that the trends shown in the statistics are likely to become worse.

The profile of the children at risk can be drawn in broad strokes by focusing on a single year. Of the 4.1 million babies born in 1992, 1.2 million, or 30 percent of the total, were born to unmarried women. When we realize that in the past twenty-five years the number of children born to single parents has increased by two and a half times (up from half a million in 1977),[1] the outlook is discouraging. Single parenthood is not by any means a precise predictor of school failure, but it is a fact that many children born to single parents (whether or not they are working or on welfare) will not do well in life. Most single parents have a poor education to begin with, and their children are usually at a severe disadvantage in starting school because they have not been well prepared socially, cognitively, physically, or emotionally.

There can be no argument that children are the future of our country. Yet the extent of the problems of children in the United States elicits increasingly pessimistic feelings about the likelihood of our being able to make any real changes to solve these problems. We are currently overwhelmed by a very large number of high-risk children, those born with health deficits, extremely poor prospects for optimal development in the first two years of life, and marginally better prospects for intervention between the ages of two and five. For most of these children the course of their lives is targeted for failure before they are old enough to learn how to read. If they live in poor communities where violence is the norm and academic achievement is an aberration, their future is even bleaker. Are we, as a nation and as individuals, to concern ourselves with all the children in the country? Clearly, the answer is yes.

At this juncture in American history, although the majority of children are doing reasonably well, they could do much better. About a third are not doing well, and most of these will probably not be doing better in the future. Frankly, because the numbers are so huge, we do not know how to improve the future of the many children born and raised in jeopardy, and their numbers are increasing steadily. On the other hand, technically, we know a lot more about the problems, and with small groups we *can* make a real difference. We have not learned to do on a grand scale what we know has been done in small experiments.

Unquestionably, American society has enough technical and financial resources to improve the outcome for nearly any individual child, but practical and political realities limit our ability to solve the myriad problems connected with improving the prospects of the hundreds of thousands of children who are born at risk each year.

Enormous scientific advances have been achieved over the past thirty years that affect our understanding of how children develop. These advances make it clear that a great deal happens in the embryonic period and in the first two years of life to influence the development of an adult. The importance of early development to the eventual educational success of an individual is immense. Based on this premise, I conclude, speaking broadly, that for the one third of all children who are not doing well their prospects have been compromised very early in their lives by circumstances that cannot later be changed.

The Cycle Begins

When I review the history of births in the United States over the past forty-five years my pessimism is great. High risk begets high risk. It is not a coincidence that nearly a third of our nation's children are in jeopardy and that a third of all births occur out of wedlock, almost all to parents who are poor. A cycle begins when a child is born to a poor, single mother and continues when the baby lacks suitable stimulation and yet begins school developmentally unprepared. It continues as a student feels unable to succeed in school and so tunes out; suffers the trauma and anxiety of inner-city life; drops out of school; and enters the world of early parenthood, perpetuating the cycles of danger and despair.

A trajectory of failure, then, begins with the high number of births occurring to poor, unmarried women in the United States. For troubled families and vulnerable children, a cycle of poverty involves irresponsible sexual behavior on the part of adolescents, both male and female. For the offspring of uncounseled sexuality, healthy childhood development is in peril.

Poverty is almost always the way of life for children born to single parents. A report of the National Commission on Children, *Beyond Rhetoric* (1991), projected what lies ahead for many of the 5.5 million preschool-age children who are growing up in families below the official poverty level, 24 percent of all children under the age of six. When compared with children growing up in families above the poverty level, these children are more than twice as likely to fail in school and to present serious discipline problems for their teachers and parents. Moreover, low achievement, grade repetition, and unruly conduct in the classroom are often the precursors of school drop-out, adolescent parenthood, delinquency, and joblessness. Poor children exhibit the early symptoms of failure at rates that are double those of children who are not poor.

RISKING THE FUTURE:

THE INTERGENERATIONAL TRANSMISSION OF RISK

The trajectory of failure is intergenerational. Babies at risk are conceived, gestate, and are born to mothers who are unprepared for their responsibilities as parents. The mothers are often too young, too poor, too uneducated, and too isolated to cope successfully with another life. It is precisely when the stakes are the highest—during pregnancy, childbirth, and infancy—that the fewest supports are available from either the girl's family, the community, or the government.

We would all agree that every child is entitled to loving parents who really want their children to succeed. Yet every day thousands of children are born who were not intended and are not wanted. Their births constitute an enormous problem. Furthermore, because of the punitive attitude of society, most states, thirty-one out of fifty, in effect, tell mothers that the taxpayers are angry with them and want to punish them.

In one study (*Chicago Metro Survey,* 1994) the question was asked of fifteen hundred respondents in metropolitan Chicago, "If an unmarried, pregnant woman on welfare wants to have an abortion, should the state pay for the abortion?" Fifty percent said yes; 42 percent said no, because they felt it was the woman's fault and responsibility, and therefore she should pay for it. In other words, 42 percent wanted to punish the woman for her pregnancy. The next question was, "Which do you think would cost the state more, to pay for the abortion or to pay for the birth of the child?" Only 17 percent said they thought the cost to the state would be more for the abortion than for the birth; 75 percent correctly said the birth would cost more. In fact, the costs of prenatal, medical, and hospital care together are six times the costs of abortion. The next question was, "If the unmarried mother and child remain on welfare, which do you think would cost the state more, the abortion or delivery and welfare?" Ninety-one percent said delivery and welfare would cost more. To the question, "In your opinion, what would improve the chances of an unmarried, pregnant woman getting off welfare and living a more productive life?" 62 percent answered that if the woman had the abortion, she would be more likely to get off welfare; 23 percent said that she should give birth and raise the child. Question: "Consider an unmarried woman on welfare who becomes pregnant. In your opinion, what are the chances of her baby living a healthy, productive life?" Twenty percent said good or excellent; 80 percent said poor. Then the question was asked again, "In your opinion, if the state paid for abortions for women on welfare who want an abortion, would society be better off or worse off?" Fifty-eight percent said better off; 26 percent said worse off.

The prospects for improvement are gloomy. As a nation, we have refused to confront the issue of children at risk until the trajectory produces successive generations of children with problems that show up in the schools and on the streets. Only when children have grown up to be truants, delinquents, addicts, or pregnant teenagers do we move to take action. By then the patterns of behavior and motivation are set and militate against successful intervention. The adolescent is hard to reach and even harder to change. Trying to change the attitudes or education of a fifteen-year-old is difficult, and the babies of failed adolescents do not stand much of a chance of doing any better than the parent.

The Impact of High-Risk Children on the School System

Harris's law: The problems presented by learning-impaired students in schools are contagious and infect all members of the class.

Because the problematic behavior of these children is contagious, spreading through the classrooms of our public schools, the chaos caused by learning-impaired students infects everyone in the class; the teacher's control of the class erodes; the learning environment becomes a casualty. Classmates are exposed and also start to fall behind. As mentioned in the introduction, generally teachers are skilled enough to handle one child in a class who is not ready for school without shortchanging the whole class, but two or three such students require too much attention being taken from the rest of the class. With six to ten students typically not ready to learn, it is no wonder that teachers are forced to shortchange classes every day, every week, and every year, year after year.

The shortchanging of children in school certainly goes a long way toward explaining why Head Start cognitive gains, which were visible when children were four and five years old, washed out after the children had been in elementary school for a few years, as Westinghouse (1969) found in its major assessment of Head Start. It was the consequence of the consistent shortchanging of students in all grades when more than one or two children were not ready to participate fully because of a learning inability. Even those children who were ready to enter kindergarten were held back, day after day, by those apathetic or disruptive classmates who demanded too much time, were inattentive, or just could not learn at the normal speed of the class (Zigler and Valentine, 1979).

NOT-READY CHILDREN

It has been traditional in America that it is the responsibility of parents to bring up their children to be ready for school at age five. That task has been regarded as a civic responsibility. The implicit contract made between the school, the teacher, the parent, and the child is that the child will be ready for school and want to learn. Unfortunately, the school system cannot function when many parents have little capacity to prepare their children for school in large part because they are undereducated and living in poverty.

Poverty is obviously a handicap and a terribly stressful condition, but it is by no means the sole problem, nor is it always a problem. Some children without economic advantages will thrive nonetheless; some will have extremely good mothers and fathers, who bravely, against all odds, defeat poverty and give their children a good start. These children will be successful, whether the cause for their success is pure genetics, very good and brave parents, or luck. Some mothers who are unwed and live in poverty do, in fact, effectively nurture their children from birth onward and get them ready to learn. Some upper-income, two-parent families fail to nurture their infants in ways essential to their success. School readiness depends on an ongoing partnership between a child, her parents, and the school. It starts before pregnancy and clearly requires appropriate stimulation and nurturing after birth if the child is to succeed in the lifelong educational process. The child's needs encompass not only cognitive elements, but also physical, social, and emotional elements, all of which are prerequisites for being ready to learn. Since healthy early childhood development requires an involved, attentive, nurturing family, a program addressed at school readiness must seek to strengthen families: to help them do the best possible job of getting their children ready to learn from the time of their conception until formal schooling starts. Good educational outcomes depend on early attention to developmental needs.

Ten years ago the principal of DuSable High School in Chicago told me one day that the president of the student council was an able young man who wanted to attend the Illinois Institute of Technology (IIT) after graduation. Without telling the principal or the student, I took it upon myself to call the director of admissions at IIT and said I was interested in this young man and would be glad, if necessary, to supply a scholarship for him. I asked him to check into the application. He called me back a day or two later and said that he was disappointed to tell me that the young man, despite being president of the student council and generally regarded as a good student, in fact tested at the seventh-grade level, at least five grades below what IIT required for college admission. The director further said that had the student been only one or two grade levels behind, IIT would have been willing to let him make up the deficiency with tutoring, but because he was so far behind, there was no chance of this happening. This illustrates just what shortchanging means in an individual case.

Assume that 90 percent of children born to single parents will arrive in kindergarten not ready for school and that 10–11 percent of children born to married parents will arrive in kindergarten not ready for school. This would mean the following totals: In 1970, when 400,000 children were born out of wedlock, 360,000 were not ready for school in 1975; of 3.3 million children born to married parents, 340,000 were not ready for school in 1975. This meant that a total of 700,000 children were not ready for school in 1975. Assume that in addition a like number of their classmates (700,000) were seriously shortchanged by the schools. Then it should be no surprise that in 1988 an estimated 1.4 million children (37.5 percent of the cohort) failed in school. Their schooling was affected adversely in a major way by most of the 400,000 children born out of wedlock in 1970. Most children born to young, poorly educated, unmarried parents will be brought up in poverty and generally in an environment that is anything but conducive to later success in school or in life.

I estimate that in 1980, 600,000 children born to single parents were not ready for school in 1985; in that same year 300,000 children born to married parents were not ready for school. A total of 900,000 children, therefore, were not ready to enter school in 1985. Assuming that a like number of their classmates (900,000) were seriously shortchanged, in 1998, then, an estimated 1.8 million children (50 percent of the cohort) will fail in school, either by dropping out or by "graduating" function- ally illiterate.

About 1.05 million children born to single parents in 1990 were not ready for school in 1995; 300,000 children born to married parents were not ready for school in 1995. Thus, a total of 1.35 million children were not ready for school in 1995. Assuming that a like number of their class- mates (1.35 million) will have been seriously shortchanged in their schooling, a total of 2.7 million children (64.9 percent of the cohort) will turn eighteen functionally illiterate.[2]

If the trend of births to single parents and the high number of divorces continue (although the numbers could change as a result of causes we cannot foresee), it might mean not only that more than 1 million of the 1.2 million babies born to single parents in 1992 will fail in school, but that perhaps an additional number, as many as 1.4 million, will also fail. What is unthinkable is that 65 percent of all eighteen-year-olds in the United States may soon be functionally illiterate.

Our society does not begin to know how to help children whose par- ents do a totally inadequate job of nurturing and stimulating their child in the critical first days, months, and years of life before children go to school. The symptoms of impairments in children appear to teachers in the form of language delays, a low span of attention, hyperactivity, a propensity to violence, and various other learning disorders.

In 1994, the American College Testing (ACT) program, a broadly used measurement that is nationally normed, tested seniors in 5,400 high schools. Of the 64 Chicago high schools tested, 35 were in the bottom

54, which is the bottom 1 percent (Weele, 1994). *Shortchanging,* as a figure of speech, was not hyperbolic; it was true.[3]

Any proposed cure, even popular ones, will not work when the cause of the problem is misunderstood. City schools are infected with the contagion of too many problematic students who are unable to learn. The various cures proposed—firing the superintendent, getting rid of the school board, or blaming the bureaucrats—simply do not work.

A student's motivation to learn is, in fact, established or killed off in the first twenty-four months of an individual's life. Curiosity, an open mind, and the ability to trust and admire parents and teachers and get along with fellow students and teachers are things children either learn or do not learn before the age of two.

Suppose the problem occurred in business. Suppose that machine components purchased from outside sources have high rates of defects. Would changing the supervisor affect the quality of the component? Or getting rid of the labor union? Or is the solution to inspect incoming materials carefully and use only zero-defect components so that you can produce zero-defect assemblies?

Making the full circle, we need to be informed about the way the world really is rather than the way some people think it is. The world is not flat, it is round. I hope that people who set public policy will recognize that attention to the very early childhood development of our newborns is crucial to the survival of American society.

Poor Outcomes: Drop-out, Delinquency, "Unemployability"
More than a decade has passed since the Commission on Excellence in Education (1983), formed by Terrel Bell, secretary of education under President Ronald Reagan, published its report, *A Nation at Risk: The Imperative for Educational Reform.* Yet the United States remains "a nation at risk." In our big cities, in particular, far too many children grow up lacking the skills and knowledge needed to be productive in the workplace and informed in the voting booth. The picture of failure, drawn in statistical terms, looks like this: in many major cities, half of all poor and minority students routinely drop out of school with inadequate skills, few job prospects, and limited opportunities to improve their lot in life.

The outlook is not always brighter for children who remain in school until they graduate. The National Assessment of Education Programs (NAEP; USDE, 1994b) has reported that half of all seventeen-year-olds in the schools of major cities lack the necessary skills in reading, writing, mathematics, and problem solving even to get through the doors that might lead them to jobs in business, higher education, professional training, or government service.

Judging by U.S. Department of Education (1994b) statistics, almost three out of eight eighteen-year-olds, or 35 percent, can be described as functionally illiterate. It is no wonder we see so much unemployment and unemployability, that American business has difficulty competing in the world, and that in the last presidential election 45 percent of all Americans eligible to vote did not do so. Some states did much better than others: Maine, Minnesota, Montana, North Dakota, South Dakota, and Wisconsin all had better than a two-thirds voter turnout. Is it just a coincidence that these states have much better graduation rates and better educational systems than the other states in the union?

It is not only in the United States that many people, because of poor education, are being cut out of the employment field. This phenomenon is also going on to an important extent in Germany, France, Italy, the Latin countries, and throughout the world. In most industrialized countries, however, the problem is not as acute or as extensive as it is in the United States.

The modest gains that disadvantaged students have made on Scholastic Aptitude Tests since the 1970s and 1980s have still left them far short of where middle-class, nonminority students stand. According to NAEP, in 1990, while 48 percent of seventeen-year-old nonminority students still in school could read well enough to understand complex written information, this was true of only 20 percent of seventeen-year-old African-American students and 27 percent of Hispanics.

Socioeconomic Costs: The Cost of Intervention and the Cost of Failure
At an economic conference convened by Bill Clinton in Little Rock, Arkansas, when he was president elect, Bruce Ratner of New York spoke. As a partner of Forest City Enterprises in the Metrotech Project

in New York City, he made a telling point. He said that the economic costs of the disaster of poverty and hopelessness in the inner city are much greater than most people realize. Ratner's advised estimate of the costs of poverty in the Aid to Families with Dependent Children (AFDC) program, the welfare system, Medicaid (whose costs are fast escalating), the court system, prisons, probation officers, insurance premiums, and losses attributable to crime is more than $200 billion a year.

What Ratner did not include in his testimony was any computation of the cost to our school systems of having so many children start school not ready to learn. Later, as these children continue their education, not only do they cost the school system a huge amount of money in special education and counseling, they also make it impossible for the 65 percent of those students who could learn in school to do so effectively. The lost potential in life and work skills becomes expensive for society as a whole.

This discussion caused me to recollect that some fifteen years ago I had pondered the costs and benefits of prevention, and I recognized that, logically, before the government could be asked to spend money on prevention, any proposed program would have to be justified by its cost-effectiveness. To determine this one must compute the cost of successful intervention and what it costs when prevention is not achieved.

Multiplying the cost of a particular intervention by its success ratio gives an estimate of the cost of successful intervention. If the cost of intervention is $5,000 a year for one high-risk child for each of three years, for a total of $15,000, and if the success ratio is 50 percent, that means that for a cost of $30,000 you could prevent the failure of at least one high-risk child.

What *is* the cost when prevention is not achieved? How much does it cost society when one child fails socially and economically in life? Fifteen years ago, I estimated that some 600,000 children were being born each year at high risk and that 50 percent of them would end up in failed lives. What would be the cost, considering the expense to society of schools, courts, welfare, AFDC, and mental hospitals? For each failed child with a life span of thirty years, the cost, at $10,000 a year, would be $300,000. When I explained this reasoning to a number of professionals working with families living in poverty, most said they thought my reasoning was right but that my estimates were low, both with respect to the percentage of children who would fail if born at high risk and also with respect to the cost of failure. They felt that the cost would be higher than $10,000 a year and the time involved longer than thirty years.[4]

Today, I would revise the computations I made in 1980. Using the figure of 1.2 million babies now being born at high risk, I still estimate that half of them, or 600,000, will end up as social and educational failures. Moreover, the work I have done over the years indicates that the cost today for each failure exceeds $300,000; today I estimate $400,000 to be the minimum cost. Thus, the probable current cost of the annual disaster of failing to bring up children to be successful is $400,000 times 600,000 failed lives, or $240 billion.

Furthermore, even with good intervention the odds of a child succeeding are perhaps only one in three, not one in two, which increases the cost of saving one child to $45,000 versus my former estimate of $30,000. Nevertheless, if successful intervention costs $45,000 and saves $400,000, it is still the most profitable investment for our society to make, with a nine-to-one payback.

The costs of social and educational failures go beyond matters that can be calculated in economic terms. In fact, the failures threaten the survival of the United States as a broad-based democracy. This reality was stressed by Bill Clinton when he was governor of Arkansas and has been stressed anew by him as president. He has noted that for forty years we waved the banner of democracy in the world. Yet now, with Communism finally discredited in Europe, American democracy, ironically, is threatened by a breakdown from within. The cause for that threatened breakdown is the widening gap between high-income workers equipped by their education to function productively in the new technological order and the growing underclass of poorly educated workers, chained to menial low-paying jobs when they can find jobs at all.

The babies born in 1970 who turned eighteen in 1988 represented an important cohort for the future of our country. For 1.4 million of these young people the future did not look good. Their education was faulty. The consequences were that they had trouble getting jobs. Some did get jobs, but many did not. The jobs they were able to get did not pay well. For these 1.4 million undereducated teenagers, their future is bleak, living as they do in a high-tech society.

Fifty years earlier there were lots of jobs for young men and young women who had strong backs and willing hearts—willing to launch a career wherever the job was. In 1988, however, employers were competing in a tough market against companies based in Germany, Japan, Korea, Singapore, and Taiwan whose products were world-class, high quality, and inexpensive. To compete, American companies continuously had to seek out the most modern and the best technology and train their employees to perform new tasks on sophisticated and complicated equipment. This usually involved new training manuals and employees who could learn new jobs fast.

Unfortunately, these jobs required good reading skills, which meant good comprehension and the ability to work with numbers, often requiring a knowledge of algebra and calculus. In particular, jobs in quality control and other technical jobs (such as those that exist in the medical-care field, one of the few areas of increasing employment) called for these skills. Not all jobs require reading and numeracy skills, but the good-paying jobs, those jobs with a future, do. The 1.4 million eighteen-year-olds who graduated functionally illiterate or who dropped out before graduation missed the boat. Their future in the job market is not good. Some could study and work to get a general equivalency diploma (GED), but even that, it turns out, does not help much. James Heckman of the University of Chicago's School of Public Policy Studies published the results of his research (Cameron and Heckman, 1993), which showed that in the job market people with GED's were no more likely to get jobs than were drop-outs without a GED; those GED holders who did have jobs were not receiving more compensation than other drop-outs. This is indeed a bleak outlook.

Was the birth cohort of 1970 an aberration? How about those babies born in 1980? Were their future prospects better? Unfortunately, they were worse. The outlook for babies born in 1980 is that by 1998, not

37.5 percent, but 50 percent will be undereducated. Most of them will be unemployable or employable only in minimum wage jobs with few prospects for the future. Contemplate the year 2008, when more than 60 percent of all American children born in 1990 will turn eighteen undereducated for the world of work as it is today. Most will be unemployable or employable only in minimum-wage jobs with poor prospects for advancement. They will be competing in a global economy against better-educated youth in Asia and Europe.

No significant across-the-board improvements in education have occurred, despite the heavy financial investments that have been made with that end in view. In 1986, for example, as a nation we spent $264 billion in public and private funds for education from kindergarten through graduate school. That number grew to $418 billion in 1991, an increase of $154 billion in just five years, with no commensurate gain in educational excellence. In 1995 I estimate we will spend more than $500 billion, still with no evident gains.

BUSINESS: THE ABILITY TO COMPETE

There has been growing concern among Americans in business, such as those represented by the Committee for Economic Development (CED), about the ways in which the failure of public education threatens the capacity of American business to survive increasing world competition. They know that after the end of World War II, when the United States industrial plant—alone among five or six major industrial nations of the world—was intact, the pursuit of quality did not have to rank high among United States manufacturing objectives. The reconstruction needs overseas were so huge and the pent-up consumer demands at home were so great that buyers often scrambled to get whatever United States industry produced.

People in business have since learned, sometimes painfully, that uneven quality is no longer acceptable. Today more than twenty major trading countries effectively compete with the United States in American domestic as well as overseas markets. All have access to advanced technologies, and many technologies—such as those involved in steelmaking, electronics, shipbuilding, motor vehicles, camera eyes, and robots—have proved surprisingly easy to transfer. Quality and service now lie at the crux of global competitiveness. These in turn depend fundamentally on a public school system whose graduates bring to the changing world of work the qualities of literacy, self-discipline, and a respect for first-class work.

In today's high-tech world, where job requirements change about once every five years even for long-term employees, it is absolutely essential for people to be able to read new manuals and accommodate themselves to new technology. It is essential, that is, if they are going to stay employed by the same company. Unless short- and long-term employees can read and comprehend what they read, employers find it cost-effective to terminate and replace them with people who can learn new jobs with relative ease.

International tests periodically conducted by Michigan psychologist Harold Stevenson (Stevenson and Stigler, 1992, 30–51) continue to show that American public school students rank below those of our major international economic competitors in virtually all realms of achievement, but especially in math and science. When the Stevenson team recently tested hundreds of first- and fifth-grade students in five cities—Chicago, Minneapolis, Beijing, Taipei, and Sendai (Japan)—the disparities in achievement were marked. For example, only 2.2 percent of Beijing's first-grade students scored as low as Chicago's average students in math, and by the fifth grade, only 1.4 percent scored that low. Yet American mothers were more satisfied with their children's performances than were Chinese or Japanese mothers (ibid., 28–30).

The governors of various states, for their part, have learned firsthand that failures in public education can show up not only in a low level of competence among public employees, but they also can undercut plans for economic development. When governors, for example, try to induce a company to choose their respective states as the site for a new plant, the chief executive officers they contact—whether they are American, German, or Japanese—say they have only a secondary interest in the low taxes offered as an inducement. Their main interest is in the quality of present and future potential employees.

This is true for two compelling reasons. First, if they are going to build a plant that will last forty years, they want to know where the labor supply is coming from twenty and forty years from now. Second, with technology advancing throughout the world, they know they will need well-educated human resources now and in the future. Employers commonly expect that the average new employee who remains with a company will have to learn at least five new jobs over twenty-five years in order to stay abreast of changes in technology. The costs of retraining come high.[5] Yet even to participate in the changing technology employees must be able to read, write, and compute so that retraining can take place. No longer is that strong back and willing heart a guarantee of continued employment in a company that has to compete against the technology of Germany, Japan, and Korea.

As long as we have so many disadvantaged children entering our school systems, we will be unable to empower graduates to compete internationally with workers whose education and skills are superior. This will in turn adversely affect our standard of living and diminish our role in the world as a first-class power, and we will continue to deny too many of our children their birthrights to the best and healthiest opportunity to succeed.

CAN SOCIETY BE SALVAGED?
PUBLIC AND PRIVATE ACTION

American society is negatively marked by alcoholism, drug abuse, community violence, crime, and family dysfunction. There are other symptoms, symptoms that are equally, if not more, horrifying. We have all heard about them, from the front pages of newspapers and from our next-door neighbors: child abuse—physical, emotional, and sexual—as well as child neglect; infant morbidity; in the schools, general insubordination, a failure to learn to read, truancy, and drop-out; and teenage pregnancy. The list goes on: a failure to do homework, an inability to handle responsibilities in the home or in school, and an inability to be trained for a good, steady job—and consequently becoming a public charge and certainly unable to raise a healthy family or become a productive and satisfied member of society; bouts of depression, feelings of loneliness, uncontrollable bursts of anger, suicide; purse snatching, assault and battery, and homicide. Many researchers and social thinkers agree that these symptoms have a common cause.

Everyone has been alerted to our public school problems. Many people say we need more money. Politicians, people in business, and parents are all in the act to straighten out the quality problems of public education. Although this involvement is welcome, we must recognize that public school education will not be fixed by money alone. Despite huge expenditures already made, nobody is arguing that the problem has been fixed.

Many proposals have been made for quick-fix remedies to deal with our poor educational outcomes: Require high school students to work harder. Make core courses mandatory for all students, starting in junior high school. Deny automobile licenses to students who drop out of school. Deny welfare payments, as Wisconsin does, to parents whose children have more than two unexplained absences during a semester. Reorganize school boards, and give more power to local school councils. Abolish the existing public school system, and let educational decisions be made in the "free market," where parents will receive vouchers and be able to choose which schools their children attend. Have a corporation or local college adopt a public school. Although all such proposals are made in good faith, these strategies obscure the complexity of both the problem and the potential solution.

What are we to do? Our society really has only two choices. The first is the familiar strategy of doing nothing or as little as possible. This is the strategy that we as a nation have chosen for the past twenty-eight years, ever since we failed to heed the prophetic warnings of the Kerner Commission report (1968): "No American—white or black—can escape the consequences of the continuing social and economic decay of our major cities. Only a commitment to national action on an unprecedented scale can shape a future compatible with the historic ideals of American society." We are three decades into that future, one generation plus later, and we are paying the price for not having made a commitment. The outlook for a nation that cannot educate all its children as it enters the twenty-first century in a highly competitive world is indeed dismal.

The other choice is to confront the issue of preventing babies from being conceived and born to families that lack the resources to nurture and care for their children properly. This strategy entails encouraging adolescents both to postpone pregnancy until they are better able to cope with parenting and at the same time to develop their own potential so that they will have the economic income and parenting education needed to be better parents.

Prevention and Intervention

We must try much harder than we have to reduce drastically the number of unintended births to poorly educated women if we are to get a handle on the public school education problem in this country. We must train more teachers to work with infants and young children. As experienced teachers know, teaching a two-year-old or a three-year-old is different from teaching an eight-year-old.

The most cost-effective prevention would be adequate counseling, better contraception, and abortion when necessary. There the intervention success ratio is one for one, and the cost less than $400 versus $400,000, or a 1,000-to-1 payback. Having universal Head Start would help some, and we should have it immediately. In a nation that can spend $500 billion on education from kindergarten on, it is absurd to say that we cannot find the $8 billion needed for universal Head Start, including programs for children zero to three years old. We found the $100 billion to bail out the savings and loan industry. Our nation could survive without that industry, but it will not survive without fixing our educational system.

When Education Should Start

Sally Provence's work at Yale is relevant. She took seventeen low-income infants and for the first two and a half years of life gave each one everything she could in the way of appropriate stimulation through child development specialists, social workers, and pediatric care. All but one of those children (one who had a learning disability, probably since birth) later did well in school. In fact, their school attendance record was above average. Ten years later, only two of the mothers were not self-supporting (Provence and Naylor, 1983, 8–25, 144–46; Seitz and Apfel, 1994).

HEAD START IS NOT ENOUGH: DROP-OUT BEGINS IN THE CRADLE

Head Start was and continues to be a good idea, and it merits the kind of support that President Clinton sought in his request for additional funds. It was our country's first attempt to prevent the stunted physical, cognitive, psychological, and social growth that so often plagues the children of poverty. The long-range results in the main have been positive: measurably fewer school drop-outs, fewer later arrests, fewer teen pregnancies, and more employment. To its credit, Head Start has probably prevented the rate of failure from being worse. This is a significant achievement, but it is not the decisive solution to the problems of failure in school.

A great deal of the literature on educational outcomes is based on the Perry Preschool Project, an extremely good program somewhat better Head Start and carried out in Ypsilanti, Michigan. The wealth of such research in child development published since Head Start began indicates that children develop a significant portion of their cognitive skills before they become eligible for traditional Head Start at age three or four. Child development experts now agree that the period before three years of age is a singular and extremely important time for the baby. The weeks and months of early growth, understanding, and reasoning can never be brought back and be done over again. It is not a rehearsal. It is the main show.

In view of that reality, 97 percent of Head Start, as now constituted, may be another example of what is too little and too late. The first year of life is the time of greatest growth of the brain itself. Hence, the new research indicates that the concept of Head Start must be extended backward to the earliest days, weeks, and months of a child's life. That approach in turn shifts the focus back to the family as the primary source of influence and socialization. The most successful models of early childhood development programs introduced twenty years ago, such as those carried out by Sally Provence at Yale and the Family

Development Research Program in Syracuse, started in the first year of life and included a strong component of family participation, where, in a relatively benign environment, parents had a chance to learn more about their children's development and how they could help them. In May of 1995 President Clinton signed the Head Start reauthorization bill, carving out 3 percent of the first year's budget for programs for children ages zero to three. In 1996 that number moved to 4 percent, and in 1998 it goes to 5 percent.

> If we could first know where we are and whither we are tending, we could better judge what to do and how to do it.
> —Abraham Lincoln, 17 June 1858

The words with which Abraham Lincoln began his House Divided speech serve to introduce the task I have set myself. Against the background of the education and job-training aspects of President Clinton's plan for the renewal of the American economy, I want to do three related things: First, assess where we now stand after a decade of debate and experimentation regarding ways to improve American public schools. Second, note what scientific research has brought to light about the process of child development since Head Start was initiated in 1965. Third, propose what must be done at a very early hour in getting children ready to learn if the hopes for the future that depend on improvements in American public schools are to be fulfilled.

Programs that attempt to improve radically children's health, education, and overall their well-being must start as early as the prenatal period. Still, we must be realists. These programs are difficult and costly to implement. They must be done and done right, and they will require many, many trained people. At the present time there is an enormous shortage of well-trained public health nurses, social workers, and early childhood development specialists. Part of this shortage results from low salary scales because we do not value early education. We pay teachers in child care and preschool much less than we pay janitors.

My argument is simple. Until we recognize where the problem is—child development long before age five—we will continue to see schools fail.

2

SUCCESSFUL INTERVENTION
AND ITS LIMITS

THE WAR ON POVERTY, 1965–1995

IN 1965 THOSE INVOLVED in President Lyndon Johnson's War on Poverty recognized the critical importance of getting children ready to learn before they entered kindergarten. The original intention was to have the program cover at least all three- and four-year-olds, but the funding was always below what would have been adequate to cover all eligible children. In 1990–92, because of raised but continuing limits imposed on funding, the $2.2 billion allotted in 1992 for the Head Start program was able to reach only 80 percent of eligible four-year-olds and only a tiny percentage of eligible three-year-olds.

To most Americans, babies and early childhood development are of minor interest in the total scheme of things. The problems of contraception and the availability of abortion for poor women are seen by most people as specialized problems, of interest to only a few reproductive rights radicals. The $500 billion we spend annually on education in this country for children and youth ages five to twenty-five; the economic and social costs of crime, violence, and prisons; and the huge costs, both economic and social, of our welfare system are almost never considered as closely related to public policies on babies, contraception, and abortion. They *are* closely related, and our ability to compete internationally in business, our standard of living, and economic costs exceeding $1 trillion a year are involved—surely enough to make these issues important public policy matters.

In the first half of this century, this nation's population doubled, from 76 million in 1900 to 152 million in 1950, which is a huge increase. Now, just forty-six years later, we have added still another 110 million people. These monumental increases in population, particularly in our metropolitan centers, have profoundly changed the way we live as individuals as well as the way we function collectively in the larger society.

Our public policies obviously have not kept pace with the increasing complications we face. We must continually rethink many of our premises and, when necessary, restructure our organizations and redirect our efforts to respond to the needs of today and tomorrow. Listening to a speech by Robert Fogel, the 1993 Economics Nobel Laureate, I was astonished to be reminded that in the year 1700, life expectancy in what is now the United States was only thirty years. By 1900, that number had increased to forty-five years. Now, life expectancy is at least seventy-six. Imagine that. In the brief period of three centuries the life span in the United States has increased by a factor of more than two and a half times. A changing world and new conditions require changing social arrangements.

One continuing problem that confronts policymakers has been that most important decisions are made by people who have been out of school for at least twenty-five years. Many of their beliefs were developed during their university years. Their fund of knowledge, which might have seemed correct twenty-five or more years ago, might not be factual today. This is not to say that all knowledge changes every twenty-five years, but some things do change. One of these major changes is our new and increasing knowledge about early childhood development. Another is the impact on child development when suddenly more than half of all mothers of one-year-olds are in the work force and out of the home.

There is no way that we know of to substitute state care for the healthy nurturing, love, and special interest a parent or close relative brings to a child. Every state in the United States has an agency that tries to cope with the most obviously bad cases of child abuse and neglect. None of the states does it well. Ours is a society in which most parents do a good job of raising their children. If only an occasional child needs a lot of help and the family cannot provide that help, our society is organized well enough to meet the need. The fact is, however, that today our social safety net is overwhelmed, and we do not begin to have the human resources or coordinated facilities to handle all the problem children that are currently being born in the United States.

In tiny experimental programs our child development experts have learned to help children in need. A major program in Prince Georges County, Maryland (at the Mental Health Study Center of the National Institute of Mental Health), worked for four years with forty-seven children born at high risk to mothers who had failed abysmally with their first child. It was clear that without intervention at least two thirds of those children would not make it. With skilled, intensive work, however, the vast majority of these children were put on a path toward mental health and success in school (Greenspan et al., 1987).

When the home environment in our country was characterized by strong families vitally interested in educating their children, the traditional public school of two generations ago did reasonably well in teaching basic and advanced academic skills. Typically, children came from two-parent families where the mother worked in the home. The student population was relatively uniform in the level of preparation for schooling, and children's lives for the most part were stable and secure. Parents respected their part in the tacit social contract with schools. They had their children ready to learn when they entered kindergarten. What is more, parents, teachers, and the community at large had high expectations for children and tended to hold them to high standards of achievement, and most people concerned themselves with all the children—their neighbors' as well as their own.

Public schools today, however, function in an environment that is radically different from traditional schools of forty years ago. In major U.S. cities, many of the children who enter kindergarten are born and reared in financial poverty. Even more important, they are born into a deprived environment, one that lacks necessary positive nurturing and stimulation. The pattern of their lives is chaotic, and the children suffer a multitude of debilitating health, emotional, social, and cognitive problems. Their parents, many of whom are themselves school drop-outs, feel alienated from the school system, and their expectations are that their children will not succeed. If you look critically at the failure in our educational system, then, you must conclude that the child's failure and the schools' failure are largely determined before the child enters kindergarten.

The results of a study by Lucile Newman of Brown University and Stephen Buka of Harvard's School of Public Health were published in 1991. The authors found that before reaching kindergarten, 12 percent of American children were already learning impaired owing to seven preventable causes: maternal alcohol abuse, child abuse and neglect, maternal drug abuse, lead poisoning, low birthweight, malnutrition, and smoking during pregnancy. The authors observed that although there were other causes of impedance to brain development, these seven preventable causes accounted for an average of three of every twenty-five babies in the United States being learning impaired by school age. The signs of limitations in children appear to teachers in the form of dyslexia, hyperactivity, low attention span, and other learning disorders, as well as hearing and vision impairments and a propensity for violence. The average number of three children in twenty-five being learning impaired is not uniformly true. In the healthiest populations, for example, in magnet schools or affluent suburbs, kindergartners who are not ready may constitute one or none out of twenty-five children. In the inner city and some rural schools it is not uncommon for six to eight students in classrooms of twenty-five children to be learning impaired. Such a high proportion of learning-impaired children appreciably affects those children in the class who *are* ready to learn, too often distracting the teacher's attention from the more ready students.

The extent of America's problem with school readiness was confirmed nationally in the 1991 formal report prepared under the direction of Ernest Boyer of the Carnegie Foundation for the Advancement of Teaching, *Ready to Learn: A Mandate for the Nation* (1991). That report, based on a survey of seven thousand kindergarten teachers nationally, indicated that 35 percent of the children in the United States were not ready for school when they entered kindergarten.

In the fall of 1985, Governor James Thompson settled a pending teachers' strike in Chicago by agreeing to the terms of a new contract that provided for salary increases. When the state legislature granted the necessary additional funds, it was on condition that the board of education of Chicago be held accountable for the results of its school system. Beginning in 1986, Chicago was required to use the nationally normed ACT test to evaluate its high school students.

Typically in Chicago between 30 and 65 percent of the senior classes take the test annually.[1] Of those who take the test, the scores are decidedly poor. ACT accepts scores as credible when at least forty students in a high school take the test. The ACT scores confirmed the exceedingly poor results found by Designs for Change in its 1984 report.

In 1987, the second year of testing, 33 of 58 Chicago high schools taking the test scored in the lowest one percentile of the ACT universe. In 1989, of 64 schools tested 31 schools fell in the lowest one percentile.

As Designs for Change found in 1984, for every one thousand first-year students who entered these high schools, approximately 40 percent remained in school to graduate. On average, only twenty-four students, or 6 percent of those graduating, could read at the twelfth-grade level. Today, without a good high school education, it is notably difficult to qualify for advanced training, which is required in today's market for any job that pays a living wage.

Imagine trying to teach a class where more than half the students are going to fail the course. In 1986 the *Chicago Tribune* published a report by the Chicago board of education that stated that in Chicago's worst fifty-eight high schools more than 50 percent of the class failed two or more courses each year. In two Chicago high schools the rate was 75 percent.

Another, more recent, illustration is the story of twin girls in Chicago that was reported by the *Chicago Tribune* (6 September 1995). These twins attended Chicago's public elementary schools, and later they attended Orr High School. "Homework was simple and rarely assigned, but they did it religiously."They were both honor students. Upon graduating they applied to Malcolm x College. Much to their chagrin, they failed the entrance examination.They could not read beyond the sixth-grade level; they could not read well enough to distinguish written opinion from fact; they could not read to understand the meaning of such words as *inaccessible* and *realize;* and they lacked enough basic math to get a job that required the quick tabulation of several three-digit numbers.

The story of these students is "all the more grievous in that Malcolm x is one of seven City Colleges of Chicago ... known for lenient admission requirements." It has traditionally served as a training ground for students aspiring to transfer to four-year universities. The experience is not unique. It is merely the most recent to have been reported in the press.

Parents and their communities feel powerless to improve their children's educational chances. It is not possible for traditional public schools to educate an incoming tidal wave of so many neglected children, who, in addition to impairment symptoms, low attention spans, hyperactivity, and hearing and visual problems, have few or no expectations for success in school.

For children who are unable to learn at the pace for which most parents have prepared their children when they come to kindergarten or first grade, what will their educational results be as eighteen-year-olds whose learning has been slowed because of classmates who are much slower learners? In 1970 in the United States 3.7 million children were born. In the normal course of events, these children would have started kindergarten in 1975 or 1976, graduated from elementary school in about 1984, and finished high school in 1988. Many did, but many did not. In June 1988, alluding to the cohort of babies born in 1970, Ann McLaughlin, the secretary of labor under Ronald Reagan, gave a speech in which she pointed out that 700,000 children would "graduate from high school unable to read their diplomas. An additional 700,000 [would] not graduate, having dropped out earlier."When you add those two numbers together, you get 1.4 million individuals. Another way to say this is that in 1988, 37.5 percent of all 3.7 million eighteen-year-olds in this country could be described as functionally illiterate.

Most existing school-based strategies designed to bring these children up to par through intervention programs often come too late and have the difficult mission of trying to help many children deprived from birth of the emotional, physical, and moral support that a stable, nurturing family normally provides a child.

EARLY CHILDHOOD DEVELOPMENT

Outcomes depend on early attention to developmental needs. If the problem were that Americans were too short, and you wanted to increase the height of children, I doubt that anyone would seriously think we should spend a lot of money to improve the eating habits of sixteen-year-olds in order to try to increase their height. Common sense tells you that most of a child's growth has already occurred before the age of sixteen. In fact, most of us have attained one half our mature height by the time we are two and a half years old. That is surprising but true. If you are six feet tall now, you were already three feet tall when you were two and a half. So, if you really want to increase a person's height, the most effective time to improve her nutrition and health is from the time of conception until age two and a half. That is when the growth is greatest, and it is also the critical period for getting children ready to learn. This critical period of development—and particularly brain development—is the link to children's later school performance. There is a need for a fundamental shift in our nation's educational philosophy.

The United States has become a great country by being practical and by solving problems. To solve our educational problems we must go way back to the very earliest days of life. That is when education really starts. That is when brain architecture, intelligence, learning ability, and the motivation to be curious are shaped. Our public schools also need to be ready for children. No doubt school reform and more money can improve public schools, but they cannot help children before their second birthday. Unfortunately, that is the time of their development that is most crucial to later school success.

Not-Ready Children and Shortchanging

It is absolutely clear that in order to accomplish the goal of having all American children ready for school at age five, we must change the circumstances under which pregnancies occur and children in utero are cared for. If we are to get all children of five ready for school, we must pay much more attention to high-risk babies. We must radically change the prospects for proper nurturing and loving care to occur as a matter of course, and for the appropriate stimulation and consistent care each baby must receive in the first two years of life, when the child's brain is being developed. Fortunately, most babies are wanted, most are well nurtured, and most are ready for school by age five. Although many suburban schools do quite well in the job of educating, big-city public schools and some suburban and rural schools are plagued by the students who are not ready.

We now spend vast sums of money every year to educate children from age five through graduate school, but we fail to do enough for children early enough to make a lasting difference in their later lives. Too little, too late seems to be the golden rule for American education. Unless we recognize that the problem is in school readiness, in the development of children long before they enter kindergarten, we will continue to see schools fail. If a child appears in school at age five apathetic and unable to learn with the rest of the class; disruptive and prone to violence; or suffering from a severe learning disability, the teacher cannot be expected to perform miracles.

Zero to Three

At Stanford University Dr. Ruth Gross (1990) reported on a carefully designed study of premature children born at low birthweight (funded by the Robert Wood Johnson Foundation). Stanford supervised eight programs conducted by eight different medical schools. Each identified 135 low-birthweight babies, of whom, at random, 45 were put into an experimental group and 90 were left as controls.

The treatment for the experimental group was weekly home visiting for the first twelve months, followed by nursery school five days a week in the second and third years, with a ratio of four children for each teacher, and bimonthly parent support group meetings. Obviously, this resulted in considerably more stimulation and parental support than the children would normally have had. The results were gratifying. For the sample of children born weighing between 4.4 and 5.5 pounds, the mean gain in IQ was 13.2 at the age of three, enough to move many of those children from being rated as retarded to normal.

In the children born weighing less than 4.4 pounds, the results were only half as good, but nonetheless they were positive. Those programs, if expanded, would not only be expensive, they would also require a huge increase in trained and talented individuals in order to provide the therapy involved. (In Illinois, for example, nearly eighteen thousand low-birthweight babies are born each year.)

There are some important questions to be asked: Do the children in child care programs for working parents also need education? Do children in Head Start and state pre-kindergarten education programs also need child care? What do all programs need in order to provide comprehensive high-quality care? Perhaps the answer lies in the concept of *Educare*. Introduced by Bettye Caldwell, professor of pediatrics at the University of Arkansas School for Medical Sciences, Educare refers to comprehensive child care that involves three components: family-based social services, education, and health. You cannot truly educate children unless you care for them; you cannot care for them without meeting their needs for intellectual stimulation; and they cannot learn if they are not healthy.

An experiment that was initiated by Caldwell and Julius Richmond and executed by Ronald Lally at the Syracuse University Family Development Research Program (1987) involved eighty children, all of whom were poor. Between 1969 and 1975, using well-trained, competent staff, they offered comprehensive services to 108 low-income families with healthy children between the ages of six months and five years. (As the research continued, 28 families dropped out.) The central goal was "the support of child and familial behaviors that sustained growth and development after intervention ceases." By age five, the children in the experimental program—both boys and girls—showed statistically meaningful gains in their cognitive functioning when compared with the eighty control children. Neither social nor emotional gains were measured, because they were too complicated to gauge. After age five, the eighty program children, all of whom were clearly ready for kindergarten, were scattered among numerous public schools close to where they lived and not concentrated in any particular school. This meant that the children constituted less than 10 percent of the classes in which they were placed.

From the longitudinal study undertaken when the Syracuse children were fifteen years old, it was clear that the program girls retained their superior records, but the program boys did not. Lally concluded that for the program boys, the peer pressure from their classmates had militated against their continuing to do well cognitively.

At age fifteen the principal measurable difference for the program boys was in their functioning in society. Of the sixty-five experimental program children who could be found ten years later, only four had been placed under the supervision of the probation department. Of fifty-four control children located, twelve, or 22 percent, compared with 6 percent of the program children, had been placed on probation. This result translated to an estimated cost to society for court processing, probation services, supervision, and detention of $186 per child in the program group compared with an estimated $1,985 per child in the control group, or more than ten times as much.

Not only did the incidence of juvenile delinquency in the control group far exceed that of the program group, so did the severity of the offenses. The four program children on probation were mainly described as ungovernable, while the offenses charged to the control group were more serious: second-offense burglary, second-offense assault, robbery, attempted assault, sexual abuse, criminal mischief, violation of probation, and petty larceny. In other words, the difference was not only a tenfold higher cost in dollars to the probation system, but a clear warning of much heavier costs to come from later prison sentences. The current average cost of imprisonment for juveniles is reported to be $30,080 a year in Illinois.

PRENATAL NURTURING

The health of unplanned and unwanted children, especially of those born to mothers who began their childbearing unexpectedly as unwed teens, is often adversely affected by the failure of the mother to nourish herself properly during pregnancy. Many babies suffer brain damage in utero owing to the mother's addiction during pregnancy to drugs, alcohol, or smoking, and sometimes the mother has multiple addictions. Because health and educability are intertwined, brain damage and developmental delays can create serious educational problems for the baby even before she is born. After she is born, often the life that awaits the baby is one that is dominated not merely by the grind of poverty, but by neglect, physical abuse, humiliation, and exposure to a violent environment in the home, on the streets, in the playground, and in the neighborhood schools.

In Chicago, for example, of the fifty-nine children in 1992 who were killed by gunfire or were burned, beaten, or stabbed to death, thirty-one were under the age of four. At the same time, police made ten thousand arrests for serious crimes in or near schools, including the possession of guns, lethal knives, and ice picks. Nationally, in the years between 1987 and 1991, the number of murder arrests of children seventeen years old or younger who killed other children or adults increased by 85 percent— from 1,226 to 2,476. In this kind of environment, the attention required for learning comes in second best in a contest with environmental insults: witnessing the beating of a mother, the sight of a relative being shot, the shattered head of a friend killed by a bullet, the invasion of police cars and ambulances and their sirens, and later the funeral cortege.

Thus, children at risk face numerous problems that defy simple solutions. Even very good programs, such as Head Start, are no panacea. Yet we must offer new program initiatives based on the child development research of the past twenty years if we are to succeed in preparing children for school.

These realities lay behind what the Committee for Economic Development stated in its 1987 report, *Children in Need*:

Learning is a cumulative process that begins at birth. The educational problems of disadvantaged children are especially obvious long before they begin formal education. It is less costly to society and to individuals to prevent early failure through its efforts directed toward parents and children alike from prenatal care through age five. Such efforts should include:

• Prenatal and postnatal care for pregnant teens and other high-risk mothers and follow-up health care and developmental screening for their infants.

• Parenting education for both mothers and fathers, family health care, and nutritional guidance.

• Quality child care arrangements for poor working parents that stress social development and readiness.

• Quality preschool programs for all disadvantaged three- and four-year-olds.

A few model programs are already in place to reduce the number of dysfunctional families (see list of agencies, appendix A). In addition to providing basic information on child development, they offer activities for positive parent-and-child interaction and for opportunities for parents to share concerns. They assist with the daily living problems families experience and help link them with other community services they may need—health care and special services for children, food and clothes, job training, and employment services—in the same way that churches, extended families, and communities once did. Resource programs help build the self-confidence young families need to manage their lives and rear their children.

There are great truths in the following quotation from the preface of *Responsible Parenthood,* a book by Gilbert W. Kliman and Albert Rosenfeld:

> The book became emphatically addressed not only to parents and would-be parents, but also to nonparents. It makes a real difference to you whether my child turns out to be, say, a dedicated teacher or a narcotics peddler. If my child is retarded or delinquent, you—without having any vote in the matter—help foot the bill or could be one of his or her victims. All children are everyone's children, or should be; and all adults, in addition to being specific rearers of their own biological offspring (or those they choose to adopt), are in a real sense surrogate parents for all children.

CHILD CARE

Most mothers, when they select a child care setting, wonder, "Where will my baby be safe so that I will not have to worry?" Most mothers are unaware that these early weeks and months are vital to the baby's brain development. The building blocks of educability are being put in place. For the baby to be safe is of course essential, but the baby's early learning to trust, to feel loved, to be encouraged to explore, to be read to, to become curious and learn, to be able to work well later with a teacher, and to get along with other children in a classroom—all vital elements of child development—are adversely affected by inadequate day care and by insensitive caregivers.

In spite of widespread public concern about the integrity of many day care providers, the training requirements for day care workers are minimal in most states. In Arkansas, for example, caregivers at a center serving infants and toddlers are required to have only a high school diploma and thirteen hours of staff development each year. Individuals who provide family day care in their homes are not required to have a high school diploma, and the requirement for in-service training is only six hours.

There is such a thing as good child care, but it is expensive and rarely available. For infants and toddlers, good child care requires one teacher for every three or four children. The teacher must be talented and well trained. Child care at a price of $60 a week for each child produces an annual fee of $3,000, which works out to an income of about $10,000 a year for the caregiver (assuming an average of three and one third children in care). Head Start pays about $11,000 a year for a teacher. Such salaries are totally inadequate to attract and keep good people in the profession. A minimal budget for an Educare provider who is a qualified teacher should include a $20,000 annual salary, plus $4,000 for insurance and rent, for a total of $24,000.

If there are four children in care, then the annual cost for a provider (based on an annual salary of $24,000) would be $6,000, or $120 a week. If a mother is earning $8 an hour, or $320 a week before Social Security deductions, insurance, and transportation costs, it is unlikely that she can pay $120 a week for Educare for her young child. She will seek care that costs less. Given this scenario, it is no wonder that there is a high turnover of teachers and that the day care field is characterized by people who have inadequate training. Yet what infants and toddlers need most is consistent, qualified caregivers.

Existing child care certainly shortchanges helpless children. Unfortunately, we still tend to think of day care primarily in terms of the benefit for the mother: its principal purpose is to allow the mother to be in the work force. There is much too little concern for the child's development and education. Simple babysitting or custodial group care does not primarily concern itself with the vitally important tasks that every child faces as she strives for optimal development. Children put on hold for five to ten hours a day, five days a week, risk serious impairment of their potential brain development, their emotional development, and their social development. The child's development in these very early years is vital to her later education and ability to learn.

HOW EARLY IS TOO LATE?
THE ROLE OF HEALTHY BRAIN DEVELOPMENT

A great deal has been learned by scientists in the past five years about brain development in the fetal period and in the first two years of life (Kotulak, 1993). Four months into pregnancy, infants already have in their brains the 100 billion neurons allotted for their lifetimes. That is all they will ever get. From that point the wiring of brain cells is in constant development, and growth proceeds rapidly. In a healthy mother, the baby's brain develops particularly fast in the last five months of pregnancy, and in the first two years of life, its 100 billion neurons form trillions of connections, joining together in dendritic chains and synapses. In writing this book, I am working with the neurons that were given to me more than eighty-five years ago—an awesome thought.

Very Early Brain Development

Over the past few years, it seems that at least once every six months there is news of more knowledge about how the brain develops. I knew a full-term baby at birth can see, can hear, and has other capacities, but I had never given any thought about what a baby's capabilities are when that baby is born two months premature, weighing only two pounds. Heidelise Als (1994), working in Boston at Harvard University, recently did a study involving only babies who were born weighing less than two and a half pounds. Of the thirty-eight babies she chose for her experiment, the average weight was actually less than two pounds. The following information is from her report:

Objective: To investigate the effectiveness of individualized developmental care in reducing medical and neurodevelopmental sequelae for very low-birthweight infants

Design: Randomized controlled trial

Setting: Newborn intensive care unit

Patients: Thirty-eight singleton preterm infants, free of known congenital abnormalities, weighing less than 1250 g, born before 30 weeks' gestation, mechanically ventilated within 3 hours of delivery and for more than 24 hours in the first 48 hours, randomly assigned to a control or an experimental group.

Intervention: Caregiving by nurses specifically trained in individualized developmental care; observation and documentation of the infants' behavior within 12 hours of admission, and subsequently every 10th day; developmental care recommendations and ongoing clinical support for the nurses and parents based on regular observation of the infant by developmental specialists; and the availability of special caregiving accessories.

Als and her nurses were able to reduce the number of days spent in the nursery from 151 days to 87 days. She cut costs from $189,000 to $88,000, a savings of $91,000 for each infant. Als' method achieved better results than did the routine training of Harvard Medical School physicians and nurses at Brigham and Women's Hospital in Boston. The report states, "The infants in the experimental group appeared significantly more well-organized, well-differentiated, and well-modulated than the infants in the control group" (p. 857).

This experiment proved the point that brain architecture is well developed before birth. After birth, the rapid pace continues. In the first two hours of life, memories of a mother's voice and smell develop in the infant's brain. Sight develops rapidly; so do hearing, smell, and the tactile senses. Over a period of several days University of California researcher Michael Leon experimented on forty newborn infants. For ten of the babies, his control group, he did nothing on day one. For another ten of the forty babies he stood at the back of the crib and, in front of each baby's nose, held a cotton swab that had been dipped in orange juice concentrate. That was all he did; he held it ten centimeters from the baby's nose for ten seconds. He did that ten different times and then removed the cotton swab. For the third cohort of ten babies, after each cotton-swab presentation, he rubbed the baby's arm. For the fourth cohort, he presented the cotton swab and simultaneously rubbed their arms, the same simultaneous olfactory and tactile stimulation Leon had seen was effective with monkeys. On day two all forty babies, asleep or awake, were presented again with the orange-soaked cotton swab. Leon got no reaction from thirty of the babies, but from the ten who had had the concurrent touch and smell stimulation, the reactions went off the charts. Their arms and legs flailed, reflecting, apparently, their pleasure at remembering the fragrance of the orange odor.

Of course, when a mother nurses her baby at the breast there is a great deal of concurrent olfactory and tactile stimulation, and it is without doubt a wonderful way of appropriately stimulating an infant. There is no doubt that very early stimulation is extraordinarily important in mammals generally. If the brain's neurons and synapses are not developed early, nature sloughs them away. Use it or lose it.

This is the time when talking to a baby in loving tones is so important. Parents must cuddle their baby and understand the cues the baby gives about distress, wanting to eat, wanting to be cleaned up after soiling a diaper, and wanting to be held and comforted by words of reassurance. The importance of maternal instincts, affirmed by scientific findings, is that the baby who is loved is the baby who learns to trust and who can learn many things quickly. He learns how to make purposeful and indicative sounds and to exchange cooing with the mother while being diapered, held close, and played with.

In this connection, T. Berry Brazelton of the Children's Hospital Medical Center in Boston says he can tell at eight months of age whether a baby can be expected to succeed or fail later in life just by watching the way the baby approaches a task. The observation involves offering two blocks to a seated eight-month-old and demonstrating that he is to place the two blocks together. The baby, who is accustomed to the approval and encouragement of the adults around him, shows signs that he expects to succeed and in fact does so by placing the two blocks together. The baby who has an untreated learning disability or who comes from an environment too chaotic or too hopeless to reinforce in him a feeling of success, will not only demonstrate an expectation of failure, but will fail the block test by pushing the blocks past each other.

Recent scientific discoveries, then, point to the importance of healthy pregnancies and the need for appropriate nurturing and stimulation during the first two years of a child's life in order to optimize the development of the brain architecture that serves us all our lives. Increasingly it is recognized that in the brain early memories are the fundamental building blocks of curiosity, motivation, logic, understanding of right versus wrong, empathy, socialization, and self-esteem. All are at least partially developed by age two. We know that during the second year of life, let us say from twelve months to twenty-four months, toddlers are learning how to communicate in an organized way, using complex gestures. They are also learning how to read the gestures of others so that they can figure out whether they are being respected, approved of, threatened, and so on.

If babies receive the nurturing and care they need during these critical first two years, they will be off to a good start. They will face many formidable barriers later in life, especially if they are poor, but if they get optimal nurturing at the earliest stages, they will face those challenges well equipped to strive, learn, and succeed. Unfortunately, the converse is also true. If babies do not get the care and nurturing they need from the fetal period through age two, they are starting out at a tremendous disadvantage. A lack of consistent nurturing can have devastating effects, ones that are difficult to change after two years of age without expensive and skillful intervention.

Developmental Delays

From the earliest moments, a baby must learn that the world is friendly and dependable and that people can be trusted. A depressed mother or a mother who is highly stressed is probably at a severe disadvantage in conveying these crucial messages of safety and trust. This is especially true if she is basically alone, with no one consistently available to help with the constant needs of a baby. Although it is true that in many cases family members pitch in to help, it is likely that a poor, single mother—especially a teen mother—who starts off with low self-esteem, lacks financial security, and has few people to trust, may find it difficult to teach the baby through consistent caring and interaction that the baby is safe and loved and will be taken care of. Babies who are not talked to and held do not learn to trust, do not become socialized, and do not learn empathy and affection. Sadly, the absence of positive lessons can be just as damaging as negative lessons.

Permanent brain damage or learning impairment can occur long before a baby's second birthday. It is true that the brain cells have plasticity, especially early on. Although some plasticity remains, after two years of age adverse developmental structures that are already in place may last a lifetime. Although preventable, this type of brain damage is difficult to reverse.

Are the experts saying that the future of children is determined at birth? Is it all over for these children as soon as they are born? How can we write off a whole generation? These questions are often asked. My answer is that we should do as much as we can to help all children born into high-risk environments, that is, those children that we can make meaningful contact with. We *must* try to help them. Still, reality is reality. Most children born into high-risk environments will get too little help too late.

It is my feeling that poor public education, the roots of violence and crime, and high socioeconomic costs clearly all flow from our failure to recognize the importance of very early childhood development. The situation reminds me of a medical dilemma I once read about. In the nineteenth century, when the British surgeon Baron Lister came along,

English hospitals were experiencing frightening levels of infection followed by death. It was much safer for a pregnant mother to take a chance and stay at home than go to a hospital because of the high risk of getting infected and dying in the hospital. Most physicians then believed that poison was in the structures of these hospitals, sort of a Legionnaire's disease. The solution they seriously proposed was to destroy the infected hospitals and build new hospitals in different places. Lister said that was nonsense. He said that it was the doctors, who, because of their habit of not washing their hands (rubber gloves did not yet exist), were actually transporting bacteria from a sick patient to a well patient. The patient was thus being contaminated by the doctor with the infection of the last patient the doctor saw. If Lister had not then and there discovered antisepsis and convinced other doctors of its importance, the United Kingdom would have had a lot of new hospitals, but the proposed cure would not have worked.

We used to think that intervention programs could reverse or make up for early developmental delays, and to some extent such programs are able to do that. Yet for many, many children three years old is too late to start.

I once told Dr. Brazelton that I had made a claim that he could examine a newborn baby for fifteen minutes, talk to the baby's mother for fifteen minutes to assess her interest in and capacity for nurturing her baby, and then predict, with a 90 percent chance of being correct, whether that child would graduate from high school eighteen years later. His response was, "Of course I could do that. *You* could do that, easily." The next day I asked Dr. Stanley Greenspan, who has studied infants and young children intensively, the same question. Could he predict a child's outcome with some confidence? He had exactly the same response: "Of course I could do that. *You* could do that." I do not know whether the prediction certainty would be 90 percent, but I bet it would be close.

Stanley Greenspan is clearly disturbed by how important the feelings of humiliation are in poor populations. They keenly feel any lack of respect. That feeling of being insulted can be traced to insufficiently developed patterns of communication during the toddler phase. The word *diss,* a shortened version of *disrespect,* is a key part of the vocabulary in some parts of the inner city. If an individual believes he has been "dissed," it can sometimes lead to murder. Psychiatrists who have studied this phenomenon are convinced that the distortion caused by misunderstanding other people's intentions often stems from preverbal levels. In the critical phase between fifteen months and thirty months of age, the child's transition from acting out feelings and frustrations to putting those feelings and frustrations into ideas normally occurs. When a two-year-old is obviously angry and starts kicking and screaming "Mommy, Mommy," she should say, "Honey, I know you are angry. Can you tell me why you are angry? What do you want me to do?" If the child just kicks and perhaps is also hit as punishment, he will fail to learn that his anger has a cause and can usually be remediated once the anger and its cause have been named and communicated. This transition is often missing in our high-risk populations, where understanding fails to develop both between children and their parents and in the family communication pattern.

There are those of us who believe that very early experiences are of vital importance to an individual's development. When we try to convince others of the importance of these years, one of the hurdles we face is our inability to portray convincing case histories that penetrate the consciousness of the audience. It is not difficult to talk to an audience about the importance of ages zero to three, but it seems almost impossible to get the listener to incorporate the conviction that it does make a great deal of difference how a child is reacting and is reacted to in the first few weeks and months of a child's life. Very early habits and expectations seem to become set in concrete, even when heroic interventions are later used to change behavioral patterns.

So many times children end up in foster homes, where almost immediately they start to act out in a fashion that virtually ensures their foster parents will reject them and eventually throw them out. Then they are bounced to other foster parents, and, of course, the same process starts again. The children become extremely adept at making sure nobody will like them. Then, not too long after, they end up in desperate circumstances.

In April 1993 the *New York Times* published the series *Children of the Shadows*. The stories were about teenagers. The snapshots were frightening, but the reporter, though excellent, had no opportunity to study the evolution of the tragic lives described: what the circumstances were eight months before birth, three months before, at birth, and in the first six weeks of life, when the children were two months old, five months old, eight months old, and so on. When did they start to walk? How did they feel when they achieved the milestones of standing up and learning to walk? Were they encouraged to feel proud of themselves? When did they learn how to talk? How much had they been read to? Did they ever learn to identify with an adult, a parent who was eager for them to learn? Did they ever learn to trust and to hope and to have expectations? Just how did they learn how to recognize anger in others? Was a parent available to help them learn to cope with their own anger and frustration? Were they able to develop empathy? Did they learn how to aspire, and what did they aspire to? Obviously, children ages sixteen or eighteen cannot verbalize their earliest experiences, those when they were two months old, five months old, two years old, or even two and one half.

Ninety-nine out of a hundred individuals, adults as well as children, do not usually concern themselves about the habits and ways of feeling and thinking they developed in their first forty-five months of life (nine months' gestation added to their first three years after birth). Their memories are at best hazy for those periods of time. But the habits and expectations they learned in those very early months and early years tend to persist throughout life. Their basic view of themselves and their expectations about how others will respond to them were formed during that period.

Most adults seem to view eighteen-year-olds as though they had been born at age eighteen. For example, they admire individual A, someone who has a good character, is competent, has good learning ability, social skills, and a record of certain attainments (such as good grades or graduating from high school). Individual B they condemn.

He is an eighteen-year-old viewed as a psychopathic, lazy, good-for-nothing, drug-using teenager—someone who is uncivilized, antisocial, and a menace to society.

Such snapshot perceptions are generally based on presuppositions that both the best and the worst eighteen-year-olds just *are* that way at age eighteen—terrific kids or bums. No cause or effect of their early backgrounds is considered. Likewise, most teachers of elementary school or high school tend to view their students as good kids or bad kids, smart or dumb, cooperative or problematic.

As a society, we seem to have blinders on with respect to early childhood development, at least until the age of four. In recent years increasing numbers of adults have seen Head Start as important. Their somewhat simplistic expectation is that with one year of Head Start, presto, the child will be ready for school. Most child development experts admire Head Start, but they understand that for many children even "good" Head Start comes much too late and offers much too little.

If we wait until the child is four years old, it is very, very difficult to change that child's attitudes, habits, and expectations. To some extent Head Start, with well-trained teachers, helps children when they are four. Yet many children understand early in life that they are going to be punished for almost anything they do or do not do. They learn to expect punishment. In fact, they may act in ways that elicit punishment. Even when these children are older, they tend to act in ways that elicit negative behaviors similar to the negative behaviors they experienced early in life. When these children are studied and evaluated at age six or eleven by teachers—as Byron Egeland and Alan Sroufe at the University of Minnesota have done (see chapter 3)—their behaviors are clearly seen as the consequence of seriously flawed early development. Their conduct leads to their being rejected by their peers and teachers. They have trouble making friends, and then, seeing their unpopularity, view their paranoia as justified. Nobody likes them. That is the way it has always been; and they contrive to act out in order to make sure that nobody will like them.

Brain Development

David Hamburg, president of the Carnegie Corporation, has studied chimpanzees. He points out that chimpanzees travel in troops of forty to fifty, which is really much like the troops that human beings used to travel in when we were part of a hunting-and-gathering society. Our species' survival is obviously related to our brain power vis-à-vis other species of mammals. The human brain has a fantastic capacity to be developed in different ways. Until 1700 the brain's survival tasks related to living in relatively small groups of people. Cities, of course, have always had their problems, but beginning with the industrial revolution in the late 1700s—when so many males of the species left their homes and families to work in industrial settings—the world's huge new metropolitan population centers began to develop. The enormous expansion of populations in big cities now challenges the human brain to do things it has never had to do before.

Today, more than half the mothers of children aged one are in the work force and out of the home. Those children are no longer being brought up the way children used to be brought up when they had both parents around, or at least a mother, almost full time. Today, children are being reared by peers and television. It is no wonder that we face new survival problems in our society.

A Homo sapiens has the capacity to become a full human being, but it is not automatic. Witness the thousands of psychopathic predators we read about in the newspapers. A Homo sapiens baby can be nurtured to become a human being, but the nurturing has to start very early and be consistent.

Highlights of recent research on brain development have been reported by Ronald Kotulak in a Pulitzer prize-winning series in the *Chicago Tribune* (1993). He reports how important very early brain development is in utero and in the first and second years of life. Parents and experts have long known that babies raised by caring adults in safe and stimulating environments are better learners than those raised in less-stimulating settings and that the effects can be long-lasting. Recent scientific findings provide a basis for these observations. Over the past decade, scientists have gained new insights into molecular biology that illuminate the workings of the nervous system. At the same time, they have acquired powerful research tools, including sophisticated brain scans, that allow them to study the developing brain in greater detail and with greater precision than ever before. Brain scans also allow scientists to measure the impact of the environment on brain function. This research points to five key findings, which should inform policymakers' deliberations on early childhood policy:

First, the brain development that takes place before age one is more rapid and extensive than we previously realized. Positron emission tomography (PET) studies show that the biochemical patterns of a one-year-old's brain qualitatively resemble those of the normal young adult. This is astonishing, considering the immense scale of early brain development. From a few initial cells, the brain develops billions of brain cells, or neurons, over a period of several months. Once these neurons are formed, they must migrate to their correct locations. Brain cell formation is virtually complete long before birth, but brain maturation is far from over: the next challenge is the formation of connections between the cells—up to fifteen thousand connections, or synapses, per neuron. These synapses form the brain's physical "maps" that allow learning to take place. We now know that in the months after birth, this process proceeds with astounding rapidity, as the number of synapses increases twentyfold, from 50 trillion to 1,000 trillion (Kotulak, 1993, 12 April, 12–13).

Second, brain development is much more vulnerable to environmental influence than we ever suspected. We have long understood that factors other than genetic programming affect brain development. Nutrition is perhaps the most obvious example. We know that inadequate nutrition before birth and in the first years of life can so seriously interfere with brain development that it may lead to a host of neurological and behavioral disorders, including learning disabilities and mental retardation.

Third, beginning in the 1960s, scientists began to demonstrate that the quality and variety of the environment have a direct impact on brain development. Today, researchers around the world are amassing evidence that the role of the environment is even more important than earlier studies had suggested. For example, histological and brain-scan studies of animals show changes in brain structure and function as a result of variations in early experience. These findings are consistent with research in child development that has shown the first eighteen months of life to be an important period of development.

Fourth, to achieve anything like optimal brain development, what is required is not only excellent health, but a mother who is attentive and who can nurture and appropriately stimulate her child. If the stimulation is too much or too little and does not take place in the early weeks and months of the first year, there is not a great likelihood that the child will be able to graduate from high school or eventually be able to fit into an industrialized society. Jobs increasingly require meaningful education in order to qualify. This particular observation fits in with a growing body of scientific evidence that shows that in the development of the brain, early memories are the fundamental sources of curiosity, motivation, logic, understanding of right and wrong, ethics, empathy, socialization, and self-esteem.

Fifth, how individuals function from the preschool years all the way through adolescence and even adulthood hinges, to a significant extent, on their experiences before the age of three. Researchers have thoroughly documented the importance of the pre- and postnatal months and the first three years, but a wide gap remains between scientific knowledge and social policy. This is particularly true in two areas: our policies reflect neither our growing knowledge of early brain development nor our understanding of factors that tend to protect young children or place them at risk.

INTERVENTION PROGRAMS OF THE 1960s AND 1970s

A concern over high school drop-out forty years ago led me to think that we should not wait until high school students are in the twelfth grade to attempt to convince them to go on to college. I thought we should start in the tenth grade. After a year or so of trying to change the plans of tenth graders, it dawned on me that we really had to start earlier, perhaps working with children in the seventh grade. As I mentioned previously, it was Silberman's *Crisis in Black and White* that led me to address the problem much earlier. In particular, the chapter "The Negro and the School," which begins with a quotation from Isaiah: "Shudder, you complacent ones," impressed me.

> The public school offers the greatest opportunity to break down the cultural barrier that helps block the Negro's advance into the main stream of American life. But the opportunity is being muffed: no city in the United States has even begun to face up to the problem involved in educating Negro—or for that matter, white—slum youngsters. . . . We will not begin to solve the dropout problem until we recognize that it does not begin in high school, nor even in junior high school. For that matter, neither does it begin in kindergarten or first grade, although this is the point at which schools, as they now are constituted, must begin to deal with it. . . . The dropout problem begins in the cradle—or, more accurately, at the point at which the child leaves the cradle and begins to crawl around his home, exploring his environment and developing the basics for his future intellectual development. . . . To reverse the effects of a starved environment—to provide the sensory and verbal and visual stimuli that are necessary for future learning and to teach the specific skills that are prerequisites to learning how to read—the schools must begin admitting children at age three or four, instead of at five or six. The nursery school holds the key to the future. (pp. 248, 277)

Silberman's recommendation that the cure lies in children beginning school earlier than age five seems to have been prompted more by hope than experience. Recent evidence indicates that even with excellent, expensive intervention, many deficits in a child's development between birth and two years of age cannot be entirely reversed at age three or four.

Those of us who have worked with the issue of prevention of poverty and hopelessness know that in many individual cases we can succeed. Teenage mothers, as both the victims of nonprevention and agents of inflicting poverty on their children, represent a critical population in the scheme of prevention. Those of us who are directly involved in this issue face challenging issues ahead as we seek appropriate solutions for this teen population and their children. Reviewing the Ounce of Prevention and Family Focus programs for teens and realistically assessing what we have achieved reveal the dimensions of the tasks that face us.

Head Start, 1965

The biggest intervention program, of course, is Head Start. When it was announced in 1965, I was already convinced that early childhood development and Head Start were indeed important. Yet even when it was twenty-five years old, in 1990, Head Start was still not funded at a level that accommodated more than about 25 percent of poor children. President George Bush recommended that the budget be increased from an expenditure of $1.4 billion to $1.9 billion at a time when the French, who have one fifth our population, were spending $7.12 billion on "publicly sponsored child care and education" (Richardson and Marx, 1989, 15). A 1989 report of the French-American Foundation concluded, "If the United States were to commit equivalent public resources to child care and linked health services, this would approximate $23 billion a year." Even with a new $4 billion authorization, which is slated to be reduced by the 104th Congress, the U.S. financial commitment per capita would still be only one sixth of what the French spend. The French realize that very early childhood development is extremely important to the future of their nation.

You have to invest money in the right ways. Americans have increased spending for education, both public and private, for children beginning in kindergarten, through graduate school, from $264 billion in 1986 to $500 billion in 1995. Yet public education has not improved, and the stated goal of President Bush and the fifty governors who met in Charlottesville in 1990—restated most recently by Secretary Richard Riley as America's first educational goal—is to ready all children for school by the year 2000. I see no real evidence that this goal will be accomplished, despite increased funding for Head Start.

Yet we cannot change everything in five minutes. Slowly, we have to develop momentum. I do think that we are moving in the right direction, but we still have too many children born at extremely high risk. Witness, for example, the high rate of babies born to single parents. Many of those parents had little education. The likelihood is that at least 90 percent of their children will end up very poor, without much support in life.

Interestingly, public policy in education is beginning to come closer to current knowledge about how humans learn. In 1994 the United States Congress passed and the president signed a new Head Start authorization bill that not only brings annual funding up to $4 billion, but since October of 1994, for the first time there is a 3 percent set-aside specifically for children ages zero to three. Now we have a big job to do in training the teachers who will be needed to work with eligible babies and toddlers. Training those teachers and the teachers of teachers about infancy is essential.

Family Focus, 1976

Family Focus helps parents to improve their knowledge of healthy child development and to enhance their parenting skills. Family Focus's drop-in center has been highly successful: 250 families came the first year. The percentage of low-birthweight babies was small, about 6 percent. The health of the young mothers has clearly improved. (In the inner city of Chicago, low birthweights constitute more than 21 percent of all births.)

One of the goals of Family Focus has been to encourage young mothers to wait before having a second baby. The history of Family Focus showed that the costs for intervention would not be cheap. With funding, the program could prevent damage to children. But these costs of prevention had to be justified on one of two bases, humane considerations or cost-effectiveness. If the concern was a humanitarian one, the cynics would say, "Don't look to us for money. Tap the bleeding hearts." To prove cost-effectiveness, one would have to measure the damage and learn how much that damage costs when society does nothing.

In my introduction I mentioned that, even after five years, Family Focus continued to find it difficult to get funding, and it remains difficult. The concept of the Pittway Corporation's Aurora center was a model primary prevention program and proved of interest to the state as a means of cutting down on child abuse and neglect. The Department of Children and Family Services agreed to commit $400,000 if Pittway would match it, and its board agreed. Their joint goal was to establish six experimental sites that would really test the concept of prevention. In deciding on a name for this public-private partnership, the Ounce of Prevention Fund was created.

INTERVENTION PROGRAMS OF THE 1980s AND 1990s

The Ounce of Prevention Fund, 1982

In Illinois the Ounce of Prevention Fund has been working for fourteen years to reduce family dysfunction and births to teenagers, 90 percent of whom are unmarried. We estimate that Ounce programs reach approximately 20 percent of those teenagers in need. With that 20 percent there has been marginal success. The staff of forty-eight Ounce programs finds that in most cases children born out of wedlock will not be adequately nurtured by their mothers or any other caregiver. Unfortunately, despite all efforts, the program has been able to make only a modest improvement in the outlook for the children of adolescents. This is not surprising when we are confronted with the statistics: in 1992, 33.4 percent of all births in Illinois, occurred out of wedlock (NCHS, 1994); in 1989, 29 percent of all black males aged twenty to twenty-nine in Cook County, which includes Chicago, had been arrested and jailed at least once during the year. Men who have been in jail or are likely to go to jail do not qualify as the most desirable husbands.

The Ounce has sought to determine whether it is cost-effective to attempt to prevent the range of problems we face by addressing causes. Even before the three-year experimentation phase ended in June 1985, the state enthusiastically increased its funding, and the Ounce's original six programs became twenty-eight in years two and three. In 1996, the Ounce is in its fourteenth year and continues to receive funding, even though the state legislature is now Republican-controlled. Both James Thompson, Illinois' governor in 1982, and its present governor, James Edgar, are Republicans.

The Ounce of Prevention Fund has grown. In the first year, with $800,000 this public-private venture funded six programs. In the second year, the state increased its contribution to $2.8 million, and in the third year it increased it to $4.5 million. This enabled us to add twenty-two programs. In the fourth year, with modest additional funding, we added thirteen small experimental prevention programs. Today the Ounce administers fifty-eight programs, with a budget of $14.2 million.

Initially, the agreed first target of the Ounce was to work with poor adolescent mothers who had young babies. The aim was to teach the mothers better parenting skills, which would result in good parent-child interaction, proper nurturing and development of the child, and the eventual avoidance of the roster of problems that high-risk children are subject to.

In the first eighteen months of the Ounce our focus was young mothers and their babies. We tried to keep the young mother in school, which meant, among other things, encouraging her to wait before having another baby. We knew that the cycle of poverty usually started all over again with those babies, particularly with second babies. Practically speaking, we spent most of our efforts with the mothers; little effort went into working with the children. Originally we budgeted about $1,000 a year for each family, or enough for the two thirds of problematic families not at the highest risk. From the start, we recognized that our programs would reach only a few of the hardest to reach one third of the highest-risk families.

The next stage of prevention efforts at the Ounce was to try to prevent the first birth. We looked around to find out what programs anywhere had been successful in preventing first births. The only one we could find was the comprehensive school-based medical clinic model, successfully operating in Dallas, Houston, Kansas City (Mo.), St. Paul, Minneapolis, and a very few other cities. We established a clinic at a high school in Chicago in 1985, at a time when the adolescent pregnancy rate in the high school was as high as 30 percent.

Basically, Ounce sites usually offer home visiting, provide parent training, encourage family planning, provide support mechanisms to promote healthy family functioning and prevent child abuse and neglect, and in many instances, offer developmental infant and toddler day care. The Ounce also manages nine federally funded Head Start programs for nine hundred children.

In addition to family-planning services, the clinics meet the tremendous need for comprehensive medical care within the high school population. Between two thirds and three quarters of our students' visits are medical and not related to sexual activity. The aim, however, is also to improve prenatal care for pregnant students and thereby reduce the number of infants born at high risk. Most of all, the Ounce, through these clinics, hopes to reduce recidivism of pregnancy. Although one third of teenage mothers nationally have a second baby within twenty-four months of the first, in 1984 the St. Paul clinics claimed they had cut subsequent pregnancies to 1.4 percent.

Yet the Ounce is not reaching the majority of children who are at the highest risk. These are the cases that probably require at least $3,000 a year per family to work with successfully. In Illinois, if one third of the births to teenagers are at the highest risk, 8,000 such cases in the first year would cost $24 million, in the second year $48 million, and in the third year $72 million. The number of trained therapists, social workers, and home visitors needed would escalate from 3,000 to 9,000, and this number would be in addition to those trained who would be working with two thirds of those adolescent-headed families who are not at the highest risk. There is no practical way to develop this amount of human resources and money in Illinois. The only alternative is to cut the number of pregnancies and births to teenagers.

There are many advantages to a public-private partnership, such as flexible (private) funds, recruitment opportunities, retention of well-trained personnel, nonbudgeted consultancies, and institutional memory. In 1984, an innovative proposal from the Chicago school system was turned down by the readers prescribed by the state's review system. With private funds we initiated that program in four middle schools to teach at the sixth, seventh, and eighth grades a brief but intensive course in family life education with peer support. Many of the original sixty students—seventh and eighth graders—were judged to be at high risk of early pregnancy. By 1986, not one had become pregnant. Although this result obviously could not be entirely replicated, that program is now state-supported and has expanded to ten middle schools.

With flexible funds, a one-hour videotape show about responsible sexual decision making called Choices was produced and broadcast nationally on public television. It was a corny, Hollywood-type film with a game-show format, and students loved it. "Choices" commanded their attention and pushed them to think about the choices they face or will face regarding their own sexual activity. First, the film makes the point that they can say no. If they do become sexually active, they are told the truth about the risks of pregnancy and sexually transmitted diseases. A powerful seven-minute segment portrays a true-to-life scenario about a young couple in love who have a baby while still in school and have to drop out. It dramatizes what their lives might be like a year or two later. The messages, which are clear and interesting and sometimes humorously couched, say again and again, "You have a choice. Don't let it just happen to you without making that choice." Hundreds of copies of the videotape have been sold at $19 each, and thousands of students in Illinois and other states have seen the film, often several times. Flexible funds have been important to the Ounce.

Evaluating Ounce programs has been difficult. A major problem is the factor of self-selection. Some parents choose to come in, some do not. Of those who do not, some need our help, some do not. Of those who do come in, some really connect with the program, some connect little. People who bring their children into Ounce of Prevention programs or Family Focus programs are different from the mothers living in the same neighborhood who do not get their children into such programs.

Of programs that stress prenatal intervention, some do and some do not make a measurable improvement in the lives of thousands of children born at risk. There is no way to mandate proper prenatal care, and there is no replacement for early healthy nurturing by caregivers. Without such care, the child is likely to reach age two developmentally delayed, with poor self-esteem and little motivation to succeed in school or in life.

Many people agree with Brazelton's observation that before the age of eight months a child's motivation is probably pretty well established and difficult to change as the child gets older. It is conceivable that individual therapy can substantially help in an individual case, but our society has no practical plan of how to give meaningful therapy to 1 million such children coming down the pike each year.

THE BEETHOVEN PROJECT:
THE CENTER FOR SUCCESSFUL CHILD DEVELOPMENT, 1986

> Although years of experience gave the Ounce a sense of the size of the task undertaken, what we could not fully appreciate until after our work had begun was the *intensity* of the difficulty, the *degree* of the complexity, and the reverberations of this complexity on everything we were to do: the goals we set, the program components we put in place, the people we served, and the outcomes we could expect.
>
> —"Beethoven's Fifth" (1993)

How could the Ounce attack the problems of the highest-risk cases? The final, crucial objective of the Ounce has been to prevent the developmental delays of such high-risk children through a program begun in 1986 at the Beethoven Elementary School. Children who are born to mothers living in six adjacent sixteen-story buildings of the Robert Taylor Homes in the inner-city of Chicago attend the Beethoven school. The Beethoven Project is the popular name of the Ounce of Prevention's Center for Successful Child Development (CSCD; see appendix B). It targets all those children born in the school's catchment area, many of whom are indeed at very high risk. Starting prenatally, we focus on the first sixty months as well as the fetal period. This project strikes at the heart of prevention of the cycle of poverty.

In seeking to guarantee the health, early stimulation, and proper nurturing of every child born at high risk, the Ounce's Beethoven Project has had a tough assignment, and progress has been slow. Yet because of programs like Beethoven, which spurred Senator Edward Kennedy to initiate the Comprehensive Child Development Act, there are now thirty-eight such federally funded programs across the country, although they must still be regarded as only experimental.

There have been critical variables in the program: the nature of the family and community life in a poverty-stricken inner city; the effect of bringing unfamiliar services into an area where the need for basic supports is high; the impact on families of inadequate or dysfunctional public welfare systems; and what questions should be asked in order to strengthen the program and its role in the community. The experience of the program has taught its staff several lessons:

1. Successful programs must earn the trust of participants. "The physical and emotional stresses faced by residents of the community—and the impediments to earning their trust—have proved staggering" (*Education Week,* February 1989).

2. The environment challenges families and programs with unrelenting obstacles to smooth program operation. The impact of multiple stresses on families with little income and few community resources can be immense. An abrasive place to live, the Robert Taylor Homes complex lacks sufficient telephones, laundry facilities, newspaper delivery, grocery stores, and drugstores—all common elements of a well-functioning community. ("It have me scared to go out my door or carry my kids to the playground."—CSCD participant)

3. Programs must respond to basic needs: food, milk, clothing, furniture, and housing safety and repairs. From the mundane (the need to find or afford limited laundry facilities) to the traumatizing (the threat of gunfire) high stress affects everyday decisions and often overwhelms even the most resilient families.

4. Each person evaluates her experience relative to her own history. Small improvements to some are great strides for others.

Both the increasingly violent environment and the already high mobility of the population in Robert Taylor have negatively affected CSCD's ability to provide consistent, long-term support to as many families as originally envisioned. The level of stress for the staff has created some instability: recruiting and retaining experienced staff have been difficult and time-consuming. Given the importance to the program of familiarity and trust between participants and staff, staffing decisions and patterns have a tremendous impact on program continuity. There is no promise of attendance from program participants. Because it is voluntary, enormous energy must be devoted to determining the correct atmosphere, program mix, and incentives to keep a diverse program population at a high level of participation.

In defining CSCD's success, there have been gains in children's health care; parents' understanding of children's needs; strengthened family relations; and the provision of a safe haven and respite care for parents, which makes available greater emotional stamina for parents. Children have better social skills and language development and increased confidence to pursue education and employment. There are subtler changes seen in family dynamics: there is softer speech, laughter, hugs, and hope.

Barbara Brotman and Joan Beck wrote in the *Chicago Tribune* (1992) about the first five years of CSCD. Although it is impossible to summarize five years' experience in just a few words, both writers captured important aspects of the project. Still largely untold, however, is the essence of what it took to get this project off the ground and some of the less-visible, positive results the project achieved in its first five years.

The task we undertook in 1986 was indeed formidable: to bring a prevention-oriented, family-support program into one of the most difficult, threatening environments in the nation, where the residents have had a lifetime of good reasons to be slow to trust anyone new. Even we underestimated the complexity of the challenges we were up against, which leads to the first and most essential point to be understood.

When CSCD began, it was a bare-bones operation of six home visitors and a small administrative staff housed temporarily in the Chicago Urban League offices. It was a year before a permanent site for the center could be found. It took all five of CSCD's early years to create the program components that are today offered to participants.

During all the time CSCD struggled with problems of space, licensing, and training a local work force in child development, the program provided as much as possible to parents and children. It served seven hundred families in its first five years. Some came to CSCD when all it had to offer were home visits. Many of these people have stayed and grown with the program.

One of the most important services CSCD now offers is comprehensive health care, which started in 1988. It provides free regular gynecological care, prenatal care, and education to pregnant women; well-child care to participants' children up to age eighteen, including all siblings; health education to all participants; immunizations; and regular checkups, all on site. Its successful immunization program is extremely important to the health of the children.

The CSCD program has also provided job opportunities for the community: more than half of today's CSCD staff are current or former residents of Robert Taylor. Many work as child care providers in CSCD's full-day developmental child care services for children ages three months to five years. CSCD has been able to provide care to that age range only since 1991, when full-day Head Start and a special program for two-year-olds began.

Most important to CSCD's success is its focus on the full development of the child in the context of his or her family. The center focuses on readying children for school in many more ways than just teaching them to count or know their colors.

Dolores Norton (1995) studied children in the Robert Taylor Homes, but not in the Beethoven school district. When the children turned two years old, their mothers were asked the following three questions:

1. What would you dream about in the way of good results for your child's growing up?
2. Now, let's think about the real world. What do you think your child will really accomplish in life?
3. Now make a guess. What, practically speaking, do you think your child will be doing ten to fifteen years from now?

In answer to the first question, some of the mothers said, "I would love to have my son or daughter graduate from medical school or law school." To the second question, some answered, "In the real world, well, I hope my daughter or son will finish high school. I hope she might become a secretary, or that he might go to a trade school and get some job." To question three, many women responded, "Well, she will probably be pregnant, just as I was at age fourteen, or my son will probably get killed before he gets to be eighteen. He will probably get into the drug scene." Generally speaking, they were very pessimistic.

On the other hand, a few were more confident and believed in their children. If the mother had a good level of control, she would try hard to get the child steered toward success and would say it was her intention to do everything she could to make sure her child stayed in school and did well. That mother had high expectations.

In other words, the real expectations of the mother made a considerable difference in what the child was going to accomplish. The mother's expectations also measurably reflected her own experience with life. The worse her own experience was, the less control she felt she had and the more likely it was that she would be fatalistic, believing, "I don't have any control, and my child is not going to have any control." The consequence is that the child will probably end up in a deep rut and hopeless.

After nine years, I would say that the Beethoven Project has been a qualified success. One child born at a low birthweight was kept in a crib until he was eight months old because the mother was afraid he would die of rat poisoning if she let him onto the floor. Beethoven Project staff worked a long time with the mother. Finally, when the child was eight months old, they were allowed to bring in a developmental expert, who noted the child's poor motor development. We bought the boy a playpen and showed the mother how to do a series of exercises with the child so that the child's motor development would improve. And it did; it was not too late.

When the Council on Foundations was in Chicago in 1990, a large group of Foundation executives visited the Beethoven Project. The young boy who had experienced developmental problems, now four years old, was there with his mother. He is a wonderful boy and is now a star pupil of the Beethoven school. How many more are there like him? We do not know. Some families have taken their lives into their own hands and moved out of the Robert Taylor Homes, which in a way, is a success marker, but we have not measured this sign of progress. Many mothers have had a series of new living arrangements in the nine years of the project, often going from bad to worse.

In November 1992 a retrospective analysis of Beethoven Project participants was meaningful but by no means definitive. Suffice it to say that we have helped some participants. We do not seem to have helped others much. Beethoven is difficult to evaluate; nevertheless, the idea of comprehensive child development has now become the gold standard as far as the Department of Health and Human Services is concerned. Head Start is most proud of its comprehensive child development programs, which it is currently reevaluating.

In contrast to our program, which has added a cohort each year, a

Roxbury, Massachusetts, program took one cohort and when people dropped out (as about one fourth of them apparently did), they were replaced, family for family. This plan followed the terms of the original federal grant. The result is that in five years the program has spent its investment on 120 people. There is no doubt that money is important in these programs, and the more money spent per capita, the better are the results. The law of diminishing returns, however, obviously also takes place. Yet there are many people who are richly deserving of help; they want help, and they can use help. We must help those people.

Violence and many other stresses in difficult neighborhoods create an environment of so many risks that no one program can overcome them all. A parent stressed by these conditions often finds it difficult to devote the necessary attention to her baby's developmental needs. Violence, of course, affects our program as well. At CSCD, there is bullet-proof glass for windows. Staffers must always be vigilant to the pulse of life within and outside the center's building. The center has been able to remain open, with few exceptions, despite the threatening environment in which it operates.

Given the multiple stresses in what the social workers call multi-problem families (MPFSY, pronounced muh-puff-see: multiproblem family syndrome), it is no wonder that CSCD cannot by itself help all families solve all their problems. As the center continues to struggle with success and failure, what is most troubling is the feeling that it is trying to climb up a down escalator that is going faster and faster.

Perhaps we are losing ground. Yet the needs of the children and families are enormous, and the successes of CSCD are encouraging. We have watched families transform themselves; many participants testify to the importance of a program like CSCD in their lives. It is essential for us all to help, in any way we can, those children and families able to take advantage of programs that are so direly needed.

In response to Brotman and Beck's report was an unsolicited, heart-warming letter from the principal and assistant principal of the Beethoven school. In part it reads: "Your dream of improving the lives of the residents of the Robert Taylor Homes might not have reached your expectations in terms of families who benefitted. However, rest assured that those who remained and became full beneficiaries of what the Center for Successful Child Development had to offer are better for being participants."

This story applies to where and how we focus the work to improve school readiness and performance. Infants must begin to develop empathy and learn appropriate social conduct before they are two years old. All staff people at CSCD know how important these early patterns of development are and how difficult it is for children to change when they have been shortchanged in the first two years of life. That is why CSCD has kept its focus on children's earliest years.

CSCD emphasizes that for a child to be ready for school, healthy development must encompass four areas of growth: the social, emotional, physical, and cognitive aspects. When children are delayed in any of the first three areas they will not be ready to learn, even if they have reached such cognitive milestones as recognizing numbers or being able to tie their shoes. Motivation to be curious, to develop empathy, and to be trusting are well in place by the time a child is two. Having appropriately developed with supportive family relationships, a child five years old will walk into kindergarten with respect for the teacher and eager to meet friends and explore new experiences. CSCD understands the importance of these early developmental patterns and how difficult it is for children to thrive when they have not consistently received the attention and support they need.

3

PRIMARY PREVENTION AND
THE RIGHT TO LIFE

TEENAGERS ARE ESPECIALLY vulnerable to the risks of out-of-wedlock childbearing. Many high-risk students have slightly older sisters who have already had babies, or they have close friends whose slightly older sisters have borne babies. According to *Beyond Rhetoric,* a report by the National Commission on Children (1991), "Each year, half a million babies are born to teenage girls ill-prepared to assume the responsibilities of parenthood. Most of these mothers are unmarried, many have not completed their education, and few have prospects for an economically secure future. . . . Clearly, the problems that harm children and threaten the nation have their roots in the failure of individuals to assume responsibility for themselves and the children they bring into the world."

The failure cannot be regarded solely as a series of individual failures. Collectively, we must assume some responsibility. Our society does not provide real family planning alternatives to individuals who are sexually active. We cannot expect the ultimate responsibility for pregnancy and childbearing to rest only with individuals—not unless they have been encouraged to make informed choices about issues related to their sexual activity, including abstinence, contraception, abortion, adoption, and the realistic difficulties they will face in raising their babies. These real choices and the means to act on them are not now generally available, particularly to the young and the poor.

The national commission, after a vigorous debate, decided not to discuss family planning options in its report—specifically abortions and vigorous counseling on contraceptives. This mirrors our nation's divisive disagreements over what to do about the sexual activity of adolescents. Although young Americans are increasingly outspoken about sex, many act as though they are uninformed about birth control. Some 10 percent of American women at risk of pregnancy use no method of contraception. They trust to luck alone—and are responsible for more than half (53 percent) of this country's 3.6 million unplanned pregnancies (AGI, 1993). Luck alone is not enough.

ADOLESCENT SEXUALITY AND PREGNANCY

We need to do more. Nearly 51 percent of fifteen- to seventeen-year-old girls and 76 percent of all girls under twenty are now sexually active (AGI, 1994, 23). Teenagers in the United States are more likely than any other age group not to use birth control and to have multiple partners. Although the postponement of premarital sexual activity (abstinence) is desirable, the realities of the sexual behavior of adolescents today demonstrates the ineffectiveness of existing strategies to prevent premarital sex. Internationally, American teenagers are far more likely to become pregnant than are teenagers in other industrialized countries (see figure 3-1).

We cannot afford to continue relying only on this option, which is, of course, the most palatable and least controversial. Instead, we must do much more to reach out to children before adolescence, making genuine efforts at honest, direct, up-front sex education, beginning in the early grades, when the questions first get asked and the chances for influence are the greatest. There must also be counseling about broader issues, including personal emotions and relationships, the dangers of sexually transmitted diseases, the importance of schooling, planning for jobs, avoiding drugs, and the prevalence of domestic violence.

In 1950, approximately 142,000 births, or 3.9 percent of all births in the nation, were to unwed mothers. The total number of births in the United States has not varied greatly in the past forty-six years, the figure being between 3.1 and 4.3 million annually (see table 3-1). In 1992, of the more than 1.2 million babies born to unwed mothers, 30 percent of the mothers were teenagers, and 70 percent were aged twenty or older.

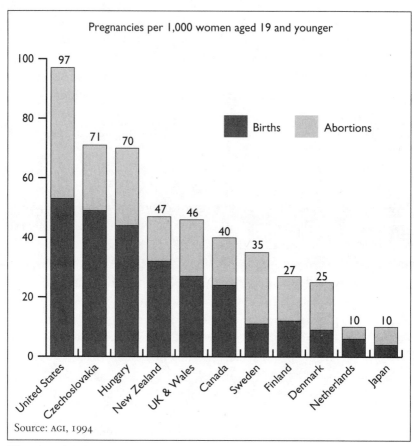

Figure 3-1
Teenage Pregnancy Internationally, 1988

This percentage is not static. Barring unforeseen changes, the trend of these past two generations points to the probability that by the year 2000 at least one third of all babies born in the United States will be born to unwed mothers. How many of these children will actually be ready to learn by the time they enter kindergarten? As things stand, a staggering number will not be ready, and the adverse consequences will be felt into the farthest future.

The sad fact is that on average the outlook for all the babies born to

Table 3-1
Total Live Births and Births to Unmarried Women:
United States, 1950–1993

YEAR	TOTAL LIVE BIRTHS	BIRTHS TO UNMARRIED WOMEN	
		#	%
1950	3,632,000	141,600	3.9
1951	3,820,000	146,500	3.8
1952	3,909,000	150,300	3.8
1953	3,959,000	160,800	4.1
1954	4,071,000	176,600	4.3
1955	4,097,000	183,300	4.5
1956	4,210,000	193,500	4.6
1957	4,300,000	201,700	4.7
1958	4,246,000	208,700	4.9
1959	4,286,000	220,600	5.1
1960	4,257,850	224,300	5.3
1961	4,268,326	240,200	5.6
1962	4,167,362	245,100	5.9
1963	4,098,020	259,400	6.3
1964	4,027,490	275,700	6.8
1965	3,760,358	291,200	7.7
1966	3,606,274	302,400	8.4
1967	3,520,959	318,100	9.0
1968	3,501,564	339,200	9.7
1969	3,600,206	360,800	10.0
1970	3,731,386	398,700	10.7
1971	3,555,970	401,400	11.3
1972	3,258,411	403,200	12.4
1973	3,136,965	407,300	13.0
1974	3,159,958	418,100	13.2
1975	3,144,198	447,900	14.2

(continued)

Table 3-1   *(continued)*

YEAR	TOTAL LIVE BIRTHS	BIRTHS TO UNMARRIED WOMEN	
		#	%
1976	3,167,788	468,100	14.8
1977	3,326,632	515,700	15.5
1978	3,333,279	543,900	16.3
1979	3,494,398	597,800	17.1
1980	3,612,258	665,747	18.4
1981	3,629,238	686,605	18.9
1982	3,680,537	715,227	19.4
1983	3,638,933	737,893	20.3
1984	3,669,141	770,355	21.0
1985	3,760,561	828,174	22.0
1986	3,756,547	878,477	23.4
1987	3,809,394	933,013	24.5
1988	3,909,510	1,005,299	25.7
1989	4,040,958	1,094,169	27.1
1990	4,158,212	1,165,384	28.0
1991	4,110,907	1,213,769	29.5
1992	4,065,014	1,224,876	30.0
1993	4,039,000	N/A	N/A

Source: HHS, NCHS

Note. In 1980, of approximately 3.6 million total births, 2.9 million were to married mothers. In 1989, of 4 million total births, 2.9 million were to married mothers. Over these ten years almost the entire increase in total births resulted from additional births to unmarried mothers, which increased from 666,000 to 1.1 million—an increase of about 428,000. Note also the persistent increase in the number and percentage of births to unmarried women between 1950 and 1993.

unmarried teenage mothers is indeed poor. It is doubtful whether even one of every four of these children will graduate from high school or be employable at a living wage. As a nation, we simply cannot afford each year to take on an annual, ongoing liability for the welfare and failed education of more than 900,000 babies (more than 20 percent of all children born each year). They are likely to turn up later in statistics on increased school drop-outs; the unemployed and unemployable; the victims and perpetrators of child abuse and neglect; and criminals in and out of jails, and contributing to an increasingly unsafe environment.

In preventing teenage pregnancy, we have hard choices to make and taboos to overcome. We must continue to find ways to help teenagers say no in order to reduce the level of sexual activity among those too young to evaluate the consequences of their actions. Yet despite our efforts to reduce teenage sexual activity, success is likely to be limited. Logically, therefore, we must also radically increase contraception availability, which means both informing teens about contraception and making contraception available, and using community pressure to stimulate participation in prevention programs.

Sex Education and Parents, the Schools, and the Puritan Ethic
There is no evidence that candid sex education encourages promiscuity, yet the myth persists. Evidence does exist, however, that shows that although American teenagers are no more sexually active than their counterparts are in other developed countries, American teenagers have significantly higher rates of pregnancy, abortions, and births. These higher rates reflect the failure of American teenagers to use effective contraceptives consistently.

There are some parents who believe that only married people have the right to have sex and that people who engage in sex outside marriage should be punished by being forced for a lifetime to care for a child who was not planned or wanted. These parents regard their teenagers' sexual activity as an offense and feel that their children cannot be permitted to ignore the parents' or society's rule against extramarital sex. Such attitudes are sometimes based on the parents' concern over their son's or daughter's "wildness." Even if a daughter becomes pregnant, some parents strongly oppose abortion. "It serves her right," one mother said of her disobedient daughter. *It* was the daughter's insistence on her right to engage in sex, which she refused to believe to be subject to her mother or father's control. "It serves her right" expressed the hope that the daughter would be punished for her disobedience; having to raise the baby would be the punishment for her sin. Occasionally, a parent, father or mother, will throw a pregnant daughter out of the house, sometimes physically. But most parents, when apprised of their unwed daughter's pregnancy, would choose abortion rather than compromise their daughter's education and consign her to become a reluctant mother.

IS SEX SINFUL?

As reflected in public opinion polls, there is clearly little agreement among parents, politicians, and voters on the subject of teaching about sex in the schools or about having school-based medical clinics. However, most politicians side with a highly vocal minority of parents who oppose sex education, contraception availability, and abortion. There is little consensus in public discussions of either contraception or abortion.

I experienced adolescence before 1930. Since then there has been a monumental change in the attitude of Americans toward sex. Sixty-six years ago premarital sex was probably less common, and it was kept secret; then most members of our society frowned on premarital sex. Certainly in the 1930s some couples who were not married lived together, but it was rare and generally clandestine. One hundred years ago, sex except for the purpose of procreation was widely regarded as sinful, a view still held in some quarters.

Although the sex-is-sin ethic no longer represents a consensus, it still seems to control the teaching of sex education in our public schools. This mind-set also undergirds the militant efforts made by some Americans to prevent the establishment of school-based medical clinics, and it colors arguments about abortion. These citizens also sincerely believe that sex education and discussions of sex education will lead the young to sin, increasing sexual activity among teenagers. That is quite a tall order. For example, in 1986, before the Ounce established its first of three school-based comprehensive medical clinics in Chicago, one high school principal said that in her school, which had a student body of a thousand girls and a thousand boys, there were three hundred babies born each year. With statistics like that, any clinic-influenced major increase is improbable. Recent Ounce research indicates that 45 percent of the elementary school students who will soon enter one of the three high schools where the Ounce has medical clinics have already been sexually active before entering high school.

Most people in the United States would acknowledge that in the past twenty years there has been a sexual revolution. Undoubtedly the birth control pill and legalized abortion both have contributed to reducing a fear of pregnancy. Today, couples living together before marriage are no longer judged by most of their neighbors to be living in sin. Sex, for a majority of Americans, is no longer considered a sin. Yet some people's attitudes about abortion still reflect an outdated opinion that a woman should be punished if she has unintentionally become pregnant.

It is time that as a nation we stop and think. We should begin to adapt our social strategies to reflect this change in consensus. It is time to recognize that for most Americans—young, middle-aged, and old—having sex is usually for the purpose of pleasure, *not* for the purpose of achieving a pregnancy. Most Americans do not feel that a woman or her baby should be punished when an unexpected or unplanned pregnancy results. It is time we stopped burying our heads in the sand. We must start changing public policies about sex education, contraception, abortion, and school-based medical clinics.

TEEN PREGNANCY: THE EFFECTS OF POVERTY

Judith Musick was the first executive director of the Ounce of Prevention Fund. For the past thirteen years she has been a keen student of teen pregnancy, its causes, and its consequences. In *Young, Poor, and Pregnant* (1993), she points out that adolescents from all socioeconomic groups get pregnant, but it is overwhelmingly those from lower economic groups who elect to have and keep the children they conceive (p. 25).

It is the psychological effects of poverty, Musick maintains, that make adolescent pregnancy and parenthood so common. She provides the analysis needed to replace the simplistic thinking that holds that teenage girls "only want someone to love."

A Psychological Profile

Adolescent girls living in poverty, more often than not, come from families without fathers. Girls growing up in poverty experience more than fatherlessness; they suffer the absence of responsible, caring, and protective men in their lives. The absence of protective men fosters a particular vulnerability to male exploitation. In addition, these girls are likely to suffer the ill effects of family chaos and especially violence and physical or sexual abuse. Their mothers are frequently angry, depressed, inattentive, and emotionally unavailable. The foundation needed for healthy psychological development is usually inadequate for girls growing up in poverty.

During adolescence, according to Musick (1993, 59), mainstream adolescent girls wrestle with such questions as: Who am I? Do my parents understand me? What should I do about my sexual attractiveness to boys? How do I feel about sex? How do I balance my social life and my school life? Where will I go to college? Will I have a career, or will I marry and raise children, or do both? But disadvantaged girls are still grappling with questions grounded in early childhood: Who cares about me? Whom can I depend on or trust? Where and how can I find security and safety?

The History of Sexual Abuse

Sexual abuse is prevalent among poor teens who become pregnant and keep their babies. Musick cites a 1989 Ounce of Prevention study in which 61 percent of the girls participating in a program for pregnant and parenting teens had been sexually molested, beginning at age eleven and a half on average. Almost two thirds had been abused by someone they knew (p. 87; see chapter 5).

Research about sexual abuse suggests that its female victims are more likely to then engage in voluntary sexual intercourse, to have more sexually permissive attitudes, to be younger at the occasion of first intercourse, and to have sex more frequently than similar girls who have not been molested.

Musick explains that when a girl has been unprotected in her family and socialized into sexuality prematurely and inappropriately it is not surprising that during adolescence she feels helpless and unable to control that aspect of her life. Her sense of personal boundaries has been radically altered, leading to later failure to resist sexual advances. She confuses love and sex (pp. 97, 99).

The pregnant teenager may not be consciously aware of them, but motherhood has psychological benefits: extending a dependent bond with her mother through the baby; receiving the emotional sustenance she did not receive as a child; assuming adult status without having to become independent of her mother; developing a new identity as a parent; and finding opportunities to demonstrate competence in the valued role of mother. Given the psychologically damaging experience of poverty, early sexual activity and childbearing meet the adolescent girl's need to feel close to and cared for by a male and to feel similar to people in her life.

Long-term studies of teenage mothers show that roughly two thirds of them complete school, stay off welfare, and noticeably improve their employment status after twenty years. However, the children of teenage mothers appear to have more school and behavioral problems, particularly as they reach adolescence. This "developmental disadvantage" translates into a higher likelihood of their becoming teen parents themselves. The negative effects of adolescent childbearing, Musick says, are made worse by additional births. Within two years of giving birth, 40–50 percent of teenage mothers have become pregnant again, and 35 percent give birth. Musick believes that teenage mothers are not sufficiently motivated to prevent a second pregnancy.

The Implications for Intervention Programs
Programs designed for pregnant and parenting teenagers should address such domains as education, work, parenthood, child development, parent-child relationships, reproductive behavior, relationships with men, and victimization. Typically, however, they tend to emphasize only one domain, such as finishing high school, getting a job, or acquiring parenting skills. They rarely focus on the reproductive-behavior domain. Because existing social support programs fail to provide adequate attention to all relevant

domains, Musick judges them not to be a sufficient response to problems of adolescent childbearing.

Programs that focus exclusively on improving self-esteem or increasing opportunities cannot be effective, according to Musick. Teenage mothers need both programs and more. The best programs have clear expectations, help teens internalize consistent guidance and support, set high standards, and reinforce positive values. They also link expectations with tangible means of achieving them. An example is the Ounce of Prevention's Heart-to-Heart Program, which emphasizes parenting, victimization, sexuality, and relationships with men.

No strategy can make a teenage mother into a sexually and socially responsible individual, Musick warns, until it provides realistic alternatives as psychologically satisfying as are the modes of feeling and behaving of her mother, her sisters, and her friends.

THE CONSEQUENCES

Every year more than a half million babies are born in the United States to teenagers, and most are out of wedlock. Data on births to teenagers in the United States published by the Alan Guttmacher Institute are surprising and uneven. Of 48,040 teenage pregnancies in 1988 in Illinois, 48 percent resulted in births; in New York state, of 76,950 teenage pregnancies, only 34 percent resulted in births; and in California (despite a heavy Hispanic Catholic population) of 156,210 pregnancies, only 38 percent resulted in births.

Research on children and poverty has been conducted at the University of Minnesota under the leadership of Alan Sroufe and Byron Egeland. They have been intensively studying 151 children born in 1975–77 in Minneapolis.

The subjects were part of a prospective longitudinal study of families from lower socioeconomic backgrounds. The sample of first-time mothers in their third trimester of pregnancy was recruited from prenatal clinics sponsored by the Minneapolis Bureau of Maternal and Child Health. In general, because they are poor they are considered to be a population at high risk for later caregiving problems. At the time of delivery, the mothers ranged in age from twelve to thirty-seven, and 62 percent of the mothers were single. Forty percent had not completed high school, and 86 percent of the pregnancies were unplanned, 80 percent of the mothers were white, 13 percent black, and the remaining 7 percent were Native American or Hispanic (Egeland and Brunnquell, 1979).

Although the research team found no mothers taking drugs, the children were poor, and most were poorly nurtured. For various reasons, over time of 267 mothers 116 dropped out of the follow-up studies. Of those who remained in the study, most of the 151 babies had disappointing outcomes: by the third grade, 109 (72 percent) had been referred for special education. In one way or another, they were failing in school. These students attended ninety different schools, and thus it appeared unlikely that the schools were responsible for the increased failure rate. Sroufe and Egeland's conclusion was that the failures were largely attributable to inadequate nurturing in the first three years of life. The study indicates that a major consequence of births to poor mothers is the high probability of those children—white, black, or Hispanic—having learning problems in school. Many of these children were simply not prepared to enter school when they were five.

Unwilling Parents

What happens when contraceptives are used incorrectly or fail, as they did for some 1.7 million women in 1988 (NCHS, 1988)? That year there were altogether more than 3.6 million unintended pregnancies out of a total of 6.4 million pregnancies. The number of unintended pregnancies resulting from contraceptive failure or misuse was almost as high as the number resulting from using no contraceptive at all. Contraceptive failure or misuse resulted in 47.3 percent of all unintended pregnancies, while intercourse without contraception led to 52.7 percent of all unintended pregnancies (Forrest, 1994). Society must listen to the pregnant woman who does not want to have a baby and then make it possible for her to end the pregnancy, whatever her financial circumstances. Access to safe and affordable abortion should be provided to any woman who chooses to terminate an unplanned, unwanted pregnancy.

Women choose to have abortions for multiple reasons (Torres and Forrest, 1988): more than two thirds point to financial difficulties; 30

percent say they are too immature or too young to have a child; and 51 percent have problems with a relationship and want to avoid single parenthood. In fact, unmarried women accounted for 79 percent of all abortions performed in the United States in 1990 (CDC, 1992). The need for access to abortion is based in large part on a concern for children born unwanted. Their being unwanted is more likely to lead to lifelong hardships, as has been documented in studies that analyze the effects on the woman and the child of a denied abortion. In a review of these studies for the *American Journal of Psychiatry*, Paul K. B. Dagg (1991) concludes:

> Relatively few of the children are put up for adoption, and the majority born of unwanted pregnancies are raised by their biological mother. A significant minority—about 30%—of the women examined in the few long-term studies continue to report negative feelings toward their child and difficulty adjusting. Finally, the most disturbing part of the whole issue is the evidence of significant negative effects on the child ... subsequently raised in the situation that the parents had tried so desperately to avoid. (p. 584)

The conclusion of the negative effects on the child is based on several well-designed prospective studies done in Scandinavia and eastern Europe in the 1960s and 1970s. Dagg evaluates the research:

> In a classic study that continues to have relevance today, Forssman and Thuwe (1966) compared, up to age twenty-one, 120 children born of unwanted pregnancies with control subjects matched by date of birth. They found that the study group had a more insecure childhood, more psychiatric care, more childhood delinquency, and more early marriages and were more often young mothers; all these findings were statistically significant. Even after socioeconomic class was controlled, fewer of the study subjects have more than secondary education and fewer were without defects of any kind, when all these problems were grouped together. (p. 583)

THE EXAMPLE OF CZECHOSLOVAKIA

The difficulties confronting children born unwanted are further confirmed by research in Prague, Czechoslovakia (David et al., 1988). Calling it "the most ambitious study to date," Dagg summarizes the results of the study, which compared a group of 220 children born in Prague in 1961–63 to women who were twice denied abortion for the same pregnancy with a control group of 220 matched for socioeconomic class, sex, age, birth order, number of siblings, and parental marital status:

> Early findings in 1970 found that the study subjects were less likely to be breast fed, had more acute medical illness, were more likely to be reported as difficult when they were preschoolers, were more likely to be rejected by friends and teachers, had poorer school performance, and were less adaptive to frustration; boys were more likely to be affected. At ages fourteen to sixteen, 216 of the original 220 were still being studied. School performance in the study group continued to deteriorate, and various indicator scales showed this group had more negative relationships with their mothers. Current studies of the children in their early twenties show an ongoing propensity for social problems that remains markedly prevalent in this group. The study subjects had more job dissatisfaction and fewer friends and reported dissatisfaction with life (all significant findings) and less education, more criminality, and more registration by the authorities for drug and alcohol problems. (p. 583)

What they found was that the unwanted children fared much worse in life than those whose mothers did not seek abortion twice. Their research showed that, among other things, at age nine the unwanted children generally had fewer friends and less developed language skills than the other children had. By their midteens, more of the studied subjects had sought academic or personal counseling; as a whole, they were more hyperactive and less sociable. Fewer went on to secondary school, opting for vocational schools or a trade. In their twenties, twice as many of the unwanted children, that is, 23 versus 11, were sentenced in a criminal court, and usually for more serious crimes. Psychiatric disorders were more common among the unwanted, as were marital problems and a general dissatisfaction with life. The authors concluded: "The child of a woman denied abortion appears to be born into a potentially handicapping situation."

Social and Economic Costs

Responsible, hard-working citizens increasingly find that the schools they support no longer work, that it is dangerous to live in our cities, and that America's competitive ability in the world markets continues to deteriorate. Hard-working people are increasingly being asked through taxes to support more poor children, more people on welfare, and more retired people. Those of us who pay the bulk of the taxes and do all the work are fewer and fewer and constitute a diminishing percentage of the total body of Americans.

The number of children under fifteen is not changing much; the number of people over seventy is increasing; the percentage, male and female, of Americans who are working is shrinking; and the load we are carrying is heavier and heavier. No wonder our middle-class standard of living is decreasing. No wonder violence keeps increasing. No wonder the number of people out of school, out of work, and out of the job market continues to rise. We must stop this trend.

There are real dollars-and-cents implications of current reproductive health policies. Although it may appear callous to consider the economic consequences of denying family planning, contraceptive services, and abortions, the effects are simply too vast to be ignored. If, through a change in public policy, Illinois were to increase its funding for family planning and contraceptive services and provide public funding for abortion—as do sixteen states, including California and New York—and if the costs for this policy were similar to the costs for New York, Illinois would have to spend $60 million instead of the current $17 million. In 1992 New York's family planning expenditures enabled it to decrease the percentage of births to teenagers to 7.5 percent of all births in the state. If Illinois' per capita spending had met New York's level of family planning expenditures by spending an additional $43 million in 1992, the results would have been 10,246 fewer births to teens, at an estimated savings to the state of $101 million.[1] If we include similar decreases in births to unmarried women over twenty years old, who account for more than two thirds of unmarried births, the estimated savings would triple, to $303 million. (In fiscal year 1992, New York spent a total of $20.5 million for abortions and

$70.8 million for family planning and contraception services, or $317 for each live birth.)

The longer-term costs for unwanted babies after birth are more difficult to assess. They include extra costs for some premature babies, multiple visits to the hospital for children who are sickly, and such costs as AFDC. In this connection, Douglas Besharov of the American Enterprise Institute wrote in the *Washington Post* (Besharov, 1993):

> After almost a year of study, an administration working group has prepared its initial report on how to fulfill President Clinton's promise to "end welfare as we know it." The report starts in exactly the right place: the 30-year growth in out-of-wedlock births, especially among teenagers, and its relation to persistent poverty.... The bulk of long-term welfare recipients are young, unmarried mothers, most of whom had their first baby as teenagers. About 50 percent of unwed teen mothers go on welfare within one year of the birth of their first child and 77 percent within five years, according to the Congressional Budget Office. Almost half of those on the rolls for three or more of the past five years started their families as unwed teens.

THE RIGHT TO LIFE

The right to life is everyone's right to the best and healthiest opportunity to succeed in life. As a child and family advocate, I support a range of programs designed to improve the physical, emotional, and financial well-being of children and families.

In the United States, babies born to women who wanted to end their pregnancies but could not afford to do so face challenges that may be even greater than those confronted by the children followed in the Scandinavian and Czechoslovakian samples. They are likely to be exposed to the interacting risks and consequences of poor health, poverty, drug use, sexual victimization, adolescent pregnancy, child abuse and neglect, and out-of-home placement.

For a child to be born poor not infrequently means to endure narcotic withdrawal in its first few weeks of life, to be neglected, punched, or victimized—being burned with cigarettes, spanked so hard that bones are broken, or actually murdered. These kinds of problems seem to be of no interest to right-to-lifers, who are confident that God wills these fetuses to live. Do not the majority of Americans pray to God and believe that their God does not will that a fetus become a human infant when God knows that infant will be born with Down's Syndrome or with AIDS? Is it certain that God believes it is worse for this fetus to be aborted than to die slowly and painfully over the next ten years or sixty years?

Although comprehensive programs and early intervention approaches designed to assist families with young children to overcome multiple obstacles to their healthy development are indispensable, primary prevention approaches constitute the first line of defense. Abortion is never a first choice for preventing unwanted childbearing, but it should not be denied as an option, merely for financial reasons, to a woman who is trying, through her reproductive choices, to assume personal responsibility for her own and her family's future.

Children's advocates do not usually talk about abortion. But the time has come for us to face reality and the statistics. No one doubts that poverty hurts kids. Slightly less well known, but no more debatable, is that single parenthood is closely correlated with poverty. Obviously, marital status does not determine whether someone is a good parent, but the fact is that parenting without a partner is excruciatingly difficult. When poverty is added to the mix it becomes all the more difficult—and most of the time poverty *is* added to the mix. For instance, 43 percent of all mother-only families are poor compared with 7 percent of two-parent families (NCC, 1991, 83).

So what do we do? The answer is, we should do everything that works. Along these lines, we must first do all we can to prevent unwanted pregnancy. This means that if couples will not abstain, we must provide safe, affordable, reliable, and accessible birth control to anyone who wants it.[2] When birth control methods fail, as from time to time they unfortunately will, we must provide access to safe and affordable abortion to any woman who chooses to terminate an unplanned, unwanted pregnancy. I stress the word *unwanted*. Nobody should be allowed to play God. No one should have the right to declare which women may choose to have children and which women may not, but we are tolerating a set of government policies that does just that. Today in America, privileged women have access to an array of birth control methods, and they also have access to abortion. In most areas of this country, however, poor women do not have any such options. Thanks to unfair and dangerous federal and state government policies, we are saying to poor women and girls, *you* do not have the same right that wealthier women have to decide whether and when to have children. It is time that this inequity, this terrible unfairness, be ended, for the good of women, for the good of children, and for the good of society, the schools, and the criminal justice system.

In 1976 nearly half a million babies were born out of wedlock in the United States (14.8 percent of all births). In 1977 Republican member of Congress Henry Hyde was able to sponsor and pass an amendment banning federal funding for abortions. In 1992, the number of babies born out of wedlock was 1.2 million (30 percent), compared with nearly a half million in 1976, an increase of 153 percent. This increase, in part, was the consequence of the suspension of federal funds for abortions for the poor women who sought them. (See chapter 5.)

PRO-CHOICE: ENSURING WILLING PARENTS

It is common wisdom in America today, among Catholics, Protestants, Jews, Muslims, and atheists alike, that the outlook is usually bleak for a baby born to a single parent. Most single parents are not well educated and have poor employment prospects. To quote the recent report of the bipartisan National Commission on Children (1991):

> Children do best when they have the personal involvement and material support of a father and a mother and when both parents fulfill their responsibility to be loving providers.
>
> Because families are the cornerstone of children's development, the National Commission on Children recommends that . . . parents share responsibility for planning their families and delay pregnancy until they are financially and emotionally capable of assuming the obligations of parenthood. . . .
>
> Families formed by marriage—where two caring adults are committed to one another and to their children—provide the best environment for

bringing children into the world and supporting their growth and development. Where this commitment is lacking, children are less likely to receive care and nurturing, as well as basic material support. Research on the effects of single parenthood confirms that children who grow up without the support and personal involvement of both parents are more vulnerable to problems throughout childhood and into their adult lives.

When abortion is denied, the unwanted pregnancy usually leaves a debilitating legacy for the mother and child.

I am well aware of the political problems involved in discussing abortion. I clearly understand that while the economics of abortion may be persuasive, voters must first consider the moral and religious aspects of the decision to terminate a pregnancy. But after appropriate emphasis on the morality of choice versus the right to life, there is still a huge problem for society. The distressing life ahead for unintended and unwanted babies born to poor, uneducated single parents is an outlook that seriously affects the educational system and eventually the criminal justice system—in other words, society as a whole.

Reproductive Choices

There is an urgent need for the primary prevention of unintended and unwanted pregnancies. The number of adolescent pregnancies is not surprising: the Centers for Disease Control (CDC) in Atlanta reports that in 1988 three out of four nineteen-year-old young women in this country had been sexually active (CDC, 1991), and 53 percent of all high school students had had sexual intercourse (CDC, 1995). Encouragement of sexual abstention will not by itself significantly reduce unwanted births. Safe, affordable, reliable, and accessible birth control should therefore be provided to anyone who wants it, and especially to adolescents.

The Constitution and the Individual's Freedom to Choose

The issue of social responsibility is about more than fulfilling financial obligations; it is about giving women the opportunity to assume personal responsibility for what is perhaps the most important decision they will ever make. It is also about fairness to all women, regardless of income. As the debate about including abortion services in any national health care package unfolded, the concerns of poor women became the concerns of all women.

A major question in forming public policy is involved in deciding whether a poor person should have the right to have an abortion paid for by the state, by Medicaid, or by whatever other government sources there may be. For some reason, the debate about abortion is almost always joined on one or more of the following three questions:

1. Does religion dictate that it is immoral to take the life of an unborn fetus? When does a fertilized egg become a human being?

2. Does a woman have the freedom to determine whether she will carry a pregnancy to term?

3. Does the U.S. Constitution preserve an individual's freedom to have an abortion even though a majority enacts a law limiting that freedom?

I am not arguing that every pregnant woman must abort. She should be allowed, if she wishes, to carry her fetus to term, assuming she is willing and anxious to care for the baby for life. She should have this privilege, but no state has the right to impose on a woman the requirement that she bear an unwanted child. In one case, a ten-year-old girl who had been impregnated when she was raped went to the hospital with her parents asking for an abortion. No funds from any public source were available to pay the $250 needed in their state to pay for it. The social workers and nursing staff came up with the money.

Unless we can drastically reduce the number of infants born into high-risk environments, we will continue to need more prisons and more hospitals for the retarded, to have more illiteracy and less ability to compete industrially in a highly competitive world, higher taxes, more flight from our cities, failing schools, frightening cases of child abuse and neglect, drug addiction, and alcohol abuse. Or we can mount efforts to prevent many of these problems. We know how. Do we have the will?

Should we allow a tyrannical minority—comprising the religious right, the organization of the Catholic Church, and the radical antiabortionists—to set public policy in these matters? This sort of public policy is not only illogical, it is bizarre. We also can and should start seriously to advocate adoption as a preferred option for unwanted children born into high-risk environments—again, not as a requirement, but as a public policy to be encouraged.

The Catholic Church: A Dialogue

In 1988 the director of the Ounce of Prevention Fund came to consult with me when the Illinois state legislature was furiously debating whether to continue public aid funding for half the costs of our three school-based medical clinics, which were distributing condoms and birth control pills in Chicago high schools. The director had been informed, perhaps unreliably, that Joseph Cardinal Bernardin was personally calling members of the legislature to encourage them to vote against the funding. The director suggested that I should try to set up a meeting, one-on-one, with the cardinal to convince him of the merit of the clinics. I agreed that although such a meeting would be difficult and perhaps impossible to arrange, it might be useful.

The next morning I took a plane to a meeting in Washington, D.C. My seat partner was Cardinal Bernardin. I glanced upward briefly to thank the Lord for having heard my silent entreaty of the previous day and then proceeded to engage the cardinal in what proved to be a most amiable conversation, one that began with a discussion of the funeral of our former Chicago mayor Harold Washington, which had taken place the previous day and at which the cardinal was one of the officiating clergy.

We then went on to talk about news reports regarding a recent letter from the American Catholic bishops that criticized contraceptive services to adolescents because of a fear that it would cause increased promiscuity. The cardinal acknowledged that we were on different sides of this argument, but he said he would appreciate knowing my reaction to the specifics of the bishops' letter. We subsequently had a most civilized discourse about the subject by mail over the next two months. The following letter is the first of two I wrote to him.

Dear Eminence,

Thank you for sending along to me the statement issued in November by the National Conference of Catholic Bishops on the subject of school-based comprehensive medical clinics.

The statement includes a very careful assessment of the overall problems, and I find myself in strong agreement with many of the thoughts expressed; for example, the words of the Holy Father, "Not only does the future belong to youth, but the future depends on youth," and, "The youth of today must be prepared to take moral responsibility for the plans and actions that will build or endanger the world of tomorrow." As we [at the Ounce] see it, our comprehensive school-based medical clinics are trying to prepare youth to recognize individual responsibility. We encourage young people to take charge of their lives, to abandon the philosophy that we as individuals are victims of fate and therefore have no control. We agree that "youth is also a fragile time when the spark of hope in the future must be nurtured, harmonized with intellectual development, and channeled toward service to one another in love. Whether this occurs in an individual case will depend to an incalculable degree on the ways in which parents, schools, churches, and society at large are willing and able to challenge young people to live up to their own God-given human dignity." We believe that we are acting in the role of society at large in this endeavor.

We concur that we should refuse to accept the "continuing high pregnancy rate among unwed teenagers . . . as a hopeless situation."

While it is true that the problem has worsened since the federal government and other public and private agencies began spending millions of dollars annually on family planning services, we regard this as a coincidence rather than a demonstration of cause and effect. For example, many more children are born today with severe handicaps than was true twenty years ago. Twenty years ago, as a nation, we started building ramps to public streets and public buildings to assist the handicapped. Nobody believes that the building of ramps to the streets or to public buildings has caused an increase in the number of children born with handicaps. Again, this is coincidence, not cause and effect.

We agree with William Julius Wilson's concept set forth in *The Truly Disadvantaged* [Wilson, 1987]. In the past fifteen years high levels of unemployment resulting from structural change in manufacturing in major U.S. cities have greatly reduced the male marriageable pool of young, black men. This in turn has made marriage an unrealizable option for many young, black women, and this in turn has been a major factor in the increase of out-of-wedlock pregnancies and births. The economic phenomenon of increasing unemployment, the job losses in the auto and steel industries, for example, were not caused by or related to increased spending on family planning. In the Northeast between 1960 and 1980 the Male Marriageable Pool Index dropped for sixteen- to nineteen-year-old blacks from 31.2 to 22.7, for twenty- to twenty-four-year-old blacks from 59.1 to 48.1. In all areas other than the West similar drops were reported. The index shows the number of black males employed per one hundred black females of similar ages. In the inner cities these ratios became much worse between 1960 and 1980.

. . . We agree that there has been a big increase in sexual activity and that this has given rise to a similar increase in teenage pregnancy, despite the increased access to contraceptives. Clearly, if we could discourage premarital sexual activity on the part of youth, it would eliminate out-of-wedlock births to teenagers. When we can learn how to do that we will both be pleased, and the problem will be solved. However, until we have learned how to discourage early sexual activity out of wedlock, we must rely on additional efforts to stem the increase in births to teenagers because the resultant births are frequently a beginning of a disastrous life, not only for the mother and father, but almost invariably for the baby about to be born. . . . Of the supportive counseling available in clinics on the use of contraceptives . . . that counseling also includes strong advice to young women to say no to sex. Our counselors are trained to encourage young women to say no. On the other hand, if they are going to say yes, then they are urged to contracept.

. . . You note that some systems reward contraceptive use by having students earn points toward school trips and other perquisites. In Chicago, we do not do any of these stunts to encourage contraceptive use.

. . . The statement [in your letter] deals with the need to respect the dignity of teenagers and their parents and their teachers. Our approach is the same. We do teach respect for the dignity of teenagers and their parents and their teachers. The need for counseling goes way beyond our refusal to accept a promiscuous life style as the norm. Through our counseling we also try to have a favorable impact on gang-related conduct toward sex, which is by itself a tragic situation. . . . In many of the schools in the inner city (and most of them do not have clinics) approximately one half of all freshman girls will have a baby before they graduate from school. We certainly applaud the efforts of all ministers and churches working with teenagers to lessen this likelihood.

But so far, all the efforts have had no visible results—or at least they are not reducing the percentage of girls who are sexually active and having pregnancies. One of the most common syndromes that we encounter is the attitude of the young women when they learn that they are pregnant. Very frequently, their reaction is, "This is no big deal." It underlies their expectation that it is their fate as teenagers to bear children out of wedlock. When they say they are considering becoming sexually active, we are doing everything we can to encourage them to be prepared to assume the responsibility of parenthood and, therefore, to avoid sex entirely or if they will not postpone sex, to at least be responsible by contracepting.

. . . The statement reads, "Moreover we note that many non-Catholic parents and religious leaders have raised objections similar to our own." In general, you are correct, but 90 percent of the parents in the school districts [of two Chicago high schools we surveyed] have approved of the clinics. And besides that, no students are allowed in the clinics unless they have written parental permission to become patients at the clinic.

As the statement continues, we also believe in the "inalienable right to education," for all human persons of every race, condition, and age. Unfortunately, school drop-out, which frequently results from pregnancy, works against this inalienable right.

As you know, under the Reagan Administration, the Office of Adolescent Pregnancy Prevention has funded a good many programs encouraging abstinence rather than contraception. To the best of my knowledge none of these programs has been effective.

In our conversation on the plane, I mentioned that a great deal more is needed than simply offering contraception. We have programs in the school to encourage readiness for jobs, thinking seriously about career opportunities, building self-esteem, saying no to sex, and a whole roster of counseling efforts to go along with the offer of a contraceptive. It is shocking to recognize how prevalent the attitude is among inner-city teenagers that there is no alternative to fate. Among the first 46 pregnancies that we encountered in our Beethoven Project in the Robert Taylor Homes, 16 were first-time pregnancies, 12 were second pregnancies, 6 were third pregnancies, 5 were fourth pregnancies, 2 were fifth pregnancies, 2 were sixth pregnancies, 2 were seventh pregnancies, and 1 was a tenth pregnancy. Needless to say, in the surroundings of the Robert Taylor Homes, these generally unwanted births are not likely to result in those children growing up to be self-respecting adults who can live out a life of human dignity.

. . . As the statement points out, "The most prominent killers of teenagers today are drugs and alcohol, automobile accidents, homicide, and suicide." Our comprehensive school-based medical clinics and the counseling we provide address these problems as well. There are many instances in which we have been able to achieve favorable results as a consequence of our counseling.

. . . The statement reports the conclusion of National Academy of Science researchers. They conclude that "we currently know very little about how to effectively discourage unmarried teenagers from initiating intercourse." One of the problems in this connection is our finding from interviewing 450 adolescent mothers in Ounce of Prevention programs that 61 percent of these young women had been sexually abused as children. A child who has been sexually abused is likely to have low self-esteem, and low self-esteem seems to go along with a feeling that the individual has no control over her life and that pregnancy is "no big deal"—compared with the other indignities that life has already heaped on these individuals.

. . . The statement recognizes the need for young people to have solid reasons for hope. We have several programs in our Ounce of Prevention group which do focus on preparing students for jobs and helping them get jobs. The Harris Foundation has . . . contributed $100,000 over two years to set up in Chicago programs called Career Beginnings for students in the eleventh and twelfth grades to give them the experience of a mentored opportunity at a job. We also provide career counseling in the sixth, seventh, and eighth grades, working both with young men and young women in an effort to improve the outlook for these students as far as their career choices are concerned. In the Beethoven Project we are trying to improve the health care of mothers who are pregnant, looking forward to healthier babies resulting from better nutrition and better prenatal care, as well as avoidance of drugs, alcohol, and smoking. All these are necessary to try to combat the difficult conditions of the underclass. . . . You point out that the best way to impart values to children is for parents to transmit high values to their children. Unfortunately, many of the parents that we are discussing are themselves damaged. The parents themselves have led lives that include being unwanted, out-of-wedlock babies and frequently also having suffered from very early sexual abuse as children. Without prevention it does not seem probable that these "damaged parents" will themselves be successful parents who can introduce their children to good moral values.

To conclude, I agree that moral values and self-esteem and human dignity are extremely important, but I am also aware that approximately one third of the young women who have their first baby out of wedlock while they are still in high school will have a second baby within twenty-four months. Most people agree that it is not a good idea for a high school student to have her second baby out of wedlock while still in school. We hope that our clinics will reduce this likelihood. Furthermore, our clinics seem to have increased the health of the students who did become pregnant. Of the first twenty-four young women at [Chicago's] DuSable High School who were pregnant and treated in prenatal care, not one of them had a low-birthweight baby. Under normal circumstances, probably five or more of the twenty-four would have been born at a low birthweight. Furthermore, every one of the twenty-four girls who had been in our prenatal care did go back to high school. And, though the data are difficult to come by, it is clear that there is a reduction in the number of pregnancies and the number of births to students at DuSable concomitant with the beginning of the clinic's operation.

. . . There clearly are many points of view . . . about how as a society and as moral human beings we can work together to reduce the number of young women who become pregnant out of wedlock and the many serious social problems resulting therefrom. . . .

P.S. In 1751 Benjamin Franklin wrote, "The number of marriages . . . is greater in proportion to the ease and convenience of supporting a family. When families can be easily supported, more persons marry and earlier in life."

Alternatives to Abortion

For pregnant, unmarried teenagers, still in school and without jobs, we have to be more open to the alternatives of abortion or giving the child up for adoption. These options should be open to teens, and if they choose to terminate their pregnancy or choose to give the baby up for adoption, we must be prepared to offer the intensive counseling that such options would require, both before and after these difficult decisions are made.

The choices are not easy for young people to face, and they will not be resolved quickly or without considerable, painful debate. They are issues that must be raised if we are to begin to move ahead in breaking the cycle of poverty that holds so many of our people in its grasp.

Professionals are convinced that in most cases the teenage mothers and fathers and the infants born out of wedlock into poverty and hopelessness would be better off if their lives could develop without the economic, educational, social, and emotional handicaps of having to cope with deprivation, lack of education, and joblessness. These young people can still have babies when they have finished school and have jobs. They will be better off, and the adopted babies will be much better off.

Who Is Responsible

We could all call ourselves thoughtful citizens; we observe our surroundings; we see things we like and things we would like to do away with. Of course, we do a good job of not seeing some things because we just do not like what we see. First we deny that the thing is there; then we say, well, it is there, but it is someone else's fault or someone else's problem. Yet it does not go away, and painfully and slowly we begin to say, well, the thing *is* there. It is not going to go away by itself. *We* have the responsibility for solving the problem. Some will even say, "I think I know how to solve this problem." When that statement is in the form of a lead editorial series in the *Chicago Tribune,* as it was during the last week of 1984, that's news.

> These are children who grow up without ever being close to someone who has a job, who never sees the relationship between learning and earning. In them, the normal adolescent quest for independence often leads to a street gang and crime or to teenage motherhood and a welfare check. And so the hopelessness gives birth to more hopelessness. . . .

The issue, then, is to make vital mental nourishment available to all young children before school age—not just those from well-to-do homes. . . . Many children lack adequate mental nourishment; their parents are too young, too uninformed, too troubled by their own problems to provide well for the needs of their offspring's growing brains. These youngsters will already be behind when they start first grade. And their failures to keep up in school will make them more vulnerable to drug abuse, delinquency, premature pregnancy, unemployment—and inability to escape from poverty. . . .

Every dollar spent today on early childhood education would reap long-term savings in money for remedial education, dependency, crime, teenage pregnancy, and a host of other problems associated with the underclass. . . .

There is a way to break those chains [of dependency, bitterness, and despair]. Using techniques already tested, it's possible to succeed where all the massive, costly social programs of the last two decades failed. It's possible to transform the doomed children of the underclass into productive, self-sustaining young people. What works, and has been proved to work in hundreds of research projects and tens of thousands of lives, is early childhood education. . . .

The dollar costs to the nation of school failure, remedial education, delinquency, crime, premarital pregnancy, and welfare dependency are staggering. The human costs are even greater. The evidence is clear that early childhood education can prevent at least some of these problems from ever occurring—and save considerable money doing so. The time has come to act on this compelling evidence. . . .

. . . It doesn't matter whether the president and his administration are moved by the misery of the poor. All that matters is that they have the brains to understand that the chains binding the chronically poor are also strangling the nation. . . .

Even if you live a hundred, a thousand miles from one of the staggering cities that has lost taxpaying homeowners and businesses and gained generations of tax dependents, you're paying for that exchange. In this fiscal year, federal aid to the poor will total more than $44 billion, despite the Reagan cuts. The entire nation pays, too, through the failure of American industry to keep pace with productivity gains of its foreign competitors. If you live in a state like Illinois, whose 5.1 million workers help support more than 1.1 million public aid recipients, the burden on your pocketbook is even greater. . . .

Chicago and other big cities have always had gangs and poverty and illiterates. But in decades past, the numbers were tolerable and the status was not permanent. It's the specter of permanency and the accelerating lurch into violence that separates today's underclass from the poverty of the past, and also from the bulk of today's low-income families.

That a major newspaper recognized the problem and the solution is significant. That many individuals in Congress, as well as governors, realize that we must and can invest money in infants and children if we are to prevent passing on problems from one generation to the next is leadership. There are a growing number of people in Congress, Democrats and Republicans—for example, Senators Nancy Kassebaum and Edward Kennedy—who see the problem and want to help.

The bad news—or perhaps it is just *challenging* news—is that it is now up to us to develop more programs that work and grapple more successfully with the problems we know are there. In Illinois, for example, Ounce of Prevention programs are now getting more than $14 million a year. That is a good beginning as far as money is concerned. Now, we must improve our programs, learn from what good programs have accomplished, and try out new ideas that look promising.

4

THE COST OF FAILURE

A STORY TOLD by Reginald Lourie, one of the founders of the National Center for Clinical Infant Studies, speaks to the matter of intervention, also called secondary prevention. One bright, sunny afternoon, a group of friends gathered on the bank of a stream to have a picnic. They had just finished their preparations for lunch when someone shouted, "There is a child out there in the center of the stream." One of the men kicked off his shoes and ran into the river to rescue the child. Just as he got back to shore and put the child on dry land someone else shouted, "There's another child out there now." The same man ran into the river for the second time and, out of breath, soon came back with the second child. While friends made sure that both children were dried off and covered with towels before finding them warm blankets, the rescuer, who was just starting to take off his wet clothes, suddenly heard someone shout again, "There's another child out there now." Instead of rushing in for the third time, he said to his friends, "Someone else go in this time." With that, wet clothes and all, he slipped on his sneakers and started to run up the path that went along the edge of the stream. The others said, "Where are you going?" The man replied, "I'm going to run up around the bend and find out who is pushing those kids into the river."

He was asking the right question: "Who is pushing the kids into the river?" Unfortunately, the answer is: "We are." As a society we are pushing our kids into the river at an alarming rate. We do this by tolerating the prevalence of desperate poverty, even though we know there are things we can do to help. We know that decent housing and access to medical care would make a difference. We also know that more programs like Head Start would make a difference.

More on point is that we know that if we ensure that women who do not want to have children have options like family planning and access to safe and affordable abortion, it will make a difference. To understand precisely how we have been "pushing kids into the river" and why reproductive choice issues are so closely related, it is important to understand the early development of children, especially their brain development (see chapter 2).

THE COSTS

How much is it worth to us to prevent illiteracy and retardation and their lifelong costs? What about the long-range costs of juvenile delinquency coupled with substance abuse; the associated costs of police, burglary insurance, probation, and the criminal justice systems; and lifelong penitentiary sentences?

The perpetrators of violent crime are increasingly younger. A 1992 study by the Office of Juvenile Justice and Delinquency Prevention shows that the number of juveniles arrested for murder increased 51 percent in a four-year period, while the figure for adults was up 9 percent. The result is that the United States has a homicide rate that is three to sixteen times higher than in other industrialized countries. (See figures 4-1 and 4-2.)

The social and economic costs of crime are astronomical. In Illinois, it costs the state each year around $16,000 to keep an adult in prison—versus about $4,200 to keep one child in school.

Crime is closely connected to educational problems, as a 1991 study, "Education and Criminal Justice in Illinois," showed. The Illinois Criminal Justice Authority (CER, 1995) found that 72 percent of the prisoners were high school drop-outs, compared with an average drop-out rate of 22 percent for all Illinois high-school-age residents. Almost one quarter of the prison drop-outs left school before tenth grade, and the average inmate had the educational skills of an eighth grader. Similarly, there are strong links between learning disabilities and juvenile delinquency, with learning disabled boys having a 220 percent increased risk of delinquency, even when socioeconomic factors are considered.

Newspaper headlines call our attention to the increasing rates of violent behavior. These headlines from the *New York Times* and the *Chicago*

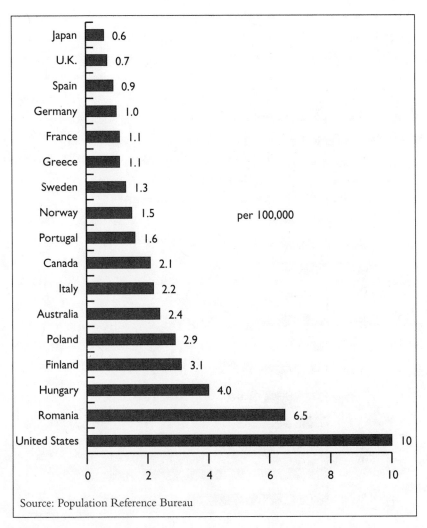

Figure 4-1
Homicide Rates for Selected Nations, 1992

Tribune are typical: Child Homicides Soar in City and Suburbs; Reports of Child Abuse, Neglect Up 4% in 1990; U.S. Is by Far the Leader in Homicide; City's Top Crime Rates Still Haunt Poor Areas: Study Links High Drop-out Rate to State Prison Overcrowding; and 30% of Young

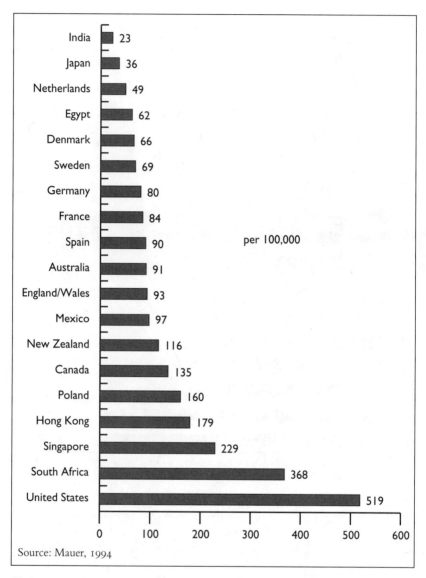

Figure 4-2
Incarceration Rates for Selected Nations, 1992–1993

Black Men Face Jail: Study, U.S. Expands Its Lead in the Rate of Imprisonment.

What the headlines do not tell us is that these problems did not just suddenly happen. Violence and criminal behavior represent the cumulative toll taken on children growing up in profoundly hostile and uncaring surroundings. The process usually begins with violence within the home. The evidence is compelling that in families where force rather than dialogue resolves most differences of opinion babies are brought up to be violent, and they will grow up to be violent, acting-out adolescents and adults. No decent society can tolerate increasing violence. According to the Illinois DCFS, more than 136,000 children in the state were reported as victims of child abuse or neglect in 1994. Credible evidence of abuse or neglect was found for nearly 50,000 children. Seventy percent of these victims were abused or neglected by their natural parents. There were more than 3.1 million cases of child abuse and neglect reported in the United States in 1994.

Our federal, state, county, and city governments spend much of our tax money trying to cope with a flood of human disasters. The huge numbers alone defy systems of efficient case management. A 1994 *Chicago Tribune* investigatory series reported on the situation of the Illinois DCFS, which is charged by law with trying to cope with the 818,000 calls made to its hot line. "It's an impossible mission that the state has assigned its Department of Children and Family Services" (Leroux and Schreuder, 1994). There is no way the state can succeed with each of the more than 47,000 children in its care, "no matter what its legal duty or how skilled its caseworkers or how much money the legislature provides. A state bureaucracy is not a family. Nothing ever makes up to a child for the failure of his own mother and father to raise him well. Many children are too badly hurt to be completely healed in a foster home, however loving, or a treatment center, however skilled. Caseworkers may make a careful judgment to return an abused child to his own home to avoid the problems of foster or institutional care." They find that it not infrequently leads to the youngster's death. These are high-risk cases. No public agency can guarantee a happy ending.

As we face this incomplete list of economic costs, we have to ask:

What can we do to prevent some of these disasters? (I exclude the human costs, which are so great that none of us will subject ourselves to study and empathize with the agony of all these human tragedies—being hooked on drugs, living in prison, life for a retarded person, living disabled, being illiterate, and so forth.) The answer is: A great deal. Some prevention opportunities are immediately obvious. If we have the will to make the necessary financial investment, we can reduce the number of children born at high risk. We can do this by expending more effort.

It is not that when children are born poor and at high risk nothing can be done for them and their families. For the past twenty-five years across the nation we have attempted programs for intervention. In all, there are many more than one hundred such programs. Most involve high costs, and all require highly trained and highly motivated professionals. All these programs have had success with some of the families they have tried to help, but there are many others they have tried to reach but have failed. Unfortunately, there is a colossal shortage of resources available for these programs and an even greater shortage of the highly skilled personnel needed to make them work.

CHILDREN IN NEED

All our intervention programs target children and families who live in highly stressful environments, environments that adversely affect optimal child development twenty-four hours a day, seven days a week. Stability is known to be a critical component of healthy child development. Yet these environments are crippled by the tremendous instability of everything from human relationships to housing, and by the domestic and community violence that characterize them. We are just beginning to understand the destructive effects that witnessing violence can have on a child—for example, watching one's mother physically beaten or stabbed—let alone physical violence against the child. If that were not enough, there is malnutrition, homelessness, racism, AIDS, and a lack of hope. Sadly, the list goes on. Each factor is a formidable one. A new war on poverty is needed now more than it was in 1965. We must recognize, however, that even with widespread replication such intervention programs alone will not win the war.

Even where successful, intervention has not been and will not be enough to stem the tide of poverty and despair that threatens our inner cities and rural poverty zones. The bottom line is that the deluge of children requiring intervention programs is overwhelming and is tragically unnecessary. Many—too many—poor women are giving birth to children who were unplanned and unwanted.

Multiproblem Family Syndrome

Family dysfunction is the name we can assign to a whole set of problems that produce the same symptoms over and over again, generation after generation. Add to family dysfunction the cycle of poverty that continues to grow in the United States, and we have a festering, expanding disaster in terms of the waste of human life. Poverty and family dysfunction frequently overlap, although poverty alone does not cause families to disintegrate, and many families that are not poor function poorly.

The cycle of poverty and family dysfunction is a frightening legacy. It may describe the risk situation of a sixth or more of all American children. More than a million babies each year are added to the 5 million children below school age who are at risk, and a large percentage—perhaps as high as 50 percent—will never be able to escape from the underclass that is growing before our eyes. Further, we must realize that the whole of American society is in danger of breaking up into enclaves of educated haves and an undereducated underclass of have-nots.

Multiproblem family syndrome may be present at birth, having been environmentally, not genetically, transmitted by a mother to her fetus. The virus leading to AIDS (HIV) can be diagnosed by a blood test. MPFSY can be diagnosed 95 percent of the time by the presence of at least ten of the following indicators:

1. The mother is HIV-positive.
2. The mother is receiving AFDC, or the mother's mother received AFDC.
3. The mother is a teenager.
4. The mother was born out of wedlock.
5. The infant was born out of wedlock.

6. The mother binged on alcohol at least once during her pregnancy.

7. The mother used illegal drugs, even once.

8. The mother was a victim of sexual abuse before puberty.

9. The mother was physically abused before puberty.

10. The mother had totally inadequate prenatal care.

11. The mother's pregnancy was unplanned.

12. No nesting plans were made for the baby; for example, no layette was purchased, the home was not readied for the baby, and there were no aspirations for the baby's future.

13. The infant had a low birthweight (a baby born weighing less than 5½ pounds).

14. The mother did not complete high school.

15. The mother has had gonorrhea, syphilis, or chlamydia.

16. The mother had no regular health provider or has no history of medical care preceding pregnancy.

17. The mother lived in a neighborhood where more than 30 percent of the population is "truly disadvantaged" (William Wilson terminology; see chapter 3).

18. The mother has more than five symptoms of depression.

19. The mother smoked regularly during pregnancy.

20. Neither the mother nor the father has ever been regularly employed.

21. The baby was born with a damaged central nervous system (CNS), such as epilepsy, spina bifida, and cerebral palsy. Some CNS damage may not be evident until schooling starts, such as retardation, hyperactivity, low attention span, and learning disorders.

22. Before conception, the mother was sexually active but did not regularly use birth control.

23. The mother lived in an environment of family violence.

24. The mother lived below the level of poverty for more than half of the preceding four years.

25. The mother's residence was in an area of high crime.

26. The mother was not read to as a child.

27. The mother was raised in an authoritarian family where the children were commanded rather than interacted with.

The likelihood of preventing failure of a child born into a multiproblem family is probably one in ten. The Institute of Medicine Forum summarized the problems of the future of children born into high-risk families:

Interrelatedness of the Problems: The interrelatedness and complex nature of the problems affecting children and families defy simple, unidimensional solutions. A recurrent theme is the recognition that there is no single causal factor or quick fix to the many complex, interwoven, and oftentimes intergenerational problems of America's children. Growing up in poverty or being dependent on welfare often translates into poor health, inadequate education, or the inability to obtain employment or earn a decent wage. These deficits can be carried through the course of several lifetimes, affecting children, their families, and their children's children. Children from poor and single-parent households are more likely to be children of teenage parents and to become teenage parents themselves. (CED, 1987)

Child Neglect and Young Parents

By reducing the problem to numbers, I am attempting to describe a huge, complex problem. Not all children born at high risk have mothers who are teenagers. There are more than twice as many children born to single mothers who are twenty years old or older. There are also married mothers who have emotional problems and other handicaps, which will mean that many of their babies will not be nurtured properly. Without question a big part of the problem, however, is poverty.

The problems related to poverty can usually be traced to the earliest days, weeks, and months of a child's life. What follows is the description of a little boy portrayed in a *Chicago Tribune* (1986) series, *The American Millstone:*

Carra is two years old, and the tragedy of his household can be seen most vividly in the way the family relates to him. Times when they are patient and loving seem fleeting. His Aunt Carla, age 15, thinks something is troubling him, but she said she does not understand what it could be.

"Sometimes he just walks out the back door and sits on the back porch," she said. "He just sits there for a long time, staring off into space."

Carra, at the age of two, already calls women bitches. Dorothy (his 37-year-old grandmother) laughed one afternoon when asked how he picked up the word. "He got it from me," she explained. "Because that's what I call these girls when they are bad."

LaWanda (Carra's eighteen-year-old mother, who is unmarried and pregnant with her second child) and Carla play a game to get the boy to say the word.

"Who she?" they say, pointing to LaWanda.

"Ma," is the reply.

"Who she?" they say, pointing to Carla.

"Ca."

"Who we?"

"Bitches."

Everybody laughs, including Dorothy, the grandmother. The boy has only a few other words in his vocabulary, and when he does speak his diction is so poor he can barely be understood. He is toilet-trained "some of the time," his mother says. When he makes a mistake, no one bothers to change him, leaving him in wet shorts until they are dry.

His nickname is Fella "because he is bad," Dorothy says. Much of what this child hears is negative, in voices loud and menacing. One recent afternoon it seemed as though the household was erupting on young Carra. Dorothy was yelling at him because he stepped into her room. LaWanda paddled him because he wouldn't sit still. William (his cousin) chased him through the apartment hitting him on the back with a cord because he touched a bicycle tire he was told to leave alone. When the boy refused to put on his shirt at the command of an eighteen-year-old house guest, the girl grabbed him by the shoulder and pulled him close. Then she hit him with a belt.

Almost any child development specialist would predict that it is unlikely that Carra will escape the cycle of poverty that has already trapped his grandmother, mother, and cousin. To stop this cycle we have to invest *up front* much more than we currently do in every child born at high risk. We also have to cut radically the number of births to teenagers.

THE COST OF LATE INTERVENTION

Over the years, in reading the mail received by the Harris Foundation, I have noticed an increase in the number of grant applications from agencies and organizations that attempt to deal with functional illiteracy, alcoholism, drug abuse, family violence, the developmentally disabled—organizations that in many after-the-fact ways apply what might be called band-aids to cure the symptoms of trouble in our society.

Prevention costs are trivial compared with the potential savings from the costs of suffering and despair from child abuse and neglect; hospital costs from medical complications at birth; hospitalization costs of very low-birthweight babies (under three pounds); developmental and congenital anomalies; significant illnesses; day care; and AFDC for teenage-headed families.

• In 1986, President Ronald Reagan's Commission on Excellence in Education found that 44 percent of seventeen-year-old blacks were functionally illiterate, with even higher percentages for seventeen-year-old Hispanics. In contrast, the Japanese illiteracy rate is less than 1 percent.

• The number of drop-outs in many inner-city schools ranges from 50–70 percent.

• Unemployment and unemployability rates among male minority inner-city residents approximate 50 percent.

• The cost to society of crime, homicide, and drug and alcohol abuse runs high. In Illinois, for example, the costs of child abuse and neglect are extremely high: in 1995, the Department of Child and Family Services had an annual budget of $1.2 billion.

• Society's costs for infant mortality and infant morbidity among the poor are embarrassing.

• The percentage of low-birthweight babies born to poor mothers runs three or four times the average for nonpoor mothers.

Many, if not most, unwanted pregnancies resulting in births to elementary or high school students are catastrophes for the young mother and frequently for the young man who was responsible for the pregnancy and who may have to quit school to get a job to support his baby. Yet when most of us think about births to teenagers out of wedlock we rarely think past the problems of the teenagers: school drop-out, lost opportunities, and so on. Occasionally, some of us think further and try to empathize with the babies. We know that one of every four American children is being brought up below the level of poverty, in conditions that are frightening. Almost nothing is so certain as the likelihood that a child, born to an unwed mother of limited education with practically no reserve resources, is going to grow up poor.

There is a widely perceived consensus that babies born poor, born to unwed mothers, and living in a neighborhood where there is a high concentration of poverty will likely live in an environment in which failure in school, physical illness, and violence abound. In such surroundings, a baby's chance of making it is poor. Even our "successful" programs are not likely to help most of these children.

Yet there is really one more class of victim, beyond the unlucky mother, the conscientious father, and the soon-to-be poor baby. Society is a big loser; all of us lose. We are all victims of this continuing tragedy because our schools are being destroyed. Whether we realize it or not, the foundation of our twenty-first-century, industrialized society is broad public education. Without broad public education we cannot survive as a leading nation in today's world.

The Example of Illinois

THE PROBLEM'S DIMENSIONS

Teenage sexuality that leads to pregnancy has become a large and costly problem in Illinois, as it has in many states. The problem touches every Illinois family financially, and many families have the children of their teenage children living with them.

There were 48,000 adolescent pregnancies in Illinois in 1992. After subtracting miscarriages and abortions, there were 24,601 babies born, a slight increase over the 24,364 born in 1983. Of these nearly 25,000 births, 3,000 were low-birthweight babies. It is these low-birthweight babies who are most likely to die as infants. The infant mortality rate for the children of teenage mothers is 20.5, or twice the rate for those infants whose mothers were not teenagers.

THE FINANCIAL COST

The costs of teenage pregnancy and its aftermath are usually tallied in any accounting of miscarriages and abortions, damaged and dead infants, and stunted teenage lives. Although these are indeed the costs of children having children, there are costs of another type, which until now have not been summarized. These are the total financial costs of teenage pregnancy. In 1983 teenage pregnancy and its associated problems cost the citizens of Illinois an estimated $853 million annually. The state's businesses supported this with $154 million. As large as that amount is, individuals in Illinois—including taxpayers, the poor themselves, and the parents of teenage mothers—paid more than four times as much. Individual Illinois citizens paid at least $698 million that year, or 82 percent of that $853 million, from their own pockets or through taxes.

How much is $853 million? In 1983 Northwestern University was commissioned to undertake an extensive and expensive study of the economic costs of births to teenagers in Illinois. They reported that the cost of $853 million was close to half the annual budget of the city of Chicago. If devoted to jobs, $853 million could have paid seventy thousand people a good wage and dropped Illinois' unemployment by a sixth. The annual cost of teenage pregnancy to Illinois is huge. The $853 million in 1983 covered the expense of children born to teenage mothers only during the first five years. Because of the cutoff for children at age five, all the very substantial schooling costs and most of the social costs of this problem are excluded from the calculation. In short, $853 million was a conservative figure.

The very largest cost areas are for AFDC and Medicaid for teen mothers and children; support for children not on aid; day care for the children of working teen mothers; birth and newborn care costs for infants; and medical attention for nonaid children. In fiscal year 1994 there were nearly 36,500 children placed in foster care and about 4,700 in institutional or group homes, making a total of more than 41,000 children placed in substitute care. The total expenditure of DCFS for 1994 was almost $1 billion, and the expenditure for 1995 was even higher; Illinois' total state expenditure in 1994 was nearly $32 billion.

PREVENTION SPENDING IS LOW

One expenditure that is not large is prevention. In 1983 only $22 million was being spent on family-life education and family planning to delay or prevent pregnancy among teenagers. Current prevention expenditures remain very low.

Prevention programs in Illinois are reasonably effective, but it is fair to say that although we are clearly better off spending several million dollars on prevention than we would be without it, what we are spending is only a drop in the bucket. For every $1,000 it subsequently cost for intervention programs because we failed to prevent a problem, Illinois spent *less than $1 on prevention*. Public aid, neonatal intensive care, drug addiction centers, street crime, infant mortality, alcohol abuse, automobile accidents caused by alcohol and drugs, unemployment, and unemployability are only some of the costly disasters that result from our failure to prevent family dysfunction. The Department of Children and Family Services in 1983 had a budget of $203 million. Its current budget is six times higher, or $1.2 billion. Its mission is to provide services to children and families to protect and advocate on behalf of children and youth who are, or who are at risk of, being abused, neglected, or removed from their families.

THE HIGH COST TO BUSINESS

Of the $853 million cost for births to teenagers in 1983, Illinois businesses paid $154 million; $82 million was in taxes, most going to the state. Although people in business might doubt that reducing teenage pregnancy would lighten their federal tax burden, they would probably agree that state taxes could lessen.

Businesses also pay a hidden expense called cost shifting. The Medicaid program and the working poor pay less than the full medical costs of teenage pregnancy. Hospitals and doctors shift their undercovered costs to the employees of corporations. This shifting is estimated to be 18 percent of such medical costs and accounts for $29 million of the $154 million annually billed to business. In fact, businesses probably pay more through cost shifting than through federal taxes. The final piece of the immediate annual cost to business is about $43 million for the medical costs of the employees. The very large business "follow-along" costs of teenage pregnancy owing to illiteracy, crime, absenteeism, and added employee training are not included.

After the first five years of life, the costs really begin to mount, particularly for schools, prisons, mental hospitals, and for welfare for unwed mothers. The cost of not having invested in primary prevention adds heavily to the cost of later intervention. The Ounce of Prevention Fund public-private partnership provides a blueprint of how to prevent damage to the development of some of our children. Although Ounce programs show measurable success, the Ounce's experience has also shown how difficult it is to achieve success in an intervention program after a baby is born into a high-risk setting. Our future lies with all those of the next generation. We cannot continue to ignore the ever-increasing number of babies who are not planned, not wanted, and not nurtured.

5

THE ABORTION QUESTION

IT IS GENEROUS TO ASSUME that all parents who wanted to have their babies, whether planned or unintended, can and will nurture their babies, read to them, and get them ready for school by age five. We know that unwanted babies are at a particularly high risk of educational failure. These babies are largely born to women who, too frequently, have no plans and little capability or desire to nurture and appropriately stimulate their children, especially during the vital first two or three years of life.

Assuming that the present birth rate continues, we can expect about 4 million babies to be born in the United States in 1995. This means that there will have been about 6.5 million pregnancies. Based on the most recent report (Kost and Forrest, 1995), 57 percent of these births (2.28 million) will probably be intended. Of the 43 percent unintended births (1.72 million), it is difficult to estimate how many were "mistimed" and how many were "unwanted." The research of Kost and Forrest revealed that "although the level of unintended childbearing is high in almost all socioeconomic subgroups of women, the proportion of births that were mistimed or unwanted was 50 percent or more."

Broken down into subgroups, the percentages were as follows: ages 15–17, 78 percent; ages 18–19, 68 percent; ages 20–24, 50 percent; never married women, 73 percent; formerly married women, 62 percent; black women, 66 percent; women living below the federal poverty level, 64 percent; women living at 100–149 percent of the poverty level, 52 percent; women having fewer than twelve years' education, 58 percent; women who already had two children, 53 percent; and women who already had three or more children, 60 percent.

Despite the Supreme Court decision of 1973 to settle the issue, the debate on abortion has become more violent than ever. The contention centers in part on the question of when a fetus becomes a person: at conception, a few weeks later, or before or after three months. The considerations on both sides of the issue should include the interests of the mother and father as well as the right to life of the fetus.

If the fetus could decide, would he or she always choose to live? If the outlook for the baby promises average opportunities in life—for example, reasonably good nutrition as a fetus and fair-to-middling nurturing as an infant and then as a child—then the pros of being born would outweigh the cons. The pro-life option is attractive if the baby would be brought up by a caring caregiver, allowed to play and learn in the first few years of life in order to be ready for kindergarten at age five, and if there would be a good school system, where the child could learn to read and write and be assured of an education sufficient to give him a fair opportunity to pursue the American dream in his life.

But if the fetus is in the womb of a fifteen-year-old young woman who has dropped out of school, is functionally illiterate, has little hope of finding a place for herself in society except as a welfare recipient; if the mother-to-be smokes or drinks excessively, knows little at her age and cares less about nutrition for herself and her fetus; if she became pregnant thinking it could not happen to her, with no intention of wanting a baby or taking on the obligation to raise the baby in sickness and in health, then the choice of the fetus would assuredly be not to want to live; the baby's choice would not be pro-life.

Suppose a fetus knew she would be born weighing three or four pounds and would spend her first two or three months among strangers in a neonatal intensive care unit. Suppose she knew when she left the hospital to go "home" that no preparation for her homecoming would have been made. For instance, her mother had not married her father. It turns out that she is no longer even friendly with him. Instead, for the past three weeks she has had a new boyfriend. Suppose that neither the boyfriend nor the mother likes the idea of the baby's wanting a good deal of attention, including cuddling and regular feeding, having her diapers changed, and wanting to be talked to a lot because it is pretty scary and lonesome for a five-and-a-half-pound baby even to survive.

Suppose she does survive the next several months, grows to weigh fifteen pounds. At this point her mother has yet another boyfriend and is pregnant again. Just when she is ready to walk as a toddler, she finds she has a baby brother who takes up most of her mother's time. Suppose it never occurred to the mother that her daughter wanted to be talked to or read to, and, as a result, the daughter is very slow to speak and make herself understood. When she wants something she has to yell, cry, point, or have a tantrum. As a consequence, her mother or her mother's boyfriend smacks her "so she doesn't get spoiled." Soon she is three years old and has a younger brother, a sister, and a new stepfather, who is out of work. She has not yet learned how to talk or to ask for things she wants. She can only point and scream and get slapped a lot if her demands seem out of line to her mother or her mother's friends.

Soon she is five years old and starts kindergarten, two years behind in her development compared with where she would have been had she had the love and nurturing a child needs in order to develop. Now she has two problems: the teacher does not like her, nor does her mother or her mother's boyfriend. She becomes increasingly apathetic and frustrated and occasionally gets angry. She simply cannot rely on anyone. There is no one she can trust. She sees clearly that she does not amount to much and never will. She feels she is a "dummy" and cannot learn. She hears from her teacher and mother that she is lazy and good-for-nothing.

It is not long before she is ten or twelve years old, angry, doing badly in school, perhaps ready to do errands for the gang members who run her neighborhood. She gets caught a few times by the police, but she is too young to go to jail. The police act as though she is dumb and no good; they have the same opinion of her that she has been hearing from her teachers and her mother.

She is now fifteen and ready to drop out of school. Maybe she has found a boyfriend—a boy who, like her, has been pushed around by his mother and her boyfriend, and by his teachers. He needs affection and welcomes

attention from this fifteen-year-old girl. Then, "doing what comes naturally," she is soon pregnant and carrying a three-month-old fetus.

Let us assume that this fifteen-year-old girl could by magic go back to
the time she was a three-month-old fetus and could make a choice
about whether she would prefer life or to avoid being born. Is it clear
that she would elect to be born?

Talk to the mother. If she had not carried her child to term she could
have stayed in school and perhaps graduated from high school and even
gone further. She might have found a job and felt good about herself.
She might have linked up with a young man when she was twenty or
twenty-two who had a job. With both of them working, maybe they
could have saved some money so that when they decided to get married
and have a baby they could promise that baby a reasonably good start.
What about the mother's right to life? Should she have anything to say
about whether she can choose between a life with few options, or must
she be limited to becoming a welfare recipient? Should she be entitled to
the opportunities that lie in front of her if she is able to terminate her
pregnancy, stay in school, and eventually graduate and get a job?

The right to life is more complicated for both the fetus and the
mother than the "scientific" question of when the fetus develops a
heartbeat. The quality of life that lies ahead for the fetus and the mother
is more important than when the heart starts to beat.

DAMAGED CHILDREN, DAMAGED PARENTS: THE COST OF NOT FUNDING ABORTIONS

With all due respect for efforts valiantly made to support families with
young children, particularly poor families, single-parent families, minority families, black families, Hispanic families, and teenage mothers and
fathers, the problems of this support are escalating. The flies are conquer-
ing the fly paper. You do not see fly paper much these days. The image of
the fly paper levitating like a magic carpet as a result of the fluttering of
the wings of wall-to-wall flies has always amused me. The problem of
damaged parents having children they will bring up to be damaged, who
then become damaged parents themselves, is not so amusing.

In denying poor women access to funding for abortion, a small but vociferous minority is forcing them against their will to bear unwanted babies. That minority is interested only in the right to life of the fetus in the nine months before birth; after birth, its interest ceases. The results of this unfairness are infants born with extremely compromised opportunities to live a productive life. As they grow older, their opportunities diminish because they are usually sent to schools where they cannot learn. Many later drop out of school, frequently become juvenile delinquents, and sometimes end up in prison. What is more, these children begin, too soon, to have babies of their own. We then have the increasingly familiar phenomenon of the intergenerational transmission of poverty. This is an unwelcome and unforeseen consequence of our present policies of banning federally funded abortions for Medicaid-eligible women.

A stark example of the outcome of a lack of understanding of the real costs involved in *not* funding abortions is perhaps demonstrated by right-to-life legislative successes, particularly those related to requiring parental approval before abortions are granted for minors. The Centers for Disease Control has shown in recent years a significant drop in the percentage of abortions for women nineteen years old and younger. In 1976, women in that age bracket accounted for 32.1 percent of all abortions. By 1990 that figure had dropped to 22.3 percent. Because of the rising birth rate among unwed women, such births soared in the period from 1970 to 1992 by more than 207 percent (Saluter, 1994; figure 5-1).

The economic and social costs of America's current policy on federal funding for abortion need to be thoroughly understood. It is quixotic for our society to continue with its present strategies to cope with the problem. There is really only one answer, and we cannot wait any longer to give that answer. Difficult though it may be politically now, we must radically reduce the number of babies born to those damaged individuals who are unlikely to be able to nurture a child to become a productive member of society.

According to the Census Bureau, 6.3 million children, or 9 percent of all children under the age of eighteen in 1993, lived with a single parent who had never married—up from 3.4 million in 1983 (ibid.). The data show about 1 million children in 1976 living with single parents who had never married (Saluter, 1977). The enormous increase from 1 mil-

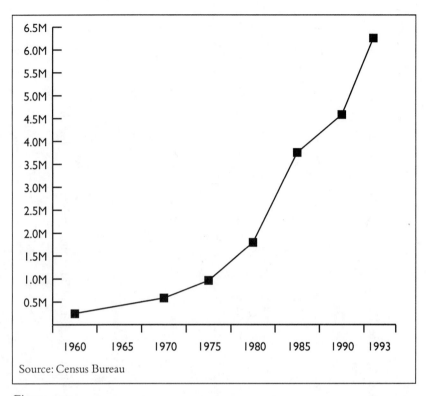

Source: Census Bureau

Figure 5-1
Number of Children Living in Single, Never-Married Households, 1993

lion to 6.3 million was partly the result of the successful efforts of Congress to cut off federally funded abortions in 1977. This legislation was devastating to women who were poor and therefore eligible for Medicaid. The restrictions went into effect on 4 August 1977.

In a Kids Count survey done by the Annie E. Casey Foundation (CSSP, 1993) only three states reported reductions in their births to teenagers: Maryland, New Jersey, and New York, all of which fund abortions for poor women. Table 5-1 makes it clear that differences in state expenditures for family planning services and public funding of abortion significantly affect birth data. The table also shows the trends in certain states of babies born out of wedlock to teenagers, which is a

Table 5-1

Live Births by Age and Marital Status of Mother, State-Funded Abortions, Public Funding for Contraception, Expenditure per Live Birth, FY 1992, Selected States

	California	New York	Illinois	Ohio	Michigan
BIRTHS TO WOMEN OF ALL AGES					
Total live births	601,730	287,887	191,396	162,247	144,089
Births to unmarried women	206,396	100,260	63,979	51,317	38,620
BIRTHS TO UNMARRIED WOMEN					
19 and younger	48,984	21,591	20,205	17,402	12,763
17 and younger	21,261	9,371	8,908	7,216	5,358
14 and younger	1,334	617	653	448	339
20 and older	157,412	78,669	43,774	33,915	25,857

The number of births to girls ages fourteen and younger is higher in Illinois than in New York, which has nearly twice the population of Illinois.

	California	New York	Illinois	Ohio	Michigan
PERCENTAGE OF ALL BIRTHS					
19 and younger	8.1	7.4	10.5	10.7	8.8
17 and younger	3.5	3.2	4.6	4.4	3.7
14 and younger	.22	.21	.34	.27	.23
20 and older	26.1	27.3	22.8	20.9	17.9
STATE-FUNDED ABORTIONS					
Number of abortions	111,196	49,700	0	0	0
PUBLIC FUNDING FOR FAMILY PLANNING AND CONTRACEPTION SERVICES[a]					
Total cost	$76.8M	$78.9M[b]	$17.2M	$20.3M[b]	$23.4M[b]
Cost per live birth	$128	$274	$90	$125	$162

Sources: Birth statistics are from unpublished data from HHS, NCHS, forthcoming in *Vital Statistics of the United States, 1992*, vol. 1, *Natality*. Information on the marital status of mothers is inferred for California, Michigan, and New York. Abortion and family planning statistics are from AGI, 1995.

[a]Only 267 abortions were funded by federal sources in the entire United States; 202,622 were funded by states.

[b]Includes costs for sterilization.

good indicator of at-risk births. That is not to say that all children born to single teenage parents are going to be societal failures or that two-parent families will have no problem children, but there is a very real likelihood that children born in poverty to undereducated single parents are not going to fare well, particularly if the babies were unplanned and unwanted, as apparently more than 80 percent are.

Do Different Policies Produce Differing Results?

If abortion coverage were restored in all fifty states, there would be an additional 750,000 publicly funded abortions annually.[1] In every year since 1977, thousands of abortions that would have been paid for by federal funds have probably resulted in births to poor women. Starting in 1978, then, each year federal taxpayers saved, at $150 each,[2] approximately $112.5 million by not paying for abortions. In the seventeen years between 1978 and 1994, a total of perhaps 12.8 million unwanted pregnancies that might have been aborted were carried to term because of the continuing impact of the ban on federally supported abortions. The total federal taxes saved (seventeen years times $112.5 million a year) amount to $1.9 billion.

Have the architects of the legislation conscientiously considered the economic consequences of their policy? From the "savings" to the taxpayers, we must subtract the payments Medicaid made for obstetricians, hospital bills, and prenatal care, which together cost about $2,000 for each uncomplicated birth. The cost of these charges to federal taxpayers was probably one half—the state pays the other half—or $1,000 each. Over seventeen years, the likely cost to taxpayers of 12.8 million uncomplicated, healthy births was $12.8 billion, or six times the $1.9 billion saved on abortions. At a cost of about $3,000 each for 12.8 million children, the larger annual cost of AFDC alone is $38.3 billion. As Senator Everett Dirksen used to say, "A billion here and a billion there, and pretty soon it adds up to real money." No wonder the U.S. budget deficit is rising so fast.

Moreover, these cost estimates do not include the expense of criminal justice and prisons, where some unwanted babies end up when they are older. There are now more than 1.5 million Americans currently incarcerated in federal, state, county, and city prisons and jails. As many as half of the adults in federal and state prisons cannot read or write; 75 percent of the adults in correctional facilities are functionally illiterate, with 90–95 percent of the inmates testing below the eighth-grade reading level. The negative results of unwanted births also include poor school performance and disastrous life consequences.

In other words, current legislation on abortion in the United States has undoubtedly added substantially to the gigantic problem of welfare as we know it and as we find it being addressed by the Contract with America. This also brings up the question of whether ethically we can now stop funding the children under eighteen born to mothers who were denied the benefit of their right to abortion. These mothers knew they would be unable to nurture and support the babies after they were born.

Supreme Court Justice Harry A. Blackmun was right when he wrote in a 1977 dissenting opinion that "the court concedes the existence of a constitutional right [to abortion] but denies the realization and enjoyment of that right on the ground that existence and realization are separate and distinct. For the individual woman concerned, indigent, and financially helpless . . . the result is punitive and tragic. Implicit in the Court's holdings is the condescension that she may go elsewhere for her abortion. I find that disingenuous and alarming, almost reminiscent of: 'Let them eat cake'" (*Beal vs. Doe,* 432 U.S. 438, 462 [1977]).

Without doubt, the economics of denying funding for abortion have been disastrous, which alone should convince legislators to change national policy. Yet there is also a fairness issue that is in many ways much more important than the economic argument. Now is the time for Congress to combine good economic policy with social justice. Legislators should stand up to the intimidating few who compel poor women to bring babies into the world they cannot nurture toward productive lives.

THE ABORTION FUNDING BAN: THE HYDE AMENDMENT

Personal responsibility is a popular phrase, but it is unpopular in public policy matters when it comes to legislation enabling women to afford abortions. The federal government's restrictions on public funding for abortions, commonly known as the Hyde amendment, have gone through various modifications, further complicated by different court rulings. The original congressional restrictions, passed in 1976 as amendments to the annual appropriations bills for the Departments of Labor and Health Education and Welfare, allowed Medicaid to pay for abortions only when the life of the pregnant woman was threatened. These restrictions went into effect on 4 August 1977. In 1977 and 1978 Congress extended the financial coverage of abortions to rape and incest victims and to women whose pregnancies would result in severe and long-lasting damage to the physical health of the mother, though the last condition was removed in 1979 (Trussell et al., 1980). Since 5 June 1981, payments for abortions have been restored in cases in which the mother's life is endangered (Henshaw and Wallisch, 1984). Under the Medicaid program, where the federal government and states jointly provide medical care for the indigent, the states have been left to subsidize abortion services to low-income women. State funds paid almost $80 million for 202,355 abortions in 1992 (Daley and Gold, 1993), but most states, thirty-one including Michigan, have followed the federal government's lead and pay for abortions only to protect the mother's life or in cases of rape or incest. Three states fund abortions under certain additional circumstances, such as severe fetal deformity or severe psychiatric conditions. The remaining seventeen states, plus the District of Columbia, pay for most abortions for poor women covered by Medicaid (AGI, 1995). Alaska, California, Colorado, Connecticut, Hawaii, Idaho, Maryland, Massachusetts, Minnesota, New Jersey, New Mexico, New York, North Carolina, Oregon, Washington, West Virginia, and Vermont fund abortions for poor women.[3] In those states there is a much lower incidence of births to single teenagers, as table 5-2 illustrates.

Voters or legislatures in some states can be persuaded to adopt punitive actions. Interestingly, when individuals are told, before they express an opinion on the Medicaid funding of abortion, that the cost of hospitalization and medical care for a birth will exceed the cost of abortion by a factor of seven to one—in other words, it will cost approximately $2,000 compared with the current cost of abortion of $300—70 percent then say that taxpayers should pay for the abortion. Clearly, in a 1988 referendum in Michigan the economics of the problem were not well understood by the voters.

Table 5-2

Births to Single Teens in Selected States with and without Abortion Funding, 1985 and 1992, as a Percentage of All Births

	1985	1992	% Change
STATES WITH PUBLIC FUNDING FOR ABORTION			
Connecticut	6.6	6.9	+4.5
Maryland	9.1	7.9	−13.2
Massachusetts	6.0	6.7	+11.7
New Jersey	7.5	6.7	−10.7
New York	7.5	7.5	—
Vermont	5.9	6.3	+6.8
STATES WITHOUT PUBLIC FUNDING FOR ABORTION			
Illinois	8.9	10.6	+19.1
Indiana	7.9	10.5	+32.9
Michigan*	6.8	8.9	+30.9
Missouri	7.8	10.7	+37.1
Ohio	8.1	10.7	+32.0
Wisconsin	6.8	8.3	+22.1

Source: Child Trends, Inc., Washington, D.C.

Note. For the seven-year period a simple average of the change in those states funding abortions was .001 percent; for the nonfunding states the average was 29.01 percent.

*Michigan stopped funding for abortions in December 1988.

Politics and the Anti-Abortion Movement

In the twelve years of the Reagan-Bush presidencies, the belief was that public discussion of sex between unmarried parties would increase promiscuity. The political climate of avoiding discussion of sex also resulted in an after-inflation drop of two thirds in federal funding for family planning services for the poor.[4]

What happened in those same years to the number of babies born to

unmarried mothers? In round figures: in 1980, 666,000 babies (18.4 percent) were born out of wedlock, and in 1992, more than 1.2 million
babies (30 percent) were born out of wedlock. An increase of more
than half a million babies (or 82 percent) took place in the twelve years
that Title X federal funding for contraceptive services was slashed 66
percent and federal funding for abortions practically abolished.

Why did Ronald Reagan switch from a pro-abortion stance when he
was California's governor to an anti-abortion one in 1976? Possibly it was
because he had simply changed his mind on the issue. Perhaps it was
because the Republican right wing—whose favorite endeavors are
encouraging chastity, discouraging family planning, banning abortion,
and regarding sex as sin—controlled as many votes as it did at the
Republican National Convention. This makes for interesting politics:
although the majority of Republicans are pro-choice, Republican
National Convention delegates disproportionately represent the anti-
abortion sector of the party.

In 1980 George Bush took his lead from Reagan and also changed his
position on abortion. When he served in the Congress, he was strongly
pro-choice. When he wanted the Republican convention to select him to
run for vice president and later for president, he switched to a pro-life
position. As governor of California Ronald Reagan signed the most liberal
abortion law in the country, which is still on the books and permitted the
state of California in 1992 to fund more than 111,000 abortions out of a
national total of more than 200,000 abortions publicly funded by states in
that year. New York state funded nearly 50,000 abortions in 1992.[5]

Many mothers who have their first babies as unmarried teenagers
continue bearing children later. More than two thirds of the babies
born out of wedlock are born to mothers twenty years old or older. The
Centers for Disease Control reports that 82 percent of the women who
obtain abortions are unmarried women. There is no doubt that in the
thirty-three states that do not provide state-subsidized abortions, many
single women are being forced to bear babies they did not intend to
conceive and, after conception, did not want to bear.

The funding of abortion for Medicaid-eligible women does help to
decrease births to single teenagers. Note particularly the 1992 percentage

in table 5-2, which for the six selected states averages 6.9 percent for the abortion-funding states and 10 percent for the six listed non-abortion-funding states—an impressive difference.

In comparing birth statistics for New York City (table 5-3), a city in a state that provides publicly funded reproductive choice programs, with Chicago, where the state does not provide such services, the statistics for 1992 clearly show the impact of adequate family planning services and Medicaid funding for abortions. Despite an overall difference in population of nearly 5 million, there were more births to girls under fourteen in Chicago than in New York. The percentage of births to women and girls under the age of twenty in Chicago is almost double the percentage in New York City.

We cannot be certain that all the differences between the two teen birth rates is accounted for by the lack of adequate family planning services and publicly funded abortion in Illinois. Yet it is equally difficult to imagine what else might cause such massive statistical differences. The difference in abortion policies has a huge impact. I am persuaded that in Chicago the huge proportion of births to teenagers revealed by the numbers—particularly for younger teenagers—helps to account for the continuing phenomenon of too many kindergartners not ready for school who, when they become seniors in high school, place more than half of Chicago high schools in the lowest 1 percent of the American College Testing Program universe (see chapter 1).

MICHIGAN'S DECISION TO BAN
PUBLIC FUNDING FOR ABORTIONS

Until 1988, Michigan funded abortions for poor women. In 1988, after a statewide political debate, the policy was changed. The state had submitted the question of Medicaid funding for abortion to a referendum. After several tries, the anti-abortion people carried the referendum. The following amendment became effective:

> The People of the State of Michigan enact: section 109A. Notwithstanding any other provision of this act, an abortion shall not be a service provided with public funds to a recipient of welfare benefits, whether through a

Table 5-3

Teen Birth Statistics for New York City and Chicago, 1992

	New York City Relatively well-funded state family-planning programs	*Chicago* Poorly funded state family-planning programs
Population	7,311,966[a]	2,768,483[b]
Total live births	136,002[c]	59,448[d]
BIRTHS TO GIRLS 19 AND YOUNGER		
% of all births	10.1	18.7
Number	13,795	11,110
BIRTHS TO GIRLS 17 AND YOUNGER		
% of all births	4.2	8.1
Number	5,757	4,865
BIRTHS TO GIRLS 14 AND YOUNGER		
% of all births	.0029	.0067
Number	398	401

Sources:

[a]U.S. Census Bureau

[b]Chicago Department of Planning and Development estimate

[c]New York City Department of Biostatistics

[d]Chicago Department of Health, Epidemiology Program

program of medical assistance, general assistance, or categorical assistance or through any other type of public aid or assistance program, unless the abortion is necessary to save the life of the mother. It is the policy of this state to prohibit the appropriation of public funds for the purpose of providing an abortion to a person who receives welfare benefits unless the abortion is necessary to save the life of the mother.

The legislators of Michigan were persistent in their efforts to ban publicly funded abortions. Before Public Act 59 of 1987 stopped all public funding for abortions except to save the life of the mother, the state legislature had passed similar funding prohibitions seventeen times but had been unable to override the vetoes of two governors. Finally, in response to a citizen initiative sponsored by Michigan Right to Life, the legislature once again passed a ban on public funding for abortions. Bills passed under Michigan's voter-initiative process are not subject to gubernatorial veto (Donovan, 1989). Public Act 59 of 1987 went into effect on 12 December 1988.

The People's Campaign for Choice, a coalition of Michigan pro-choice groups, mounted one last challenge to Public Act 59—a referendum to restore abortion funding. This proposal was defeated in November 1988. The key issue for voters seemed to be money. Writing in *Family Planning Perspectives* (1989), Patricia Donovan observed:

> The opponents of abortion funding in Michigan . . . assiduously avoided the issue of [the] morality of abortion. They skillfully tapped voters' fears of higher taxes and resentment over perceived welfare abuses and subtly implied that taxpayers were being asked to pay for the consequences of promiscuous behavior on the part of poor women. A Michigan ad emphasized that the state paid $6 million a year for abortions and that welfare costs have not gone up in states that have eliminated abortion funding. (p. 222)

Michigan taxpayers stopped funding abortions for poor women, and the number of abortions in Michigan dropped from more than 45,000 in 1988 to 35,138 (23 percent) in 1989 (see table 5-4). The number of births to teenagers increased from 17,000 to more than 19,000 (12.5 percent), and the number of babies born at low birthweight increased by more than 10 percent.

Low-birthweight children disproportionately later present economic costs, educational failures, and social problems. Since the funding ban in Michigan, the number of babies reported as born with congenital anomalies has substantially increased. Much of this increase can be explained not by the simplified reporting procedures begun in 1989, but

Table 5-4

Statistics on Live Births vs. Abortions for Michigan, 1987–1993

	1987	1988	1989	1990	1991	1992	1993
Total abortions	47,814	45,438	35,138	34,655	33,119	33,160	34,329
Live births	140,466	139,635	148,164	153,080	149,478	143,827	139,560
Abortions, mother under age 20	13,624	12,900	9,625	8,754	7,750	7,464	7,203
Live births, mother under age 20	17,240	17,374	19,545	20,224	19,325	18,341	17,198
Low-birthweight babies (under 2,500 grams)	10,095	10,237	11,323	11,608	11,706	10,829	10,700
Babies born with congenital anomalies	791	746	3,161	4,409	2,495	2,108	1,589
Babies born who were mother's fifth or later child	4,950	4,823	5,448	6,084	6,221	6,227	6,060
Mothers with less than twelfth-grade education	N/A	N/A	28,931	30,278	29,713	28,300	27,155

Source: MDPH, Office of the State Registrar and Division of Health Statistics

Note. Current reports of this nature are unavailable from MDPH. In December 1990 MDPH reported: "The Medicaid ban on abortion contributes to a significant rise in births to young, poor women—women most likely to have babies with less of a chance for survival, and to increasing numbers of surviving medically fragile infants. Family planning programs, which offer some solutions, are inadequately funded to meet the public demand for service."

by more low-birthweight babies (who are at greatest risk of having birth defects) having been born each year (Milli et al., 1991).

On 9 June 1992 the Michigan Supreme Court, by a vote of five to two, upheld the state's political decision to stop all public funding for abortions except to save the life of the mother. The Court's ruling stated: "The election to subsidize childbirth does not impermissibly influence the procreative decisions of indigent women. Nor does it coerce a woman into forfeiting her right to choose an abortion" (*Doe vs. Department of Social Services,* 1992). The facts in the case suggest otherwise. The plaintiff was a poor fifteen-year-old who became pregnant as a result of rape, and even though both she and her mother wanted an abortion, Michigan's Medicaid program would pay only for the teenager's childbirth expenses, not for the termination of a pregnancy that was itself coerced. Unless money was raised to pay for this young woman's abortion, a baby conceived in rape and carried unwillingly is now one of Michigan's younger citizens.

The experiences of the poor, pregnant adolescent in the *Doe* case are not unique to Michigan. In a 1989 Illinois survey of 450 teen mothers who participated in fifteen Parents Too Soon programs funded by the Ounce of Prevention Fund, 61 percent reported they had been victims of unwanted sexual encounters, and one third were younger than twelve at the time of their forced experience. These findings were subsequently confirmed in a study from the state of Washington that found that two thirds of a sample of 535 young women who had become pregnant as adolescents had earlier been sexually abused, including 44 percent who had been raped. Furthermore, compared with pregnant adolescents who had not been abused, the victims of abuse were more likely to have used drugs and alcohol and were more likely to have become abusive mothers (Boyer and Fine, 1992).

It is hard to know what the Michigan legislature was attempting to do when it enacted its policy of refusing access to abortion for women who were unable to pay. The Supreme Court of Michigan, however, made it clear in its decision in the *Doe* case denying Medicaid funding for an abortion that the state of Michigan *was* liable for providing prenatal care, paying medical bills, and for the cost of the girl's hospital stay.

It is unlikely that the state legislators understood the economic implications of the additional unwanted births they forced so many poor women to have.

There is no doubt that the punitive attitude of the voters toward poor mothers who have unintended pregnancies is costly to every state that refuses to pay for abortions for Medicaid-eligible women. The Department of Public Health in Michigan clearly recognizes the costs and publishes data about the social and economic disasters that are occurring: Before the ban, 20 percent of all Detroit babies born each year had teen mothers. After the ban, this increased to 25 percent. Births to mothers who received inadequate prenatal care rose 54 percent; babies with low birthweights rose by 33 percent.[6]

Michigan's refusal to fund abortions for poor women is unfair, particularly toward those who are victims of rape or incest or whose pregnancies may complicate existing medical conditions. In perhaps the cruelest irony of the Medicaid program, while all states pay for amniocentesis and most newer prenatal diagnostic procedures (Weiner and Bernhardt, 1990), Michigan, along with thirty-three other states, does not fund abortions after the diagnosis of an anomalous fetus (NARAL, 1992). Thirteen percent of abortion patients decide to abort because the fetus has a possible health problem (Torres and Forrest, 1988). Poor women, however, are entitled only to know they are carrying a defective baby, and most do not get financial support if they choose to abort. A 1990 Michigan Department of Public Health report links the increased number of chronically sick and handicapped babies it serves to the Medicaid abortion ban (MDPH, 1990b). Many are substance-exposed babies who spend time in expensive neonatal intensive care units.

The Monetary Consequences of Michigan's Decision

A significant question, then, and one that is seldom asked, is what did the state *spend* as a result of its ban on publicly funded abortions? Although it is simple to quantify the $3 million "saved" by Michigan in the first year of the funding ban, it is much harder to estimate the money Michigan taxpayers will have lost in a single year through Medicaid-assisted maternity care, AFDC, and food stamps; through Medicaid payments for low-birthweight babies' extended stays in hospitals or other higher costs of medically fragile infants; or through foster care for babies, unwanted before birth and abandoned or abused after birth. These costs do not magically stop after the first year, but persist and tend to increase over time.

The long-term costs associated with the funding ban are likely to be staggeringly high. Consider the impact on teenagers. After the first two years of the funding ban, there was an estimated 52 percent increase in births to teenagers whose pregnancies were unintended (MDPH, 1990a). If, then, we assume, for example, that the 2,171 additional births to teenagers in 1989 were to Medicaid-eligible adolescents who otherwise would have chosen abortion, the eventual cost to taxpayers could be as much as $100 million. Each year American taxpayers spend a total of $20 billion—including AFDC, food stamps, and Medicaid benefits— assisting families that start with a birth to a teenage mother. A teen mother who receives public assistance costs the public an estimated $121,360 over her lifetime (Hotz, McElroy, and Sanders, 1995).

Another Michigan example is the 11.8 percent increase in very low-birthweight babies (less than 1500 grams) between 1988 and 1989. Very low birthweight is the chief culprit in infant death and disability. A Centers for Disease Control study shows that babies unwanted at conception are more likely to weigh precariously little at birth, probably reflecting risky maternal behavior during pregnancy (Pamuk and Mosher, 1988). Most vulnerable and costly are very low-birthweight babies. Almost half these babies die before their first birthday. Assuming that the 238 additional very low-birthweight babies born in 1989 were born to Medicaid-eligible women denied abortions, and with the excess medical cost of one of these babies in the first year alone being $52,000 (GAO, 1992), their excess medical costs in 1989 could total $12.4 million.

Sixteen thousand substance-exposed infants are born in Michigan each year (MDPH, 1992). The expenditures for in-patient hospital care for newborns with perinatal chronic respiratory disorder, the most common reason for hospitalizing crack-exposed babies, have zoomed in Michigan since fiscal year 1988, from $840,000 to an estimated $18.1 million in

1992 (MDPH, 1990b). According to a U.S. General Accounting Office report, the social welfare cost for one of these seriously impaired children through age eighteen could reach $750,000 (GAO, 1990). If one hundred seriously impaired children of the sixteen thousand substance-exposed babies are born to indigent mothers who would have had abortions, their births alone could ultimately cost the public $75 million.

Compared with 1988, almost twenty-five hundred additional babies were born in 1989 in Michigan with congenital anomalies such as spina bifida, congenital hydrocephalus, Down's syndrome, and birth defects involving the heart and the respiratory system. The cost to the state for each such baby could easily be $100,000, for a total of $241.5 million. Another two thousand plus babies born to teenagers probably brought a cost of $51,500 each for the first five years—without calculating the costs for any additional serious difficulties—for a total of nearly $114 million.

Next, add the cost of more than a thousand low-birthweight babies. These babies will cost more than the average of $50,000 each for the first five years and are likely to cost much more when they are in school, when so many of the children at risk of school failure are found with physical and emotional damage that necessitates costly special education. The total estimated cost of $10,000 for each of the nearly eleven hundred children born at low birthweight, then, is nearly $11 million.

Although some mothers may plan to have five or more children, probably half or more of the large family pregnancies are unintentional, resulting in unwanted births to poor women. The likelihood is that these fifth or sixth children will be brought up in poverty and will cost the state of Michigan significantly in years to come. The cost of the 10,300 abortions that Michigan did not fund in 1989, at $250 each, probably saved Michigan $2.6 million, a small fraction of the additional costs noted above.

In 1990, Michigan's safety net needed to stretch even farther to hold many more babies. In that year, the second year of the abortion funding ban, Michigan had experienced a 9.6 percent increase in the number of births—the largest two-year gain since 1956. In Detroit, which has the highest percentage of children living in poverty of any large U.S. city (CDF, 1992), births rose 15 percent, which was five times the national increase.

The state's ban on publicly funded abortions coincided with nationally mandated efforts to provide prenatal and maternity care to more pregnant women through expanded Medicaid coverage. In 1988 there were almost 40,000 Medicaid-assisted births in Michigan, compared with more than 64,000 in 1991 (MDSS, Medical Services Administration, pers. comm., June 1992). Of the Medicaid-assisted births in 1990, more than 60 percent resulted from unintended pregnancies (MDPH, 1990a).

When poor women carry unwanted pregnancies to term, the public does not simply pay for routine prenatal and delivery expenses. In December 1990, the Michigan Department of Public Health issued a report, "Rising Health Care Costs for Children with Special Needs: A Budget Out of Control? or a System Out of Balance?" which states: "The Medicaid ban on abortion is contributing to a significant rise in births to young, poor women—women most likely to have babies with less of a chance for survival and to increasing numbers of surviving medically fragile infants" (MDPH, 1990b, 4–5).

When poor women want to avoid an unwanted pregnancy, especially if they are young, unmarried, have serious health problems, and are denied access to abortion services, there are costly consequences for them, their children, and society. The resentment of Michigan taxpayers over paying for abortions for poor women has resulted in a punitive and expensive policy. The money saved in direct costs is trivial compared with the enormous sums being spent each year on medical, educational, and social services for babies born unwanted.

Although it is difficult to quantify because of the dynamics of the problem, over time, the additional long-term public costs of caring for the unwanted babies born in Michigan in 1989 could exceed $300 million, more than one hundred times the direct savings realized by the abortion funding ban. Ironically, these huge expenditures do not create an effective safety net for babies at birth or as they grow up. Thus, Michigan's implicit promise to provide safe and adequate care for children born unwanted has not been kept.

The Short- and Long-Term Consequences for Infants and Families

Being born unwanted is associated with significant, if not easily quantifiable, costs—costs that continue throughout children's lives. As the longitudinal studies from Scandinavia and Czechoslovakia (see chapter 3) indicate, children born to women denied abortions are more likely to require special services, such as remedial education, counseling, and drug treatment, and have a greater likelihood of becoming incarcerated. The consequences for infants who get into the child welfare system and the special case of drug-exposed babies suggest equally grim prospects for many of the Michigan children who are born unwanted.

Michigan is not Czechoslovakia, and Detroit is not Prague. We will never be able to identify or follow the developmental effects of denied abortions on a cohort of children who were born unwanted in Michigan. Although unwanted pregnancies do not necessarily produce unwanted children, the reports from Michigan state agencies in the years immediately following the ban on publicly funded abortions raise troubling questions about the experiences that are likely to await Michigan infants whose mothers did not want to carry their pregnancies to term.

• In Wayne County, which includes Detroit, the postneonatal mortality rate, an important measure of the environmental risks facing infants between twenty-eight days and one year of age, rose from 3.9 deaths for every 1,000 live births in 1988 to 5.4 deaths in 1990. By 1993, the percentage was back to 3.9 again (MDPH, 1987–93).

• The Michigan Department of Social Services reported a 38 percent increase in confirmed cases of abuse or neglect involving victims under age one during the period 1988–91 (MDSS, pers. comm., 1992).

• Infants constitute the fastest-growing group in Michigan's foster care system. The number of Michigan infants placed "out-of-home" increased from 1981 to 1990 by 62 percent (Schwartz et al., 1994). In Wayne County, infants account for 30 percent of the children placed for the first time in substitute care in 1990, compared with 19 percent in 1985 (Abbey, Vestivich, and Schwartz, 1991).

• The University of Michigan's Center for the Study of Youth Policy (Siefert, Schwartz, and Ortega, 1994) found that postneonatal death rates among infants in foster care placement in Wayne County rose from 6.6 for every 1,000 placements in 1980–82 to 11.4 deaths in 1987–89, a rate more than double the postneonatal mortality rates for all Wayne County infants.

The authors of the University of Michigan study, the first to look at infant mortality among children in foster care, concluded that "the commonly held assumption that the child welfare system provides care and protection for children has created an illusion of security." Even before the funding ban resulted in more babies being born unwanted, infants entrusted to Michigan's foster care system were much less likely to find long-term stability than were older children. More than half the infants placed between 1981 and 1987 had no record of returning home or to a relative in the first four years following initial placement. Between 1981 and 1987, the percentage of infants having multiple placements increased from 55 percent to 73 percent (Schwartz et al., 1994). Thus, the state's implicit promise to care for the additional babies born to poor women denied abortions is not likely to be kept. Babies born unwanted cannot rely on government services for even basic protection from physical harm, let alone the continuity and nurturance of good-enough care.

Drug-Exposed Infants: A Special and Complex Case

As one thinks about public responsibility toward children and families at highest risk, the situation of infants exposed prenatally to drugs presents special and extraordinary challenges. The Michigan Task Force on Drug-Exposed Infants (1992) estimates that 16,000 infants are born in Michigan each year to women who used harmful substances during pregnancy. In fiscal year 1991, only 1,200 pregnant women were admitted into publicly funded substance abuse treatment programs.

During the period between November 1988 and September 1989, chiefly covering the period immediately after the abortion funding ban went into effect, a survey was conducted at Detroit's Hutzel Hospital, an institution that serves a high-risk, mostly low-income population. The survey revealed that 44 percent of infants delivered at the hospital had been exposed prenatally to drugs (Ostrea, Lizardo, and Tanafranca, 1992). The clinical manager of Hutzel's neonatal intensive care unit observed that many of the women who used drugs during their pregnancies would have had abortions had they been able to. The manager also reported that some drug-addicted women purposely use crack in an attempt to terminate their pregnancies but fail (*Chicago Tribune*, 1989).

A growing number of drug-exposed newborns become "boarder babies." Abandoned by parents whose own drug or alcohol problems make them unable or unwilling to care for their newborns, these infants remain in hospitals because they have no other place to go. In 1992 the Child Welfare League of America, surveying seventy-two public and private hospitals in twelve cities, found they were spending $34 million each year caring for 7,200 babies who were healthy enough to be discharged but who had no homes. Eighty-five percent of these infants had been exposed to drugs or alcohol before birth. All the boarder babies in the Hurley Medical Center in Flint, Michigan—the American city with the fourth highest percentage of children living in poverty— had been prenatally exposed to drugs.

The official state response to the desperate situation of substance-using pregnant women is tragically insensitive. In 1991, in the executive order that established the task force, Governor John Engler said: "If the problem of drug-exposed infants is not dealt with effectively, the costs to society will be staggering because many drug-exposed infants require expensive, high-technology medical care in neonatal intensive care units, are placed in foster care at a high cost to the state, and will later need special education services."

The task force report acknowledged that "many women do not learn they are pregnant until well into the first trimester, the time when the developing fetus is most vulnerable to drug-related impairment. Even if women discontinue alcohol and other drug use upon learning they are pregnant, fetal damage may already have occurred" (p. 39). The task force also noted that many substance-using women are victims of physical and sexual abuse and incest, which may, obviously, result in pregnancy. Despite this awareness, the task force recommended that "reproductive health services should be made a basic health service (teaching abstinence, family planning methods, pre- and postconceptional counseling). *Abortion counseling is not included*" (p. 71, emphasis added).

Cook County, Illinois: Reversal of a Funding Ban

The experience in Cook County, Illinois, provides compelling evidence that there is a substantial unmet need for abortion services among low-

income women. In September 1992, Cook County Hospital began per-
forming abortions after a twelve-year hiatus; it is the only county hospital
in the state that provides an abortion service and the only public facility in
Chicago that offers abortions at low or no cost. Scheduling an abortion
requires phoning the hospital's abortion hot line during a two-hour period
on Mondays only. Although the hospital received 45,000 calls in the first
six months after September, or nearly 2,000 calls a week, it was not able to
satisfy the demand for abortions. With current facilities and personnel the
hospital was able to perform at most only thirty abortions a week (pers.
comm., R. Jones, Cook County Hospital, 1993). Some women are
directed to two private clinics that provide subsidized abortion services,
but each week hundreds of other poor women in Chicago must forgo
abortions unless they can find the money to pay for them.

The economic consequences of the state's policy not to fund abortion
are costly. Three major areas of increased expenditures contribute disproportionately to the growing structural deficit in Illinois' budget:

1. Despite fewer people being eligible for AFDC and Medicaid, expenditures grew from 6 percent of the total budget in 1972 to 15.5 percent
in 1994.

2. From 1978 to 1995 DCFS increased its budget from $128 million to
$1.2 billion, an increase of nearly 950 percent. Foster care alone increased
from 14,000 children placed in 1978 to 47,000 in 1995.

3. Spending for the state correctional system increased substantially.
The number of adult inmates in prisons increased from 7,326 in 1970 to
35,614 in 1994 and continues to rise at a rapid rate (pers. comm., Illinois
Dept. of Corrections, 1993).

In 1994 these three classes of expenditures totaled one third of the
state's total expenditures. All these expenditures related in large part to
the continuing increase in births to single parents. The number of babies
born to single parents in Illinois in 1992 was nearly 69,000, or 33.4 percent of all births, which is a new high. The number of births to single
parents would have been even higher were it not for abortions.

6

THE CYCLE OF POVERTY AND VIOLENCE: A REASSESSMENT

IN THE PAST THIRTY YEARS, since the War on Poverty began, we have been learning that our nation's problems are a lot more difficult than we used to think they were. Solving them will require much better programs *and* substantial federal funding. Yet if the solutions are to merit federal funding at a time of federal budget austerity, we will have to be a lot more hard-headed about our premises and plans than has been necessary in the past.

As far back as 1908 our nation's policy toward children has been based almost entirely on humanitarian grounds. We felt that we had to, as a matter of decency, help poor children, children who for one reason or another were unlucky enough to lose one or both parents and who, without help, would suffer from nutritional, educational, emotional, economic, and social deficits. As Americans, we felt we could not stand by and see children denied the chance to live a decent life and to participate in the great American dream.

Eighty-eight years later the United States has many more children to cope with than it is currently able to handle. Society must develop the skills to give the children of damaged parents a much better chance of making it than they currently receive. Yet the only real way to begin to cope with the problem is to prevent the enormous number of unplanned, unwanted pregnancies. As I look at the broad picture, I am not optimistic; I see:

1. The feminization of poverty: comparing 1960 with 1993, the Census Bureau (1961, 1994) reports that the number of children in black,

female-headed families living in poverty has more than doubled, from 1.5 million to 4.1 million.

2. The National Center for Education Statistics sponsored a national test in 1992 on literacy levels. The results showed that only 17 percent of black seventeen-year-olds could locate, understand, summarize, and explain relatively complicated literary and informational material, as opposed to more than 50 percent of white seventeen-year-olds (USDE, 1994a). Table 6-1 demonstrates the dire consequences of an insufficient education. The 1992 U.S. Department of Education National Adult Literacy Survey shows clearly why some people worked at good jobs while many others with poor skills were either unemployed, underemployed, or were "out of the labor force" (that is, not counted as unemployed).

3. Most inner-city schools are a disaster.

4. Fifty to 70 percent of inner-city children drop out of high school before graduation.

5. Approximately 50 percent of minority young men are unemployed.

6. Violence in the subways of New York is paralleled in many cities.

7. Murder in inner-city housing projects across America is a daily occurrence.

These disparate data yield a clear conclusion: we are failing to socialize and civilize a significant percentage of our nation's children. Historically, socializing and civilizing children has been done by parents. When parents fail and the criminal problem reaches today's proportions, society has to cope with the problem, either by correction or prison. When the number of high-risk children grows faster than our ability to cope, we must recognize that we are failing to do what a viable society needs to do. Until we can correct the causes, we will increasingly be forced to suffer the consequences, and those consequences are increasingly brutal.

Our failure to do more than we have done in the past has already contributed to disappointing gains in worker productivity. It has also led to huge unemployment and unemployability, including a large number of young people who are not even categorized as unemployed but are defined by labor economists as "out of school, out of work, and out of the labor market."

There is growing resentment over paying the costs of the war that

Table 6-1

Born into Poverty: Its Relation to Education, 1992

		Literacy Level				
		1 (lowest)	2	3	4	5 (highest)
Total U.S. Adult Population		21%	27%	32%	17%	3%
Highest level of education	0–8 years	75	20	4	<.5	<.5
	High school diploma	16	36	37	10	1
	GED	14	39	39	7	<.5
	Four-year degree	4	11	35	40	10
Prison	State or federal prisons population only, local jails excluded	31	37	26	6	<.5
Region	Northeast	22	28	31	16	3
	Midwest	16	28	35	18	3
	South	23	28	30	15	3
	West	20	23	33	21	4
Sex	Male	22	26	31	18	4
	Female	20	28	33	17	3
Physical, mental, or other health condition	Any health condition	46	30	18	5	1
	Visual difficulty	54	26	15	5	<.5
	Hearing difficulty	36	30	24	9	1
	Learning disability	58	22	14	4	1
Race, ethnicity	White	14	25	36	21	4
	Black	38	37	21	4	<.5
	Hispanic/Mexican	54	25	15	9	<.5
	American Indian	25	39	28	7	1

(continued)

		Literacy Level				
		I	2	3	4	5
		(lowest)				(highest)

SOCIOECONOMIC VARIABLES

		I (lowest)	2	3	4	5 (highest)
Median weekly wages		$260	$281	$339	$454	$650
Average weeks worked in previous 12 months		19	27	35	38	44
Adults in poverty		43%	23%	12%	8%	4%
Adults in each skill level, by occupational category	Manager, professional	5	12	23	46	70
	Sales, clerical	15	28	34	30	20
	Craft or service	43	36	27	17	8
	Laborer, assembler, fisher, farmer	37	24	16	7	2
Adults in each skill level, by employment status	Employed full time	30	43	54	64	72
	Employed part time	9	12	15	15	14
	Unemployed	8	10	7	4	3
	Out of labor force	52	35	25	17	11
Adults who voted in a national or state election during past 5 years[a]		55	61	69	81	89
Adults who get information about current events from print media		68	85	89	91	92
Adults who read the newspaper	Every day	35	49	52	57	61
	Never	21	3	2	I	I

Source: Adapted from USDE, 1994a

Note. Poverty Status defined according to 1991 poverty income thresholds of the federal government. Some totals will not equal 100 percent owing to rounding.

[a]These numbers and those that follow show that because so many people do not vote, politicians can ignore the poor.

failed to break the cycle of poverty. Often we blame the victims. Yet a disproportionate share of problem students, juvenile and adult offenders, and welfare recipients really never had a chance. Too often they come from the ranks of unwanted children whose parents failed them from the start. How to break the cycle of teenage mothers bearing children who soon become teenage mothers themselves is a problem we have not begun to solve. How can we change the pattern of violence parents unintentionally teach their children, the same violence that they experienced as children?

We must drastically reduce the vast amount of sexual abuse. It is most difficult for anyone to build self-esteem and develop a nurturing, loving parent-child relationship in the aftermath of one's own early sexual abuse. The sexual abuse of children is not only widespread, it usually involves multiple incidents and multiple perpetrators.

Sexual violence and promiscuity lead to sexually transmitted diseases and AIDS. Hopelessness and posttraumatic stress disorder lead to the use of drugs, which leads to crime, careless sex, and more disease and more drugs. Existing programs that work even moderately well tend to be helpful in breaking the cycle, but we need to work on all aspects of the many factors that lead to family dysfunction, including much more attention to the emotional problems and depression that so frequently lead to self-medication by smoking too much, drinking too much, and taking drugs.

As a society organizing itself to cope with wholesale family dysfunction, our services are much too fragmented; often they are offered separately, as, for example, in helping someone to get a general equivalency diploma, child care, job training, or mental health treatment. In fact, the individuals caught in the web of poverty and despair need help on all fronts at the same time. They cannot be expected to negotiate the hurdles of different agencies in different locations, with different office hours, and complicated barriers to qualifying for services. We need more programs at one location to help comprehensively in all the areas of education, employment, housing, nurturing, and health care.

Finally, we must recognize that what we are encountering in family dysfunction is a complicated system involving all kinds of loops and feedback. For example, unemployment and poor prospects for employment among sixteen- to twenty-four-year-old males leads to fewer marriages and many more children born out of wedlock.

Our nation's huge expenditures for public and private education cost $500 billion a year. The costs of crime and violence, a high prison population, and an overloaded judicial system add hundreds of billions of dollars to taxpayer spending. Together with the economic and social costs of the welfare system, the enormity of these expenditures warrants the major funding of new prevention programs that place babies and early childhood development investments at the top of the list of our public policy agenda.

POOR ENVIRONMENT, POOR STIMULATION, POOR OUTCOMES

The National Commission on Children has addressed the problems of children born at high risk of failure and of those who grow up in dysfunctional families. It has looked at the intricate web of being disadvantaged and followed its numerous threads, including poverty, the physical and emotional health deficits of children, learning disabilities, poor school achievement, violence, and risky antisocial behavior among adolescents. Stepping back from this fabric we can discern patterns.

Family dysfunction is the name we can assign to the set of problems that produces the same symptoms over and over again, generation after generation. Add to family dysfunction America's intensifying cycle of poverty, and we have a festering, expanding disaster accompanying the waste of human life. Poverty and family dysfunction overlap tremendously, although poverty alone does not cause families to disintegrate, and many families that are not poor oftentimes function poorly. Children born to unmarried, teenage mothers or into families with one or the other parent a criminal, mentally ill, or addicted to drugs are at high risk. A great number end up as societal failures, that is, physically handicapped, mentally retarded, mentally ill, unable to get or hold a job, homeless, addicted at an early age to alcohol or drugs, chronic recipients of welfare, or as criminals. All in all, they live lives that are miserable. On humanitarian grounds alone this is a catastrophic outlook for us all.

Case Studies: Typical Children Raised in Poverty
The following case studies reveal a pattern of inconsistent caregiving during the early years of life and escalating developmental problems despite intervention efforts.

JOHN

Initially, "John" was involved in an evaluation research program with his biological mother. He lived with her until her death, when he was three years old. At that point he and his younger sister were adopted, and John's participation in the project continued with his adoptive mother.

As a participant, John was assessed for development (cognitive and motor skills, language, and personality), school adjustment, and the quality of his home environment. In addition, John and his primary caregiver have been videotaped in order to assess their interaction at various stages. John and his adoptive mother have been interested and willing participants in the project since John's adoption. Before his adoption, John and his biological mother maintained regular involvement in the project.

A review of John's records before age three suggests that his early cognitive development, including motor skills, was somewhat delayed during infancy and toddlerhood. By the time John was eighteen months old, he had been referred to the Northside Child Development Center in Minneapolis by a public health nurse. Cognitive assessments at two years of age placed John at the lower end of the average range of abilities. Early reports described John's environment as chaotic during this period. His mother was described as being ambivalent and overly hostile toward him. Parental disorganization was reported regarding child care and home management. There was a suggestion of physical abuse as well as physical and emotional neglect. John and his mother moved several times during his first year of life and periodically stayed with friends during times when they did not have a place to live. The mother's parenting skills and understanding of John were described as minimal.

At the time of his adoption, John was experiencing behavioral problems, which included overactivity, an inability to comply with simple commands, and destructiveness. He was assessed at the University of Minnesota's Clinic of Pediatric Neurology and referred for therapy at

that time. From the time of his adoption to the time he entered kindergarten in 1982 (ages three to six), John's adoptive mother made a number of significant changes to accommodate his needs for structure and
supervision. She appeared to be exceptionally sensitive to the need for
consistency in his relationships. Reports suggest that the environment
in John's adoptive home was a nurturing one in which many attempts
were made to provide John with the support he needed to maintain
adequate functioning at home and at school.

Reports from John's teachers in kindergarten and first, second, and
third grades suggest that John was experiencing problems with attention, aggression, peer relations, and possibly with depression. A standard-
ized measure of child behavioral problems completed by John's sixth
grade teacher indicates that his behavior at that time was becoming
increasingly aggressive and self-destructive. He often got into fights
with other kids and with his teachers. He once set a fire on the school
bus and once slashed the principal's tires. John's adoptive mother sought
various forms of help for him over the years, including counseling,
behavioral therapy, and Ritalin, which was prescribed to lessen his
attention deficit disorder. John is currently in a school program for the
emotional and behavior disordered and is now in foster care owing to
his behavioral problems at home, his destructiveness, and his claim that
his adoptive father physically abused him. The adoptive mother emphat-
ically denies this claim.

The most recent contact with John and his adoptive mother (in the
spring of 1993) [more than three years ago] revealed that he is still in foster care and that he had recently had a court-ordered neurological evaluation, an MRI (magnetic resonance imaging), an attention-deficit test, and
a blood test to see whether there was any evidence of lead poisoning. His
adoptive mother pushed hard to get this evaluation. Before the test
results came back, her expectation was that John would probably end up
being put on an appropriate medication for the rest of his life.

MARY

"Mary" and her mother have maintained regular involvement with an
evaluation facility in Minneapolis, with the exception of three years

(approximately from the time Mary was age twelve to age fifteen) when Mary was in foster care.

The caregiving Mary received early in her life was described by various staff members as inconsistent and sometimes overprotective. Her mother was always described as being depressed and unable to cope, and as the years went on her parenting skills seemed to diminish. Her thinking was described as being sometimes bizarre and fragmented. She did not seem to be able to respond appropriately to Mary's needs. She became more rejecting of Mary and referred several times to having discipline problems with her when she was afraid she would lose control and hurt Mary. Over the years the mother was on many different medications for different ailments, including antidepressants, and also had problems with alcohol. She constantly felt she needed counseling or hospitalization but was never able to follow through on those needs.

Mary was a very small baby at birth and continued to be overly small for several years. During home visits in the first year of Mary's life, project staff noted that she was somewhat delayed developmentally. She always seemed sickly and scrawny, and more than one interviewer described her as being a "failure-to-thrive" child. Her attention span was short and her fine motor skills were not as advanced as they should have been. She seemed to have a problem with diverging vision *(stray eye)* in one eye. At one point Mary's doctor wanted her admitted to the hospital for tests because he felt certain that she was going to be a midget; the mother refused. By that time Mary had also experienced several ear infections and colds.

At the eighteen-month visit some unusual behaviors were observed. Mary banged her head on the floor or wall when angry or spontaneously caused vomiting. She was described as clingy and whiny and not at all healthy-looking.

At two years of age Mary's verbalizations were mostly gibberish, and she was not able to stay on task for more than brief periods. On the Bayley Scales of Infant Development she did not succeed at any tasks for her age level. Her coordination and concentration were noted to be that of a much younger child. She was dirty and unkempt and was still exhibiting the head-banging behavior.

At follow-up assessments from ages 2½ to 5, Mary was still not able to stay focused or complete tasks. She was described as being disoriented, and her responses were frequently unrelated to the question asked. At age five she was described as being whiny and demanding, and her behavior was interspersed with extremely angry outbursts. She was extremely thin and sickly.

Once in school Mary finally seemed to make progress. In first grade, at age six, she was referred to a program for the educable mentally retarded (EMR) and received much individualized help. She was not able to concentrate, and she picked on other children. She looked better, though, and acted a bit calmer. In the second grade she continued to make some academic progress. During a home visit at this time she was described as being easily distracted, and her answers were often vague or unintelligible.

The Division of Child Protection of DCFS first became involved with Mary's family when she was in third grade, at age eight. There were separate allegations of physical abuse (by the mother) and sexual abuse (by the father). The allegations of sexual abuse were not followed up on, and the department apparently allowed Mary to remain in the home with the provision that the mother get help in handling Mary. That did not happen. Three years later, at age eleven, Mary indicated that there had been ongoing sexual involvement with her father over a period of many years, and he was removed from the home. She has been receiving various forms of therapy ever since.

A few months later Mary was in foster care because her mother said she was out of control and that she could not handle her anymore. A few months after that the mother was ready to terminate her parental rights, but the county refused to be hasty. Mary remained in foster care over the next three years, until age fifteen, staying with three or four different families. An attempt was later made to reunite her with her mother, but it was unsuccessful.

About a year ago things changed a little for this family. Mary's mother had fallen on hard times and was drinking heavily. Her ex-sister-in-law found her, brought her home, helped her find a job, and provided some stability in her life. The ex-sister-in-law also took custody of Mary and became her legal foster parent. They now all live together, the ex-sister-in-law providing the structure and parenting that the mother is not able to provide. The mother claims to be content with her life but says it is stressful living with Mary again.

At age sixteen things do not look good for Mary. She looks younger than she is and continues to be in an EMR class. She does not do well academically or socially and has no friends. She continues to exhibit behavioral problems in school; for example, she has called her teachers names and on one occasion threatened to kill one of her teachers and his family. She has been hospitalized twice for depression and is currently on Prozac; she has threatened and attempted suicide, and she has always had problems getting along with others. The new living situation with her aunt as legal foster parent may continue to provide the stability Mary needs so much in her life. Her relations with her mother may never improve. When asked to describe Mary's problems, her mother replied, "She's a problem child, period. I think Mary could live a decent life if she would just straighten out. It's all for attention."

In *Damaged Parents: An Anatomy of Child Neglect* Norman Polansky discusses a study that was conducted with two groups of poverty-stricken white parents in Appalachia. One set of parents either neglected or abused their children, or both, and the other neither abused nor neglected their children. Researchers found that in almost every case, those parents who were guilty of neglect or abuse had themselves been neglected or abused as children.

When this study was replicated in inner-city Philadelphia, the results were similar, leading researchers to conclude that regardless of differing environmental factors, damaged children frequently grow up to be damaged and damaging parents, thus perpetuating the cycle of neglect and abuse. "Parental personalities were found distorted to a degree that, in ordinary clinical work, presupposes damage early in their own lives, a supposition that was largely supported by the facts that were available" (Polansky, 1981, 159).

INVESTING IN CHILD CARE, LINKED HEALTH SERVICES, AND EARLY CHILDHOOD DEVELOPMENT

Whatever the level of success from prevention efforts, approximately 4 million babies will still be born each year, and at least a million of these will be born at very high risk. For these we will need more and improved intensive intervention programs modeled after successful programs. These will include one-stop services for women, infants, and children; first-class pediatric care; social worker support; home visiting; parenting education; family support; and developmental screening programs—all of which are important. Every child we help to become a successful individual in our society is important. Not only is the individual's success vital, but we now realize that delinquent individuals have a significant adverse impact on the behavior and learning ability of their peers. If we can reduce by half, from 1 million to five hundred thousand, the number of babies born into high-risk environments annually, we will have a much better chance for our intervention programs to be well staffed and successfully implemented. The remaining 3 million babies are, at the very least, equally important. Now that we know the importance of prenatal care and optimal development in the first two years of life, we should study the French system of child care for all infants. It subsidizes all families with young children, to a varying extent, depending on the financial needs of families. The French system is solidly built on highly trained, master's degree-equivalent, child development specialists and public nurses.

The authors of "Transactional Regulation and Early Intervention" (Sameroff and Fiese, 1990) discuss how the risk of psychological disorders in children increases geometrically with each additional risk factor. They list ten important environmental risk variables:

1. Chronicity of maternal mental illness
2. Maternal anxiety
3. Parental perspectives score derived from a combination of measures that reflected rigidity or flexibility in the attitudes, beliefs, and values that mothers had in regard to their children's development
4. Spontaneous positive maternal interactions with the child during infancy
5. Occupation of head of household

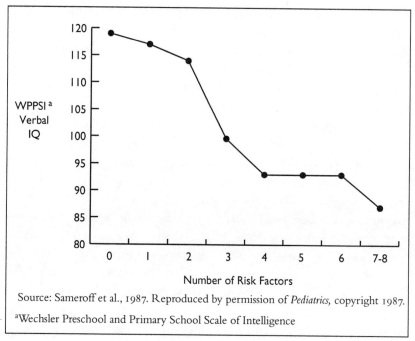

Source: Sameroff et al., 1987. Reproduced by permission of *Pediatrics,* copyright 1987.

ᵃWechsler Preschool and Primary School Scale of Intelligence

Figure 6-1
Effects of Multiple-Risk Scores on Preschool Intelligence

6. Maternal education
7. Disadvantaged minority status
8. Family support
9. Stressful life events
10. Family size (pp. 119–45)

Figure 6-1 demonstrates how quickly the risk mounts as the number of factors increases. The authors conclude that universal interventions will not solve children's problems. Rather, every situation, that is, every different combination of risk factors, requires particular, individualized interventionary tactics.

If we could assemble in one room, in their work uniforms, representatives of all the people who work on services for children and for the adolescents they grow up to be, we would see: army educators, child abuse investigators, child psychologists, detention center or jail wardens and guards, drug-abuse-center doctors, employment counselors, foster parents, Head Start teachers, health department officials, judges, mental hospital aides, neonatalogists, obstetricians, occupational therapists, pediatricians, physical therapists, police officers, preschool teachers, probation officers, psychiatrists, special education teachers, visiting nurses or nurse practitioners, school counselors, shelter personnel, social workers, truant officers, and welfare department workers. This is only a partial list of those who must cope with the casualties when a child's normal development is significantly delayed, derailed, or impaired.

Prevention is not only possible, it is now even recognized legislatively. The passage in 1986 of Public Law 99-457 provides some funds so that infancy specialists can start working from birth with infants and toddlers at high risk of developmental delay.[1] Such early intervention can improve early interaction and improve the chances that appropriate development will occur, which in turn can often prevent developmental delays and even prevent profound retardation.

Prevention programs do work, but what is sorely lacking is a clear national policy concerning children. Minimally, this policy would necessitate two major new programs: increased training of early childhood development professionals and many more experimental prevention programs. We need to increase the number of administrators and researchers as well as clinicians. At the undergraduate level, in both universities and community colleges and in graduate programs, we must rapidly increase the number of people professionally trained as child care specialists, health care technicians, nurses, occupational therapists, and preschool teachers.

New training and prevention programs cost money and will initially compete for funds with existing programs, many mandated to deal with the casualties of failed prevention after it happens. Yet a decision to avoid disaster must be established; a long-term target should be to set aside 5 percent of all human services budgets—local, state, and national. Where the victims of current disasters are begging for help and where a state or city is mandated to provide services to treat them, it is a challenge for administrators to find money for prevention. An ounce of prevention, it has been seen, will produce a pound of cure in the long term and frequently even in the short term.

A LETTER TO THE CANDIDATE FOR PRESIDENT:
A LOOK BACK

I wrote the following letter to Governor Bill Clinton in the spring of 1992, when he was a candidate for the presidency. At that time he was well behind in the Democratic Primary polls. I realized there was only a modest chance that he would read the letter or act on it. I did get it into the hands of one of his closest advisers. I do not know whether Mr. Clinton ever saw it. The letter read:

A president cannot enact laws. Congress does that. But a president can lead and propose laws.

If he leads by proposing and the Congress does not follow his lead, he is either ahead of his time or just plain wrong. If he proposes only what is safe and what everyone agrees to—what pollsters say a majority of voters want—that is not what anyone would call leading.

A real leader must understand problems, analyze them, and propose solutions that, within a reasonable time, will be passed by Congress and become law.

Here is a list of many of the urgent domestic problems we face:

1. The discouragement of young people about their future. This obviously involves jobs, the prospects for gratifying and remunerative work, long term as well as short term.

2. A health care system that needs major overhauling. Preventive health care is unavailable to more than 35 million Americans and particularly to children. Even for the people who have insurance, it is too costly. Businesses that pay the bulk of the cost of insurance find that health costs are much too high and climbing. A major reason for the lack of international competitiveness on the part of U.S. business is the huge costs that businesses pay for the health insurance of their employees and former employees. If all small businesses had to provide insurance, some would go out of business; and if new businesses had to pay the costs for insurance, it might make it impossible for some of those businesses to start. The cost of health insurance really is a social cost and should be payable through taxes on the whole of our society.

3. Public education is a shambles. Particularly in our major cities, schools are failing to educate a majority of the children attending public schools.

Without an appropriate education, these young people will not only be unemployed, but for all intents and purposes, they will be unemployable. In today's society, skill in reading and numeracy are absolutely requisite to getting a decent job. The skills of new employees also have a major effect on future U.S. competitiveness. A part of our failure to educate is the poor training that so many of our teachers have. This is particularly apparent in math and science teaching. Another part of the problem is that our system is discouraging to many able people who would like to become teachers but find it is unrewarding.

   A very important part of the solution to the education problem is to recognize the importance of and do more about early childhood development. Preschool programs [for children] from birth to age five should be developed as recommended by the Committee for Economic Development. It is now clear from research and evaluation in the past ten years that a child's ability to read and to learn are importantly affected by early childhood experiences and also by the child's health. It is estimated that 12 percent of all U.S. children arrive at school at age five learning impaired because of preventable problems. While Head Start has had increased funding in the past three years, it is, for most poor children, still a program for only one year, not two or three, as it should be. Furthermore, the average income of Head Start teachers is approximately $12,000 a year, which is too low to attract and provide for continuity in able, skilled teachers. Training programs for early childhood education are inadequate. In the United States, in contrast to France, only a relatively few of our millions of very young children have the benefit of learning from master's level teachers who have been well trained in early childhood development. It is clear that there is a close correlation between the quality of the teacher and the learning results of the students. Because of a great shortage of well-trained teachers, early childhood development programs, generally speaking, are too few and inadequate.

4. Out-of-home child care is increasingly needed because more than one half of the mothers of young children are now in the work force in occupations that take them out of the house. Finding child care for the children of working mothers is very difficult. There is no system of providing high-quality child care in most communities. There are few

standards. The quality is generally low. In most cases, the compensation of child care workers is at such a low level that it neither attracts nor retains well-trained and competent personnel. There is an enormous turnover of teachers. A young child particularly needs continuity and consistency in care. High turnover of teachers is inimical to a child's healthy development.

5. The shortage of affordable housing in the United States is an absolute disgrace. We see the results of this shortage in the numbers of homeless who are populating the streets of our major cities. Even for people who do have homes, if they are poor, it is likely that their neighborhoods are crime-ridden and dangerous. High rise "projects" breed crime. It is inhuman to force our poor to live in cauldrons of crime.

6. Violence is rampant in the United States. Not only was it visible in the rioting in Los Angeles, but nationally we have unacceptable levels of domestic violence, drug-related violence, drive-by shootings, child abuse and neglect, and a prevalence of children going to school with guns and knives. The statistics in the United States on guns and on violence are a world-recognized disgrace.

7. Our major cities are getting older. Roads, bridges, and many other kinds of structures are increasingly antiquated and dangerous. Because cities have suffered an exodus of many taxpaying individuals and companies, they are suffering from an erosion of the income needed to make it possible for them to repair their infrastructures. The successful effort by the Reagan and Bush administrations to lower federal taxes and do away with revenue sharing has increased the tax burden on the cities and states. But the cities are faced with white flight, increased violence, and bad public schools, which increase the likelihood that stable families and businesses will continue to move away from the cities, further eroding the cities' tax bases.

8. Research in medicine and in the sciences generally has made the United States the envy of the world in the past fifty years. That huge margin of superiority is being eroded day by day as funds for research are increasingly difficult to find. Many talented researchers are being kept out of their fields because of a lack of research funds. While it might seem that so much has been discovered that little remains to be discovered, this is the exact opposite of what is true. . . .

9. Because of a dearth of tax revenues and politicians' fears of raising taxes, the states are increasingly walking away from their responsibilities. The cities are not considering needed programs because of their lack of taxing power. The federal government is in gridlock. The Congress seems unable to develop any plans. What little it does propose, the president vetoes. To the Congress and most citizens, the president's plans seem inadequate, and the Congress tends to reject the president's leadership.

The nation needs a plan that addresses all the above problems at the same time. A good plan will not be a quick fix. Indeed, it will be a very slow fix. But we need broad-scale planning with a strong start to tackle these problems as soon as possible. We must begin as fast as we can and increase as fast as we can, but recognize that for any plan to be meaningful it is going to have to be at least a ten-year program [see table].

Ten-Year Goals for Public Policy

	Child Care Facilities[a]	Housing Starts[b]	New School-Linked Health Clinics[c]
1993	1,000	50,000	1,000
1994	3,000	150,000	3,000
1995	5,000	250,000	5,000
1996	6,000	400,000	6,000
1997	6,000	400,000	6,000
1998	5,000	400,000	5,000
1999	4,000	400,000	4,000
2000	3,000	400,000	3,000
2001	3,000	400,000	3,000
2002	3,000	400,000	3,000

[a]Proposed number of structures to be built, each housing 100 children on average.

[b]Low-rise, drug-free, new housing units, with 75 percent of occupants to be nonpoor working families; 25 percent for poor working families and some welfare families.

[c]Proposed number of new facilities available during school hours to middle and high school students, and, at different hours, open to neighborhood children and families not from that school.

It is possible for a new president to initiate a sensible but bold plan and for the nation to begin moving before the summer of 1993 with strong leadership from a new president. The new Congress should be willing to enact an intelligent, well-thought-out, comprehensive program. Such a plan will require national unity, enthusiasm, and confidence. Any program that sets forth targets of fewer than ten years is really unrealistic. We can no longer think in two-year terms or four-year terms or six-year terms or address our problems principally with an eye on the next election.

Illustrative, though not complete, are the following suggested goals:

In addition to infrastructures, the plan would incorporate the training of needed personnel. We must plan to train *now* the people we will need tomorrow to staff the structures I [have] outlined. . . . More specifically,

In 1994, in order to staff 3,000 new child care facilities, we will require 30,000 staff, of whom

3,000 will require master's degrees

10,000 will require bachelor's degrees

17,000 will require associate's degrees

To train the people needed to build the housing, job training, and apprentice programs will be established.

To staff the school-linked medical clinics to be opened in 1994, we will need 42,000 staff, of whom

6,000 will require master's degrees in social work

6,000 will require master's degrees in nursing

12,000 will require bachelor's degrees in social work

12,000 will require bachelor's degrees in nursing

6,000 will require bachelor's degrees in clerical and computer skills

. . . While the Congress is considering the proposed legislation, the president should invite into Washington for a series of meetings the executives of foundations, corporations, and unions.

He should also invite representatives from schools for public-policy studies to provide new thinking and new administrative structures for many of these new public programs.

He should also invite the executives of our many teaching institutions to help plan the needed training.

Concurrently, we should also begin to investigate a range of new ideas, including the retraining of math and science teachers, and initiatives such as developed by Dr. Leon Lederman of the University of Chicago.

We should build on successful programs like "Career Beginnings," which work with high school students in providing summer jobs and mentorships and encourage inner-city youth to seek careers that are consistent with their own talents, where meaningful jobs can result. We should use existing structures like Career Beginnings and counterpart programs and expand these programs nationally.

With respect to housing, we should reinvestigate various modes of producing good-quality housing at a lower cost, stressing the need for human-sized buildings, particularly when children are going to be involved. No more high-rise projects, which are so inimical to child development and make it so difficult for mothers to interact continually and consistently with their young children and to exert the steady influence that is necessary for good child development.

This plan needs to be fleshed out. It should be concrete, but at this stage, not set in concrete. I believe that the visual impact of seeing structures for child care facilities in inner-city locations, coupled with new, beautiful medical clinics linked to schools, and new housing in areas that promise to be free of drugs and free of violence, would all bring hope to the working poor and welfare recipients.

7

TRENDS IN EDUCATION, POVERTY, VIOLENCE, AND PUNISHMENT

THE FOUR ISSUES of this chapter's title are inseparable. As the quality of our schools declines, literacy plummets, causing poverty to soar. Poverty leads to violence, and violence leads to punishment. Poverty contributes to higher rates of unintended pregnancy, and attempts to punish poor women by refusing them abortions perpetuate the larger cycle of poverty.

Our nation must solve the problem of poverty if we are to continue to progress. Without a solution, we will slide into the status of a second-class nation, no longer a world leader. Competitively, we will be unable to keep up in the world, and we will be torn by dissent within our own nation. Ironically, just as Communism falters all over Europe, our own democracy is in great danger because of the imminent breakdown of our society in the form of a growing underclass that is poorly educated, with an increasing gap between high-income and low-income workers. Former Governor Thomas Kean of New Jersey quoted Thomas Jefferson, "If a nation expects to be ignorant and free in a state of civilization, it expects what never was and never will be." Owen Butler, chair of the Committee for Economic Development, has asked whether we are aware that we are about to pass on to our children, grandchildren, and great-grandchildren living conditions such as the conditions that exist in Mexico City and Manila, where in order to be safe you have to erect high walls topped with broken glass or barbed wire around your home. Then, with the help of armed guards, you can almost feel safe. In Johannesburg, South Africa, ten years ago, I was a guest in a suburban home. It was lovely, capacious, and safety seemed assured. American friends visited the same home a short time ago. Now a high fence surrounds the house, with barbed wire and broken glass on the top of the gate. Armed guards are also in place with an intricate communications system.

The real question is, what are the causes, and what can we do to correct them? When a baby is born to a woman who is poor—white or black, Hispanic or American Indian or whatever, a woman who learned early in life that she was regarded as of no account by her family and later by the schools she attended, whether that woman's first baby was born when she was thirteen years old or fifteen, seventeen, twenty, twenty-five, or thirty—in the United States the outlook for that baby is dismal.

Because babies are helpless when they are born, they need a great deal of help. The mother will be stressed by her poverty and have little or no knowledge about ways to help her baby develop. She will not know how to help her baby's brain develop, to teach the baby how to cope with life, which is something every baby needs, whether that baby is a human baby or the baby of a lion or a horse or a gorilla. Human babies need a long period—several years—in which to learn how to cope in the world. Based on her experience of life, the mother will probably have little trust in any help she may occasionally be offered from individuals or agencies. Yet babies need protection, continuing and consistent encouragement, and at least one loving parent who believes in the baby, expects the baby to be successful in life, and knows how to encourage the baby to feel that its life will be successful.

It is wholly unrealistic to blame a baby for growing up unable to cope, unable to learn, unable to do well in school, and unable to get a job and live a good life, which is what we expect of our fellow citizens. However unrealistic, we *do* blame children. And that was true when the baby's mother was a baby; she probably never had a chance.

The contraceptive pill has become widely used. Premarital sex used to be hidden; now it is the norm. Getting married just to give the baby his father's last name is increasingly being looked upon as a bad idea. If the father's job prospects are poor, the trouble of a later divorce is a bad trade-off for many young women. All over the world, not only in the

United States, women increasingly are forgoing marriage based on pregnancy, whether intentional or unintentional.

In Sweden and Denmark, for example, births to unmarried women are much higher than they are in the United States. Nearly 50 percent of the babies are born to unwed mothers. In Illinois, at 33.4 percent, the rate is also high. Yet parents in Denmark and Sweden are living together: they are unlikely to be adolescents; the baby is intended and wanted by both the mother and the father. They together bring up the baby, nurture the baby, are able to help the baby develop. The father and mother frequently later get married.

> It comes as a surprise to some to learn that premarital sex has long been common in the U.S. While the average age of sexual initiation has gone down in the past twenty-five years, a majority of men and a substantial minority of women engaged in premarital sex at the beginning of this century. . . . In the 1950s, now celebrated as the golden era of "traditional family values," close to half of all marriages occurred during the teen years, and half of those marriages were preceded by a pregnancy. Pre-marital pregnancy in the teen years was certainly no less common then than now. . . . Americans appear to be far more concerned about lowering rates of teenage sex activity than in preventing teenage pregnancy, abortion, and childbearing. (Furstenberg, 1995, 7, 8)

We are against sex, no doubt, for young people. We want the problem of sexual activity among teens to go away, but it does not go away. I doubt whether we can punish it away or change the welfare system in such a way as to make it go away.

There are major studies being done on teenage pregnancy and its costs. One difficulty of such research, of course, is that the individuals who become pregnant and have babies as unmarried teenagers are different individuals in outlook and in character from those teenagers who, even if they are active sexually, do not become single mothers or bring their babies up in poverty.

Countless studies of teenage parenthood provide only glimmers of support for the premise that parenthood is dictated by a "rational choice." . . . Far more evidence suggests that early parenthood is the result of a "rationalized choice." Very few teenagers set out to become pregnant before conception occurs. Almost none would have taken the pill for 20 days consecutively *in order* to become pregnant. Teens have sex, use birth control imperfectly, and elect not to get an abortion and merely pass the point of no return without mobilizing to terminate an unplanned pregnancy. Pregnant teens can also see many reasons why parenthood might be attractive, given the alternatives in their immediate lives and their future prospects. If they are failing in school or have already dropped out, if they experience little purpose in life, or if they imagine that parenthood will reinforce their relationship with the baby's father, having a child makes at least as much sense in their minds as not having one. (Ibid.)

Their frequent reaction is, "No big deal."

Of course, many of these adolescent parents have been sexually abused as children (see chapter 3). For far too many teenage women the problems of sexual abuse; the easy availability of drugs and alcohol; homelessness; posttraumatic stress disorder resulting from physical abuse; witnessing domestic violence; failure and feelings of hopelessness in school; and the experience of no one having any expectations for them are the problems these children face. All militate against a responsible attitude about bringing a child into the world with expectations that that child will succeed.

Joseph Hotz and colleagues at the University of Chicago have carefully examined the costs to the welfare system of births to teenagers (Hotz, McElroy, and Sanders, 1995). Hotz estimates that over their lifetimes teenagers will receive between $12 billion and $20 billion in public assistance, or somewhere between $72,000 and $120,000 for each teenage mother. He adds, however, that many of these same individuals later work and pay taxes. He concludes that the net costs to the government after the receipt of later taxes is not really significant in the total scheme of our $5 trillion economy. There are many reasons why teenage parenthood, particularly unmarried teenage parenthood, should be discouraged. But it is important to realize that the net cost to the welfare system and to taxpayers is relatively minor (ibid.).

Norval Morris (a former dean of the University of Chicago Law School) recently reported on a meeting he chaired in Bellagio, Italy, of high-level subcabinet ministers of several European countries. The purpose was to discuss the subject of drug abuse, how to prevent it, and how to lessen the harm from it. He was struck by the remarkable difference in approach of the European nations compared with our policies. The drug problems are not dissimilar, and no country is pushing for legalization. Although no one has exact knowledge of the levels of drug use and abuse, each country probably has about the same level of drug abuse. The European nations, however, respond by trying to lessen the harm resulting from drug use. Every other country, except the United States, relies on various means of trying to lessen that harm. The United States focuses on law enforcement as a remedy. Our theory is that punishment will deter. This policy apparently does not accord with human nature, at least in the United States. As a consequence, per capita we have about ten times as many people in prison for drug offenses as do the Europeans. More than 25 percent of all inmates of our state's penitentiaries are there because of drug use or a violation of laws related to drug use or sale.

All in all, using law enforcement and punishment and putting people behind bars clearly have not lessened the amount of drug use and drug abuse in the United States. As a matter of fact, it has not even worked to increase the price of drugs by making them more difficult to obtain. According to economic theory, if deterrents and punishment were working, at some point or other the price of drugs should have gone up, but it has not.

As to using punishment to change ways of living, our attitudes about abortion parallel our attitudes about drugs. We rely on laws and punishment to deter and discourage births to single women. This underlies the reasoning of those Americans who approve of the Hyde amendment, which, they claim, saves taxpayers money. They say taxpayers should not have to pay for other people's abortions. Punishment is heavily relied on to deter women from pregnancy. Availability of contraception and abortion are both discouraged in favor of economic and legal sanctions. In Europe, which has about the same amount of adolescent and preadolescent sexual activity, pregnancies among adolescents are many fewer and abortion is used much less frequently, although its availability is much broader.

Does the threat of punishment deter pregnancy? The answer is: somewhat, possibly, but only very slightly. The percentage of all births to single women of all ages continues to rise in every state in the country and in other countries as well. (See, for example, table 7-1.)

Table 7-1
Births to Single Women of All Ages, 1970 and 1991 (as a percentage of all births)

	1970	1991
United States	11%	30%
Canada	10	29
Denmark	11	47
France	7	30
Germany	6	35
Sweden	18	48
United Kingdom	8	33

Source: Manvel, 1995

How do we treat unintended pregnancies among single women? If the young woman is from the middle or upper class, her parents, perhaps after initial disbelief and frequently anger, encourage abortion. (See chapter 3.) If the individual who is pregnant unintentionally is not from the middle or upper class and lives in a poor section of the city, and particularly if she is not white or of a minority ethnic group, then our society exhibits a strong tendency in favor of punishment. People say, "They should not do this, and we ought to tell them to shape up or else."

The consequences for both drug abuse and unintended pregnancy are similar. If we punish instead of trying to lessen the harm, we seldom deter the conduct that we are trying to prevent and end up with much more damage—many more people in prison and many more babies born to adolescents out of wedlock.

A *Chicago Tribune* editorial of 13 November 1994 emphasizes the importance of early intervention and stresses the futility of punishment.

IT BEGINS AT BIRTH

When a 5-year-old arrives for kindergarten at a Chicago public school without knowing his full name, or how to count to five, or even how to properly use a bathroom, can the school system be expected to send him on to college 13 years later?

This is the season for the release of statewide testing scores and Chicago, once again, has come up short. While some schools have shown progress during the five years of the city's experiment in education reform, others have backslid. And naturally, everyone looks to flaws in the system for an explanation.

You can bet that there are plenty of flaws in the Chicago school system. But this mustn't be forgotten: When a child has been intellectually deprived for the first five years of his life, the best teachers in the world can't repair all of the damage.

For a perspective on the challenge for public schools, one had to look no further than the *Tribune's* recent series, "It begins at birth," by writers Charles Leroux and Cindy Schreuder. It demonstrated the critical developments in socialization, behavior, motor skills and other essential tools for living that occur in the months just after a child is born.

In the first year, the communications network within the brain develops at a breathtaking pace. But if the neural synapses, the bridges of that communications network, aren't exercised, they wither.

That withering impoverishes the mind and, ultimately, nourishes the cycle of poverty. Babies who are not stimulated are more likely to have developmental delays and behavioral problems. They won't do well in school, they won't obtain the skills to hold a job. They may be more prone to violence. And when they have children, they are likely to subject them to the same deficit of adult attention.

A society can build jail cells and threaten to throw people off welfare, but it won't break the cycle of poverty until it nourishes those infants who are at risk of being intellectually neglected.

Congress and the Clinton administration took a solid step when they approved legislation earlier this year to extend the Head Start program to children from birth to age 3. If done properly, at-birth Head Start will identify kids most at risk and provide nutrition, parent-skills training, and the mental and physical stimulation needed to spur development of the brain.

If done properly, the traditional pre-school Head Start will take those children at age 3 and nurture them and their parents until they head off to kindergarten, where they will receive enhanced instruction through the primary grades.

It's a daunting proposition. The country spends $4 billion a year on Head Start and $7 billion for Chapter 1, the education program for disadvantaged school-age children, and still those programs meet only part of the need.

Yet anyone who talks about breaking the cycle of poverty without starting at birth hasn't recognized the depth of the problem. By the time the school bells ring, it most often is too late.

America's public schools cannot singlehandedly make up for the delayed development of children, so many of whom arrive in kindergarten not ready to learn. More than half of all American students attend public schools in cities with more than 400,000 inhabitants, or smaller cities that have densities of more than 6,000 people per square mile.

Generally speaking, the students in these schools are less able to learn than students in wealthier suburban and private schools. On average, there is no doubt that the parents of the latter children are better educated, more affluent, and show more interest in their children's education than the parents of students in the public schools of large cities. Their children's readiness for school at age five is much superior to large city public school kindergartners. Also, per capita these wealthier parents are willing to and do pay more annually for their children's education—frequently twice as much or even more. Higher salaries and better environments naturally tend to attract better teachers.

It would be instructive to ask ourselves, what is the cost per student for education from kindergarten through high school? Let us assume that in the cities the cost is $5,000 a year. If we multiply this by thirteen years, we could assume a cost of $65,000 per high school graduate. Yet we know that school drop-out is common in the public schools of cities. Disorder in the classroom and occasional violence in the school are also much more likely than they are away from cities. The consequence is that educational outcomes are inferior and the cost of a successful outcome is much higher than $65,000.

Is a quality high school education important? In today's industrialized world, when almost all the good-paying jobs require well-trained and educated personnel, perhaps only 2–10 percent of inner-city kindergartners eventually achieve or can realistically even qualify for the post–high school, advanced technical training required to obtain these better jobs. If we judged K–12 education using cost-effectiveness as a criterion, assuming that only 5 percent (1 in 20) of the original cohort of students in kindergarten are getting as much basic fundamental education as is required to be eligible for advanced technical training, the cost for thirteen years per student would not be $65,000, but twenty times $65,000, or $1.3 million for each "educated" student.

How about the students in private and suburban schools? Let us assume an annual cost of $10,000 for thirteen years, or $130,000. If 90 percent of these high school graduates achieve the necessary fundamental education, the cost for each educated student would be $143,000. Poor public school results costing $1.3 million for each successful outcome in the inner cities are extremely expensive.

Figures 7-1 and 7-2 show the ever-widening disparity between rich and poor and the lack of any progress for the bottom 60 percent of Americans over the past fourteen years. The first graph depicts 1950–78, the second 1979–93.

BREAKING THE CYCLE

What follows is a large portion of a British report, *Unfair Shares* (1994), written by Richard Wilkinson.[1] The report concerns "the effects of widening income differences on the welfare of the young." Although its

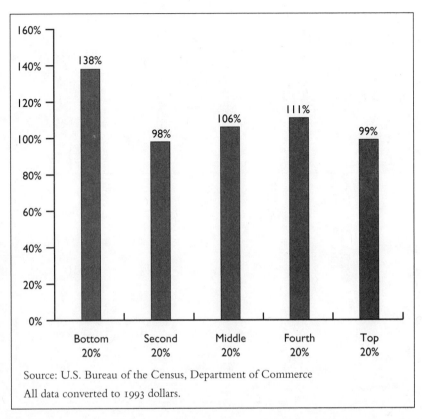

Source: U.S. Bureau of the Census, Department of Commerce
All data converted to 1993 dollars.

Figure 7-1
Growing Together, 1950–1978: Real Family Income Growth

subject reflects conditions in the United Kingdom, the views expressed are
relevant and important to us in the United States regarding our children.

AN OVERVIEW

This report presents new evidence which shows that *relative* poverty has
absolute effects and is a much more destructive social force than is generally
recognised.

It focuses on the welfare of children and young people and discusses
trends in health, depression, crime, drug abuse, suicides and educational

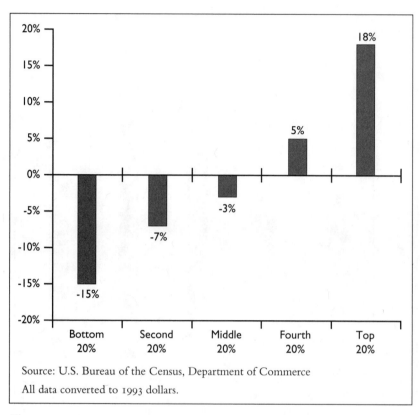

Source: U.S. Bureau of the Census, Department of Commerce
All data converted to 1993 dollars.

Figure 7-2
Growing Apart, 1979–1993: Real Family Income Decline

standards. This report shows that the growth of relative poverty in Britain
has had a major impact on these trends.

The report's purpose is not to point a finger of blame at particular
authorities or to suggest that childhood problems do not also have a host of
other causes. It is, instead, to provide a clear demonstration that there is at
least one important and remediable contributor to some of the social ills of
our society.

Why, as society becomes more materially prosperous, are there increasing
signs of social failure? This booklet shows that at least one major component
of the answer is the scale of relative poverty and income inequality in

society. Their social and psychological effects on the population have widespread repercussions.

No one doubts that economically deprived neighbourhoods suffer more than their share of poor health, crime, drug abuse, depression and other social problems. What this report adds is evidence from two new sources which show that the scale of these problems is responsive to changes in the extent of relative poverty over the years. First is new evidence from internationally comparable data on the distribution of personal income in different developed countries which allows the effects of income distribution to be compared between countries. Second, the unprecedented widening of income differences during the 1980s provides a new opportunity to assess the effects of changes in income distribution.

The damaging effects which disadvantage appears to have on the least well-off are, at most, only partly offset by the beneficial effects of increased advantage among the better-off. The issue is therefore not merely a matter of social justice: it is also a matter of overall national standards of attainment. The lower standards of health, of educational attainment, and the high cost of problems such as crime and drug use associated with increased relative poverty, are not only a human waste but an economic expense which a competitive modern economy cannot afford to accept. There is accumulating evidence that there is no trade-off between equity and economic growth. Economic growth, productivity growth and investment are now higher in countries with smaller income differences. For the sake of the economy and society as a whole, as well as of young people themselves, we need greater investment in human capital.

While children's charities such as Barnardos do their best to put young lives together, action to reduce relative poverty is a priority if we are to prevent them from being torn apart in the first place.

INTRODUCTION

It is tempting to let the eye skip over apparently dry statistics, but we cannot afford to ignore the trends in the list which follows. The figures all show adverse influences affecting children and young people during the 1980s. This period was chosen because the rapidity of change during that decade provides an opportunity to discover what lies behind them. As well as the unhappiness they record among children and young people, they affect the social fabric and the quality of life for all of us.

• Total reported crime, including juvenile crime, increased by almost 80 per cent and violent crime by 90 per cent during the ten years 1981–91.

• The number of drug offenders between the ages of 17 and 29 doubled between 1979 and 1989.

• There was between a four- and five-fold increase in the number of deaths from solvent abuse between 1980 and 1990.

• The proportion of children on Child Protection Registers almost quadrupled during the 1980s. The rates of children 0–4 years old registered after sustaining serious injuries increased by 50 per cent between 1979 and 1989.

• The number of children in care under the age of 10 increased from 1985 onwards. The numbers under 4 years old increased by 30 per cent between 1986 and 1991.

• Reading standards among 7 and 8 year olds declined during the 1980s.

• A study of school expulsions covering the period 1986 to 1991 reported dramatic increases in the use of "all types of exclusion for children in all age groups."

• The suicide rate among young men aged 15–24 increased by 75 per cent from 1983 to reach a peak in 1990. . . .

These problems should not be seen in isolation from each other. Instead of approaching them as half a dozen separate trends, as if they had only independent causes and just happened to coincide, this report starts out from the widely held view that we are dealing with a broadly based social malaise. That is to say that, as well as having many separate causes, the trends in crime, in suicides, drug abuse, depression and the increasing numbers of young children in care or on child abuse registers are also likely to have some important common causes. . . .

The simultaneous worsening in these social indicators provides a fresh incentive to investigate and try to understand what is going on. This report is prompted by two important developments which cast a powerful new light on what is happening. Both of them serve to clarify the contribution of changes in income distribution and relative poverty.

The first is that internationally comparable data on income distribution have recently become available covering a number of developed countries. As well as enabling comparisons to be made between countries at a given point in time, the new data also make it possible to look, in a limited number of societies, at the effects of changes in relative poverty over time. Suddenly we can begin to get a more objective view of the strains which a wider income distribution imposes on the fabric of a society.

The second development is that in the 1980s changes in income distribution in Britain became, for the first time, sufficiently rapid and substantial for researchers to be able to identify their social effects. Figure [A] shows the unprecedented widening of income differences during the 1980s. After slowly widening in the early 1980s, income differences widened rapidly from 1985 onwards. The proportion of children living in households with incomes below half the national average (the definition of relative poverty chosen by the European Community) increased from 10 per cent in 1979, to 31 per cent in 1990/91 (after allowing for housing costs). Such a sudden change allows its effects to be traced in detail for the first time. Previously income distribution had been too stable to identify its effects.

These developments have provided new evidence suggesting that income distribution and the extent of relative poverty have more important and more widespread effects than have yet been recognised. Most strikingly, national standards of health in the developed countries are, as we shall see, powerfully affected by how equal or unequal people's incomes are. So much so, that the best way of improving national standards of health in developed countries would almost certainly be by reducing income differences. It is much more important than, for instance, smoking or other behavioral risk factors. . . .

A Preliminary Note on Changing Family Structures
Before embarking on the discussion of the trends in income differentials and their social effects, a word about the changes in family structure. The growing number of lone parent families is often regarded as an alternative explanation of the disturbing trends in the welfare of children and young people. Although there was almost a three-fold increase in the annual number of divorces during the 1970s, the figures then levelled off and there was little change during the 1980s. The proportion of births outside marriage increased from 8 per cent in 1970, to 12 per cent in 1980, and then to 30 per cent in 1991. . . .

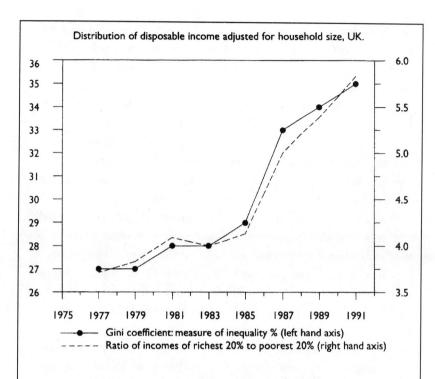

Distribution of disposable income adjusted for household size, UK.

———●——— Gini coefficient: measure of inequality % (left hand axis)
– – – – – Ratio of incomes of richest 20% to poorest 20% (right hand axis)

Fig 1 shows how income differences have widened in the UK since the late 1970s. Two different measures of inequality show the same pattern of a gradual widening of income differences which accelerated dramatically from 1984 or 1985. The Gini coefficient of inequality measures income differences, not simply between the rich and poor, but among the whole population. (The Gini coefficient can vary between 0 percent, which would mean everyone had exactly the same income, to 100 percent which would mean that one person had all the income and everyone else had none.) The other measure, shown here by the dotted line, records the growing disparity between the richest and poorest 20 percent of the population.

Figure A
Widening Income Differences

One important indicator is that much of the association between lone parenting and less good intellectual and educational performance of children seems to be related to poverty rather than to lone parenthood itself. The children of lone parents have more signs of emotional disturbance and do less well educationally. But these disadvantages do not flow automatically from having only one parent. Because environmental factors which are known to affect children's development, such as low social class, poor housing and low incomes, occur much more frequently among lone parent families it is important to separate out the effects of being brought up by only one parent from the socioeconomic disadvantages which so often go with it. At any one time some 70 per cent of lone parents are receiving Income Support to alleviate their poverty, and a higher proportion need it at some time while their children are still dependants. . . .

The possibility of overcoming the handicapping effects of poverty associated with lone-parent families can be seen through international comparisons. Among developed countries, Japan and Sweden represent the opposite ends of the spectrum of family structures. Japan remains closest to the two-parent nuclear family model, with few births outside marriage and low divorce rates, while Sweden—with over half its births outside marriage—is surpassed only by Iceland in the extent of its departure from this pattern. But, despite such a stark contrast, they do almost equally well in terms of child welfare and health. They come first and second in the international league table of life expectancy at birth and have low crime rates. That such major differences in family structure should produce such small differences in outcome is, this paper will argue, a reflection of the fact that these two countries have the narrowest income differences in the developed world. During the last generation, Japanese income differences have narrowed dramatically to become smaller than in Sweden. In Sweden, the celebrated support provided for parents ensured that in 1987, after taxes and benefits, only two per cent of Swedish children in lone parent families were in relative poverty compared with an average of 21.2 per cent for a group of eight countries in the Organisation for Economic Co-operation and Development (OECD). Among children living with both parents, only 1.5 per cent were in relative poverty in Sweden compared with an average of 5.7 per cent for other countries. Partly as a result, infant mortality rates for illegitimate babies in Sweden are as low as those for legitimate births in social classes I and II in England and Wales. . . .

LONGER-TERM TRENDS AND EFFECTS OF
RELATIVE DEPRIVATION [See figures B and C.]
. . . The House of Commons Home Affairs Committee Report on *Juvenile Crime* says "there is obviously an unquestionable link in some cases between unemployment, hopelessness and crime." . . . It goes on to say, "A range of social and economic policies would undoubtedly make young people less likely to turn to crime" and warns "it is of no use to achieve economic success if moral bankruptcy comes in its wake." . . .

EXPLANATIONS
The psychosocial impact of income distribution on national death rates testifies to the extent of the social dislocation caused by widening income differences. It tells us that human beings are more sensitive to inequality than had previously been recognised.

But the relationship between increasing income differentials and the various social problems it creates is not necessarily a simple one. A large number of different pathways are involved in the links with crime, child abuse, reading standards, school expulsions, drug taking, child prostitution and health problems of different kinds in different age groups. Because the relationships are not always clear and simple they are denied as an excuse for inaction, and the social and financial costs continue to increase. However, there can be no doubt that relative deprivation is a component in all these outcomes and has contributed to the statistical trends we have seen in recent years.

Each of the various forms relative deprivation can take have a wide variety of effects. For instance, when people fear unemployment or losing their homes because they cannot keep up with mortgage payments, the stress may result in increased domestic conflict, divorce, heart attack, depression, emotional disturbances in the children, increased use of alcohol, child neglect as parents work longer hours, social security fraud, theft and so on.

That they have some common roots is also shown by the extent to which the various different problems we have discussed overlap, and how one is a risk factor for another. The links between them are familiar. Unemployment and

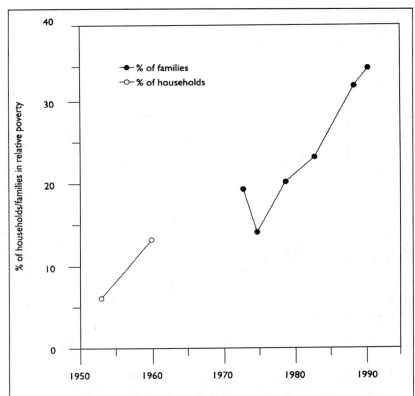

Source: Piachaud D. Poverty in Britain 1899–1983. *Journal of Social Policy*, 1988; 17: 335–49
(Updated from DSS, Households below average income 1979–1991)

Fig 13 records the growth of relative poverty in Britain since the early 1950s. The earliest two points, at the lower left, show the proportion of households in poverty. All the later figures show the proportion of families in poverty, so the two parts of the graph are not comparable. However, if earlier figures were available for families they would have shown much higher proportions in poverty initially and given the impression of a much smaller growth in poverty during the 1960s. The figures from 1970 onwards are comparable. Throughout the series relative poverty is defined as a constant proportion of average income after allowing for the number of people in each family or household. Although there has been almost a continuous rise in the proportion of the population in relative poverty during the second half of this century, the rate has been particularly rapid since the late 1970s.

Figure B

Increasing Percentage of Households/Families Living in Relative Poverty

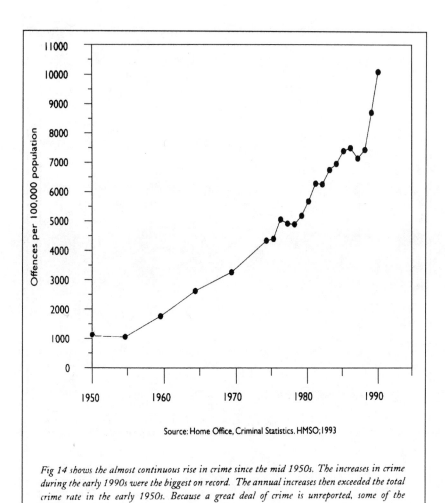

Source: Home Office, Criminal Statistics. HMSO; 1993

Fig 14 shows the almost continuous rise in crime since the mid 1950s. The increases in crime during the early 1990s were the biggest on record. The annual increases then exceeded the total crime rate in the early 1950s. Because a great deal of crime is unreported, some of the variations shown may reflect changes in reporting.

Figure C

Number of Notifiable Offences Recorded by the Police in England and Wales per 10,000 Population low income lead to increases in family conflict which increases the chances of emotional disturbance and behavioural disorders among children. A study of the effects of unemployment on marriage found that half the couples reported an increase in the number of arguments and a third said that one or other partner had left home temporarily or contemplated doing so. Social life was curtailed and their circle of friends shrank. The effect of unemployment on marriage was particularly severe among young couples with children. This, and other more direct effects of deprivation on the home environment, increase the likelihood of educational impairment among children. The parents of children on Child Protection Registers are much less likely than others to be employed. The sources of stress contributing to child abuse which are most frequently recorded by the workers who register each case were the same year after year: marital problems, debts and unemployment.

The contribution which domestic conflict makes to emotional disturbance and later delinquency among children is also well known. A quarter of all children running away from home were found to have previous criminal convictions and many had been regular truants from school. Later on we find a link between crime and mental and emotional problems. A third of 16–18 year old men given criminal sentences are classified as having "primary psychiatric disorders." The links between low income, depression and violence in adults and later delinquency in their children has recently been drawn together to show how the recent rapid increases in violent crime can be explained.

The effects of income distribution on stress in families and the emotional development of children is not confined to the relatively poor any more than it is only the poor who get into debt or financial difficulties. As well as adding to stress and domestic conflict at home, it also increases the pressure on parents— particularly lone parents—to find work, even when the hours squeeze the time left for child care. Low pay means that people with jobs tend to work longer hours where they can. The upward shift in the hours people worked can be seen during the 1980s until the trend was halted by the recession of the early 1990s. There is growing international concern about the effects of child neglect resulting from increased relative deprivation and changes in the job market. The proportion of women going back to work within nine months of giving birth increased during the 1980s from 25 to 45 per cent.

Inadequate resources, financial stress, an unemployed husband at home, or an inability to afford housing with adequate space for a family, all increase the frequency of domestic conflict and family rows. Domestic conflict is an important cause of emotional disturbance in children which in turn has immediate as well as longer-term effects. Although family rows occur throughout society, there is no doubt that they are harder to avoid as stress from other sources increases. It is, after all, easier to avoid getting angry with a child who loses a coat or breaks something if you can easily afford to replace it and have not already faced several rebuffs during the day.

Another important pathway is linked to low self-esteem, and to a sense of failure and inadequacy, to which a relatively low income predisposes people. In the eyes of society how well-off you are appears as an expression of your ability and value as a member of society: implying that poorer people are of less account. This is closely related to the notion of respectability which, for many, is synonymous with social status and looking "respectable." Self-esteem for others may be equally dependent on having the right make of trainers or tee-shirts. With the lack of self-confidence which is exacerbated by relative deprivation, comes an atrophying of friendships and the social contacts which have been found to be protective against the effects of stress. It is difficult not to suggest that a sense of depression and inadequacy, inactivity and eating for comfort, contributed to the dramatic increases in obesity among men aged 16–64 and among women 35–64 years. Between 1987 and 1991 obesity almost doubled among men and increased by about a third among the women.

As the international health evidence makes clear, it is not just a poor minority of the population whose health is affected by income differentials, and it is not just a matter of need. Though that is where the damage may start, the ripples spread much more widely, eroding social values, attitudes and social relations throughout society.

The effects of increases in relative poverty and deprivation affect the sense of security among the majority of the population. The more unemployment, homelessness, houses repossessed, and poverty there is, the greater will be the sense of anxiety and insecurity among the population at large. The sense of security which comes from knowing that there are adequate pensions, that high quality medical care is available to all, that there are job vacancies within reach, and that an adequate safety net exists to prevent destitution, is replaced by a growing sense of insecurity as these guarantees crumble. If things go wrong there is further to fall and the risks of daily life are more worrying.

At the same time, a less caring society redefines human relations. Social norms are redrawn. We become familiar with the coexistence of begging and homelessness alongside wealth and our humanity is subtly redefined. Greater insecurity obliges everyone to look to their own needs in disregard for those of others. Increasing crime means that we see others as a threat to our own welfare. People become fearful on the streets and our assumptions about how we relate to each other change. Where once the welfare apparatus of the state had stood as a clear statement of our mutual responsibilities to our fellow human beings, their decline now stands as a denial of that responsibility.

There are also problems of the perceived legitimacy and fairness of social institutions and of the social structure as income distribution widens. A law abiding society depends to a large extent on the social organisation being seen as a system which operates fairly and enables people to live satisfactory lives in accordance with its rules. Where people feel their paths are blocked, that they are denied opportunities and treated unfairly, breaking the law ceases to be a moral issue and depends instead on a calculation of risks and benefits. The gradual transformation of a society, which had at least some of the attributes of a community which cared for its members, into a collection of individuals related only through the pursuit of material self-interest, leads to further decay of the social fabric.

To dismiss issues of relative deprivation and relative poverty as the "politics of greed" or of "envy" is as inaccurate as it is insulting. The processes have more in common with the situation in parts of the world where remnants of tribal societies have become marginalised and impoverished by more powerful modern societies. As their culture and way of life is undermined and becomes unworkable, people are left without the coherent cultural system capable of providing meaningful roles and the social basis of self-respect. Those who can leave do; many of the rest sink into listlessness, despair, alcoholism and self-destruction. The effects of relative poverty in metropolitan societies are not so different.

FINANCIAL HARDSHIP INCREASES THE RISKS OF FAMILY
CONFLICT AND ALSO OF EMOTIONAL DISTURBANCE
AND DELINQUENCY IN CHILDREN.

DEBT, UNEMPLOYMENT, HOMELESSNESS, LOW SELF-ESTEEM
AND THE LOSS OF SOCIAL CONTACT IMPOSE STRESSES
WHICH CONTRIBUTE TO THE DAMAGE CATALOGUED
IN THIS REPORT.

GREATER MATERIAL INSECURITY, A SENSE OF INJUSTICE
AND A GROWTH OF ANTI-SOCIAL TENDENCIES
TAKE THEIR TOLL THROUGHOUT SOCIETY.

Conclusions

. . . The costs of failure to solve these problems are enormous. In the United
States, where relative poverty has also worsened dramatically in recent years,
the death rate in both sexes and at most ages—except the youngest—is
higher in Harlem, New York, than it is in rural Bangladesh. The greatest
single cause of the excess mortality is heart disease. Although the death rates
from drugs and violence have not yet overtaken it, both are reflections of
the antisocial forces which can arise where people feel the system has ceased
to work for them. So disabling are these trends that the control of drugs and
violence within black communities is increasingly seen by black leaders as a
precondition for political and economic emancipation.

As Donnison [1993] has pointed out, the kinds of social problems to which
a maldistribution of income give rise are likely to be shaped by a number of
factors including the demographic characteristics of each neighbourhood.
An area with a large number of lone parents will, as a consequence of their
poverty, have a lot of debt problems, higher social security fraud and
depression, and the schools will have to cope with more children with
behavioural and learning difficulties. A poor area with a high proportion of
old people will have high levels of loneliness, dementia, chronic disease and
disability, high demands for health and community services and a lack of the
social infrastructure able to provide care and support to elderly people living

alone. Areas in which there is a high proportion of young men without jobs will be characterised by high crime rates, violence and drug use.

Each kind of area and each kind of problem gives rise to its own set of needs, but without substantial increases in resources—both for the poor themselves and for the agencies trying to provide services—significant progress is unlikely. The results of working on any single consequence of widening differentials will be limited by the way each is embedded in a network of other constraints. Each problem is exacerbated by the existence of others. The problems of poor lone parents and unemployed young people are made worse by the wider setting of disadvantage: by the lack of good public transport, by the boredom of life on large estates, by high rates of unemployment, by the presence of drug pushers, by the lack of good educational opportunities and by so many other aspects of an impoverished material and social infrastructure. On many estates there are growing signs of antagonism, not towards the rich living safely [on] the other side of town, but to the teachers, doctors, bus drivers and others whose job it is to provide services.

The responses to such circumstances are, as Donnison again points out, not determined in a totally predictable, deterministic way, but are chosen and shaped by individuals, families and communities. Occasionally the social resources of confidence, energy and hope will be sufficient to lead a community out of antisocial behavior, despair and apathy, and into a more positive cycle of creative activity, self-organisation and political involvement which could build the missing social infrastructure and begin to repair the damage: but much depends on people's success in bringing new resources into their community.

Operating at distinct levels, central and local government, health authorities, employers in public and private institutions, people working in communities and neighbourhoods, all have a role in repairing the damage. We need national policies to reduce income differentials through taxes and benefits, through economic and employment policies and through education and training. Organisations which employ people can create new jobs, increase job security and provide improved access for low paid employees to education and training on and off the job; they can experiment with more egalitarian working environments and they can reduce pay differentials. At the level of local government, housing provision, public services and the quality of the environment should all be addressed as a matter of priority.

It must not be forgotten that these problems are rooted in the antisocial extent of material inequalities. Governments must bear the primary responsibility for the development of policies which can reverse the process of social waste. They need to act to bring together the social and economic costs for four reasons: to prevent the wastage of human life and human potential; because high quality human capital is now essential for economic growth; because the quality of a society's social fabric is now crucial to the quality of life of the population as a whole; and because the burden of social failure imposes an intolerable burden on public services and on the Exchequer—reflected in rising costs of health services, of crime control, of social security dependence, of vandalism, remedial education and so on.

In the short-term, income has to be redistributed through taxes and benefits. Later a better educated population and better economic performance will diminish differentials in pre-tax incomes. Where human resources are all-important, a social strategy now provides the essential underpinning of an economic strategy. Among OECD countries, those with narrower income differences tend to have faster rates of productivity growth. Similarly, among a wider group of nations, there is a statistical association between narrower income differences and higher rates of investment. All eight of the most rapidly growing south-east Asia economies reduced their income differentials between 1960 and 1980 and now have narrower income differences than elsewhere. These findings not only fit the belief that modern economic growth depends on a highly educated and adaptable labour force, but they also put paid to the idea that redistribution and growth are incompatible.

Until recently, few would have predicted the extent of the devastating social effects of a widening income distribution. As well as trying to repair the damage and making sure it never happens again, there is a deeper message to be learnt. That inequality should have such powerful psychosocial effects shows the crucial importance of the wider social dimension of human life. We are not merely economic beings, with material needs, motivated by material gain. Nor are our social needs limited to those met by domestic life and relationships. Vitally important is the way we fit into a wider structure of meaning, fulfilling roles from which we derive a sense of self-worth and experience ourselves as valued members of society. The neglect of this social dimension of life has reached a point where it blights the quality of life for all of us.

Wilkinson's analysis of the psychosocial and other consequences of disparate income levels in the United Kingdom is relevant for Americans, particularly in view of the following commentary in the *New York Times* (14 August 1995).

Poor children in the United States are poorer than the children in most other Western industrialized nations, as young Americans suffer the brunt of several trends toward greater economic inequality, a new study shows.

Only in Israel and Ireland are poor children worse off than poor American youths, according to the study, an analysis of 18 nations by the Luxembourg Income Study, a nonprofit group based in Walferdange, Luxembourg.

The results are the most comprehensive of several recent analyses, and are particularly striking because the United States has the second highest level of economic output per person of the countries examined, after Luxembourg itself, and has the most prosperous affluent children of any of the 18 nations. . . .

The United States appears to have sunk through the rankings over the last 30 years, although no conclusive data are available now, said Timothy M. Smeeding, one of the study's authors and director of the Luxembourg Income Study. The American lead in overall prosperity has dwindled since the 1960's, income inequality has risen briskly in the United States and child poverty spread here in the 1970's and 1980's, although it may have leveled off in the early part of this decade. . . .

Mr. Smeeding said there appeared to be several reasons why the United States had such extreme poverty among children.

The United States has the widest gap between rich and poor, he said. The United States also has less generous social programs than the other 17 countries in the study, which are Australia, Canada, Israel, and 14 European countries: Austria, Belgium, Britain, Denmark, Finland, France, Germany,

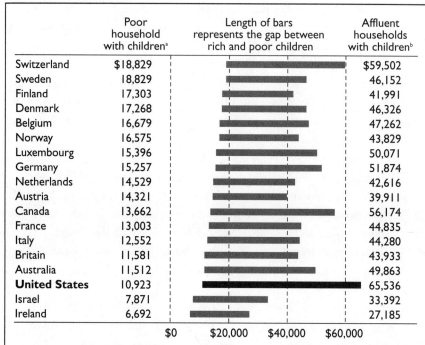

	Poor household with children[a]	Length of bars represents the gap between rich and poor children	Affluent households with children[b]
Switzerland	$18,829		$59,502
Sweden	18,829		46,152
Finland	17,303		41,991
Denmark	17,268		46,326
Belgium	16,679		47,262
Norway	16,575		43,829
Luxembourg	15,396		50,071
Germany	15,257		51,874
Netherlands	14,529		42,616
Austria	14,321		39,911
Canada	13,662		56,174
France	13,003		44,835
Italy	12,552		44,280
Britain	11,581		43,933
Australia	11,512		49,863
United States	10,923		65,536
Israel	7,871		33,392
Ireland	6,692		27,185

$0 $20,000 $40,000 $60,000

The latest research indicates that poor children in the United States are poorer than the children in most other Western industrialized nations because the gap between rich and poor is particularly large in the United States and because welfare programs here are less generous than abroad. Households with children in the United States also tend to have lower incomes than the national average, a pattern that is not true in many other nations.

The bars represent the gap between rich and poor children in Western countries for which detailed data are available. The left end of a bar is the household income of poor children; at the right end, affluent children. All figures are in 1991 dollars, with foreign currencies converted using adjustments for national differences in purchasing power.

[a]After-tax income, including Government benefits like food stamps or the Earned Income Tax Credit, for a family of four that includes children and that is poorer than 90 percent of the households in the country and more affluent than 10 percent of the households.

[b]After-tax income, including any Government benefits, for a family of four that includes children and that is more affluent than 90 percent of the households in the country and poorer than 10 percent of the households.

Source: Luxembourg Income Study

Figure 7-3
The Gap between Rich and Poor Children

Ireland, Italy, Luxembourg, Netherlands, Norway, Sweden and Switzerland. The study did not include several Western European nations, like Greece, Spain and Portugal, that have very poor children but limited data. . . .

The study compares incomes of poor and affluent households with children. The figures include not only after-tax wages and other personal income but also cash benefits from the government, like food stamps and the tax credit on earned income for low-income working parents with children. The calculations take into account differences among countries in the size of families and in the cost of living.

The figures do not include free government services, like the free medical and child-care services available in many European countries.

Sheila B. Kamerman, a professor of social policy and planning at Columbia University, said that for this reason, the latest analysis may have underestimated the extent to which poor American children lag in income. "If you were looking at in-kind benefits as well as cash benefits, the situation in the U.S. would look even worse," she said.

Professor Kamerman and Alfred J. Kahn, another Columbia University social policy professor, published a lengthy study two weeks ago reviewing social problems in Britain, Denmark, Finland, France, Germany, Italy and the United States and found that American poor children received the least help. . . .

The Luxembourg Income Study is financed by the National Science Foundation in Washington and similar agencies from 18 other governments. Its staff has been working for the last decade to develop ways to make reliable international comparisons. The group is a repository for computerized data on income distribution from 25 countries around the world, which it makes available for free to social researchers.

In addition to his work with the study, Mr. Smeeding is an economics professor at Syracuse University and one of the nation's leading experts on income calculations.

8

BREAKING THE CYCLE: A NEW WAR ON POVERTY, 1996

THE PUBLIC POLICY predicament facing our nation is delineated in the following statement from the Institute of Medicine's National Forum: "The interrelationship [between] the causal factors requires an equally integrated approach to the solutions. Throughout the reports, a recurring message is that *to find lasting solutions to the problems of children and families, it is necessary to address many issues simultaneously, including the state of the economy, the quality of education, the condition and availability of work, and the general welfare system*" (emphasis added). I would also add to the list of problems decent, safe housing; wages at least double the minimum wage; and a solution to the drug problem. To address all these issues simultaneously is more than we can realistically expect to recommend. We need to focus on the origins of these problems.

WIDESPREAD INTERVENTION IS NOT ENOUGH
Band-aids will not solve the problems of poverty and family dysfunction. Somewhere in the cycle we must intervene to prevent its repetition. Scientists and researchers have shown that the best place to begin is at the beginning: from conception. This is not to say that intervention cannot or will not work at any other point in the cycle. It is to say that focusing efforts on the earliest years of life will be the most effective and the least costly in both human and economic terms.

Secondary intervention is not enough to stem the tide of poverty and despair that threatens our inner cities and rural poverty zones. The deluge of children requiring intervention programs is overwhelming and tragically unnecessary. As former surgeon general Joycelyn Elders has said, "Young males must learn that donating sperm is not equivalent to being a father." The many, many poor women giving birth to children that were unplanned and unwanted results from unfair government policies that deny family planning and abortion to poor women. These policies have a thoroughly negative impact, and the statistical evidence of it is startling. Our current practices are pushing us closer and closer to social chaos.

Public policy should require that all parents, before conception, demonstrate that they are able, both financially and emotionally, to support and nurture a baby. In China, for example, couples are limited to having one child. The economic penalties for breaking this rule are severe. It is obvious as you tour China that it does not have the problem of unwanted children: every child seems to be wanted and planned for. In our country, too, we would be better off, especially our children, if every baby born were planned and wanted, and after a healthy birth, nurtured and supported in growing up in our complex environment. Every child should be guaranteed a healthy mother. To accomplish this perhaps we should require mothers to have a preconception examination by a doctor so they understand how important the pregnancy and healthy child development are.

THE ELEMENTS OF REMEDY: SHARING RESPONSIBILITY

Many years ago Walter Lippmann, in writing about our democracy, said that the hallmark of responsible comment is not to sit in judgment on events as an idle spectator, but to enter imaginatively into the role of participant in the action.

Unless youngsters receive, at a minimum, a quality high school diploma and are equipped to succeed, an escape from poverty is unlikely. From Reginald Clark (1983) we know that failure in school is not necessarily tied to children born to mothers who are poor, black, and single. Poor, black, single mothers who interact well with their children, who expect them to be successful, and who talk to them in a nonauthoritarian way and in turn listen to them are mothers whose children stay in school, do their schoolwork, and end up with a diploma, perhaps a degree, and a job. Mothers and fathers whose homes are chaotic, who do not know how to nurture their children, and who neglect or abuse them tend to see these children fail in school, drop out, and themselves produce too many children when they are too young to be parents, thus recycling the hopeless poverty they grew up in.

Beginning Again, Beginning Now

We must try to prevent the transmission of risk from generation to generation. The National Commission on Children's report *Beyond Rhetoric* (1991) correctly identifies early prevention as one of its guiding principles for action: "Preventing problems before they become crises is the most effective and cost-effective way to address the needs of troubled families and vulnerable children."

• We can discourage irresponsible sexual activity by individuals who are too young to have jobs and too immature to nurture an infant properly.

• If we cannot prevent sexual activity, we can try much harder to encourage responsibility for contraception, creating, for example, more school-based comprehensive medical clinics.

• If pregnancy occurs anyway and the outlook for the child to be born is bleak, we can encourage abortion.

• If abortion is not acceptable and the nurturing environment is a high-risk one, we can encourage adoption by a family that is willing and able to nurture a baby.

• If the pregnancy is to go to term, we can provide good prenatal care and motivation through parenting education.

Preventing before Fixing: Preventing Adolescent Pregnancy

We must work to prevent poverty and the potential for family dysfunction in every way we know how. But we must go further than the usual call for more and better entitlements, jobs, programs, and secondary intervention programs. As children's advocates, we must join the struggle to ensure that every couple, regardless of income, has access to family planning services and abortion. We must provide full access to information for people to assist them in making these critical but difficult decisions.

Our number one problem: To convince the religious right and the Catholic Church to recognize that in 1995 God is not served by religious leaders who say that it is God's will to increase our world's population in total disregard of the sexual reality that sees many eleven- and twelve-year-old kids sexually active. Religious leaders should not continue to ignore medical advances that have tripled the expected life span of human beings. Many nations whose food and other productive potential cannot keep pace with the combined birth and death rates face continuing starvation.

Our society has grown complex as it has become industrialized. The standard of living can be, and for many is, much higher than it was three hundred years ago, but a decent life today requires that members of society be more highly trained than formerly. There is only a small proportion of jobs for unskilled, uneducated adults. Educating a child to become a participating member of a civilized society takes more effort, investment, time, and support from parents, teachers, and peers than is possible in our many pockets of poverty. One need look not only at the United States, but also at Mexico, Brazil, Egypt, and Kenya. The social conditions of all these countries attest that too many babies, coupled with too little food, too little nurturing, and too little education, add up to a catastrophe. Can conservative religious leaders not recognize the realities of 1995?

If these leaders cannot do so, church members can. For example, a large percentage of American Catholics practice birth control, and many accept abortion, despite the contentious dogma of the church. Why are some human beings so sure that God mandated everlasting rules against contraception and abortion? Popes decided this, and they have done so only in recent years. Obviously, such rules should change. In the United States, where religion is separate from the state, politicians must face up to this problem.

It is time for all people who want our nation to survive as a successful civilization to join together and attack this cancer that is plaguing our society. It is self-destructive. In our big cities the current rate of births to adolescents out of wedlock is roughly three times the rate of twenty-five years ago. Our society does not begin to know how to cope with that birth rate. We lack not only the will but also the capability to provide sufficient day care centers, food, medical help, educational supplements, financial support, social worker support, jails, police, and all the other support systems and infrastructures we need. We simply must attack the root cause. And we must not wait.

There is no question that conscientious counseling efforts by competent people can reduce high pregnancy rates because most young people in school do not want and do not plan their pregnancies. We know more today about the problem of teenage pregnancy than ever before. We know what does not work and what does. We must all redouble our efforts to move ahead, now. We have no time to sit back and moan. For example, we should be experimenting with the idea of paying women to wait to have babies and then pay them, when they have graduated from high school and are married, much more than the $300 to $400 a month that welfare usually pays.

Although we know that women and girls do not get pregnant by themselves, they are increasingly called upon to raise children by themselves. This is unacceptable. I would encourage a major media effort along the lines of Mothers Against Drunk Driving and anti-drug-use and environmental campaigns. Learning from the success of other media efforts, we should try to make it socially unacceptable for all men and women who are not prepared to care for children to ignore the great additional risk they are creating for their children and for all children when they do not take birth control seriously.

To mobilize an intensive care program for all infants who need it, we must drastically reduce the number of high-risk children requiring extra care, and that means successfully attacking the epidemic of teenage pregnancies. To stop the cycle of poverty leading to hopelessness, poor education, poor health, joblessness, welfare dependency, crime, prison, developmental disabilities, schools that do not work and cannot work, and taxes (which are resented because the programs they support do not cure the problems), we have to invest much more in every child born at high risk than we do now, and at the same time we should aim to cut teenage pregnancies by 90 percent. Realistically, a lesser goal will not enable us to reach *all* children who need help. To achieve such a dramatic reduction in teen pregnancies requires courage and leadership.

According to the Chicago board of education, only 15,535 students graduated from public high schools in Chicago in 1993 out of 32,230 freshmen who had entered the high school system four years earlier. Only 4,194 (27 percent) of the 15,535 seniors could read at the national twelfth-grade average—that is, 4,194 out of 32,230 students who entered high school—a dramatic confirmation of the systematic short-changing of a cohort of students from the time they are in kindergarten. Prevention has to be our emphasis. Preparing our poor children to succeed with their education is the only way they will ever succeed.

I am reminded of the old vaudeville gag of the drunk who drops his keys in a very dark street. He gets down on his hands and knees in the dark, but he cannot find the keys. Thirty feet away there is an overhead lamp that casts a good light on a circle ten feet in diameter. The drunk decides that it is too tough to find his keys in the dark, so he moves over and starts looking under the light. Our key, the prevention of births to unmarried teenagers, is lost in the dark. That is where we must find the key.

A CONTRACT FOR RESPONSIBLE BEHAVIOR

The stakes are our very future. If we allow political caution to control our deliberations and if we fail to make clear what the real problem is, most of the work of special government commissions will have been for naught. Teenagers must be required to wait until they have finished their education, have jobs, and have completed the psychological tasks all adolescents face before they are adults and earn the right to proceed to marry and have children.

Focusing on Early Childhood Education: Zero to Three
We have a huge task ahead: we must radically improve the early development of all our youngsters to be sure our public and private educational systems improve their results. Only in this way can we radically improve our educational standards.

We must first do much more to assist the development of infants than merely concentrating on building a mother's self-esteem, teaching more about parenting, and encouraging mothers to go back to school. Our existing programs are appropriate and essential for one third to two thirds of young parents, but they are inadequate for the multiproblem, hard-to-reach teenagers. Rather than planning to spend $1,000 a year, these multiproblem families probably require $5,000 a year in support costs for each family and child for each of the first three years. This would make possible, in centers and homes, the kind of day care these infants and their mothers need.

To supply the highly skilled personnel who are needed, we must train many, many more, early childhood educators and public health nurses, and develop more physical facilities. We should also encourage a much higher status for public health nurses and early childhood educators. Such a system might cost $12 billion a year. When operative, it would make a substantial advance in our nation's educational goals. Twelve billion dollars spent annually may seem like a large amount, but compared with the $500 billion spent in 1994 in the United States on education from kindergarten through university, it is only 2.4 percent of the total.

We have to train many more minority people than we currently do. We particularly have to train specialists in infant care, both to assess infant delays and development and to provide therapy for them. The nation has been extremely slow in the training of sorely needed public health nurses, nurse practitioners, early childhood development specialists, social workers, and paraprofessionals in all these categories. As a consequence, even if we had all the money necessary to mount huge programs, it would take us at least ten years to prepare and train needed personnel. That does not seem to be an immediate likelihood.

We must formulate an experiment for troubled schools to identify the children in a normal classroom who are learning delayed. We must then send into that classroom one additional skilled therapist for every three or four learning-delayed children and allow the existing teacher—who is skilled enough to handle the class normally—to go about the business of teaching the twenty or so students in the class who are ready to learn. Then neither the teacher nor the students would be handicapped by the three to ten children who need special, personalized care. This solution would help in alleviating the problem of mainstreaming and avoid the problems of labeling. Expensive as they may be, solutions like this should be tried.

Head Start ought to be funded so that every poor child has an opportunity to participate, either in a Head Start program or its equivalent, funded by the state or the federal government or a combination of both. Head Start programs ought to last longer than 2½ to 3 hours, morning or afternoon. We ought to be working toward making those programs available for at least 8 hours a day to younger children at the ages of one or two, three, or four.

Funding Day Care and Trained Caregivers

Children of working parents who are in child care programs for working parents also need education. Children in Head Start and state pre-kindergarten education programs also need child care. All programs need to be guided by a comprehensive, structured, high-quality plan that provides both day care and educational support.

These suggestions are rational and practical. The present policy alternatives are so inadequate that we must try to organize a coalition of interested citizens and government employees, elected and appointed, to confront the problem.

PUBLIC POLICY AND PREVENTION: AN INTEGRATED, BROAD-SCALE PLAN

At the Charlottesville meeting in 1990 the National Governors Association adopted six ambitious goals to improve America's educational system. President Clinton, then the governor of Arkansas, had a major hand in drafting the goals, the first of which states that by the year 2000, "All children in America will start school ready to learn." In 1991 President George Bush expressed the entire body of aspirations as *America 2000: An Education Strategy.* So far, so good. But it is not enough. In that same year the Committee for Economic Development, not being entirely satisfied with any of the proposed actions to implement *America 2000,* published *The Unfinished Agenda:*

In the past, society's responsibility for providing educational opportunities for children started with their entry into school. But a new understanding of how children learn makes it clear that the nation can no longer afford to wait that long. The development and education of all our children from the earliest stages of their lives must be made a national priority, and throughout that process, the needs of the whole child, from conception through adolescence, must be addressed. Children must be better prepared for school and motivated to take advantage of educational opportunities.

We must also work in every way we know how to prevent poverty and the potential for family dysfunction. We must, however, go beyond the usual call for more and better entitlements, for jobs, and for secondary intervention programs. Advocates speaking for children at the bar of justice must strive to ensure conditions whereby every woman, regardless of income, has access to family planning and abortion services. Further, we must provide women full access to information that can assist them in making these critical but difficult reproductive decisions. As a related matter, once we have made reproductive health programs widely available, we must work to create a social environment in which irresponsible choices about early sexual activities and childbearing are widely condemned. I stress the need to reach boys and men with these messages. These messages must be driven home to boys and men, as well as to girls and women, who are increasingly called upon to raise children by themselves.

Not only should additional family planning and abortion programs be funded, but much more research must be done in the area of male contraception so that the expense and responsibility for family planning can be more evenly distributed between men and women. If we can reverse the trend of the rising number of babies born into high-risk environments, we will be better able to concentrate our efforts on intervention for other at-risk children. Of the 1 million babies born each year at high risk, perhaps 300,000 unwanted births could be averted if all women had access to safe and affordable reproductive alternatives, including contraceptives and abortion services. With much more intensive counseling and media-supported advocacy for responsible sexual behavior, we could perhaps prevent an additional 200,000 high-risk births. Although both these figures are estimates, reaching this minimal target would be significant.

Even with such successful prevention efforts, at least a half million babies will still be born at high risk each year. They will need comprehensive and intensive intervention programs modeled after some of the more successful demonstration projects currently being tested—such as one-stop access to supplemental nutritional services and first-rate pediatric care—including developmental screening and support for parents through education, home visits, and social services. By reducing the number of babies born who need such specialized services, we will be better able to provide quality programs.

Legal Abortion, Sanctioned Abortion: Funded Abortion on Demand
Only when nationwide abortion is equally available to poor and non-poor women will we be able to lower the number of unwanted babies born at very high risk. If there are now more than 1 million babies a year born at high risk, probably at least half a million are unwanted. These births could be prevented.

Separately, the issues of abortion and taxes are controversial; together they are incendiary. As a result, much heat but little light gets generated in the public discussion of Medicaid-funded abortions. Recent events, however, make it impossible to leave the debate smoldering on the back burner. The continuing debate on health care reform includes arguments on whether to include abortion services as part of a basic insurance package. This means that change is likely, either for women whose private insurance policies usually do cover abortions or for indigent women who rely on the Medicaid program, which in most states does not pay for abortions.

Our current two-tiered system of abortion services—available to women with insurance or private resources, but largely unavailable to women needing publicly subsidized care—is no accident. The Clinton administration's decision to request an end to the sixteen-year-old ban on the federal financing of abortions for poor women under its Medicaid program prompted a strong reaction from Illinois Representative Henry Hyde, for whom the amendment that instituted the first legislative check on the federal government's Medicaid coverage for abortions is named. Admitting that the ban only partially achieved his real goal—

the prohibition of all abortions—Hyde said in an interview: "I would do whatever I could to save the unborn of the rich if I could. We weren't able ever to do that, but we could save the unborn of the poor" (*Chicago Tribune*, 1993).

The emotionally charged issue of financing abortions may be framed narrowly in monetary terms. Many citizens oppose public funding because they equate such use of tax dollars with tacit approval of abortion. Representative Hyde has said that he hopes to retain the Hyde amendment by appealing to congressional colleagues "who are very concerned about the fiscal dimension of requiring tax dollars to pay for abortions" (ibid.). Yet the medical cost of abortion is only one of many economic and social costs to be considered in the abortion-funding debate. There are other dimensions that raise equally troubling questions: Does a government's denial of access to abortion implicitly promise government services to a mother and child? Is that promise kept? Because most abortion policies, and therefore any implied promises of service, are made by state governments, we must look to the experiences of states in order to understand the impact of their decisions.

Let us take a close look at the 1988 decision by the citizens of the state of Michigan to terminate public funding for abortions except to save the life of the mother. There are legitimate questions about the consequences of that decision, which was made by voters convinced in large part that they would save money as taxpayers. What has been the cost to Michigan? Clearly, the taxpayers ended up paying many times more than the few dollars they saved on not funding abortions.

Trained Professionals, Paraprofessionals, Community Workers
In 1984 Family Focus hired a researcher to evaluate its teenage program after the first five years of operation of its drop-in center in Evanston, Illinois. The researcher asked why the number of births for the teenagers in Evanston jumped from 43 to 68 between 1981 and 1982. The research revealed that in 1979 a nurse practitioner had been assigned by the Evanston Public Health Department to work at Family Focus several days a week. Her position was terminated for budgetary

reasons by the department in 1981. After she left, the number of pregnancies escalated.

We do not begin to spend enough money on prevention programs. Frankly, however, there is still too much that we do not know about how to prevent problems. At this stage money alone is not all we need. We need new ideas, new programs, and new research.

The most important problem we have to address is how to make sure that our children can have a better start through better prenatal care and better interaction with caring parents in the first several months of life. The path to success in school starts prenatally. Bad habits or developmental delays are increasingly difficult to remediate as weeks and months go along.

We are just at the beginning of trying to understand how to motivate parents to do a better job for the children they bring into the world. As for prenatal care, major obstacles exist in financial and geographic barriers, but more than any barrier is the motivational one. People seem to have an extremely strong, probably unconscious motivation to replicate their parents' patterns of child rearing even when they end up repeating the resulting disasters.

At the risk of doing an injustice to a great metaphor, I return to the story of the rescuer of the children in the river (see chapter 4). This story is an ideal tool to ensure that the message I am trying to deliver is not misunderstood and that the urgency of the task before us is appreciated. Imagine for a minute that the river represents poverty, and then remember that my remarks pertain to the prevention and termination of *unintended and unwanted* pregnancies. When these pregnancies result in births because of unfair and discriminatory policies, that is when children are *pushed* into the river, when they are *pushed* into poverty. Of course, there is no doubt that even a wanted child born into poverty faces barriers that wealthy children do not. But equally there is no doubt that the birth of each and every wanted, loved, and cared-for child enriches our nation, regardless of the economic circumstances of the family into which the baby is born.

A life of poverty and hopelessness for parents and their children is something we all want to prevent if we can. When poor women do not wish to bear children, or when they wish to delay having a family, it is indefensible for us to force them to have children based on some outmoded and paternalistic sense of morality. The current policies of states like Michigan and Illinois disproportionately affect poor, single, minority women—women who already face every other imaginable disadvantage in life. We cannot possibly believe that these women thank us for liberating them from the responsibility of making their own reproductive choices. Nor are they grateful for the resulting welfare dependency, poor health, joblessness, and despair.

Children truly are the future of our nation. We owe it to them, and to our nation, to ensure that all children are born with the best possible chance to live, love, grow, and excel. If we shirk this responsibility we will have contributed directly to the misery and suffering of generations to come. If we grasp this opportunity, we will have given the world a gift of inestimable value.

AGENCIES WORKING
FOR FAMILIES AND CHILDREN

Advocates for Youth (formerly the
   Center for Population Options)
1025 Vermont Avenue, NW, Suite 200
Washington, DC 20005
202-347-5700; *fax* 202-347-2263

American Civil Liberties Union
Children's Rights Project
132 West 43d Street
New York, NY 10036
212-944-9800, ext. 714; *fax* 212-921-7916

Annie E. Casey Foundation
Kids Count Program
701 St. Paul Street
Baltimore, MD 21202
410-547-6600; *fax* 410-547-6624

Breaking the Cycle of Disadvantaged
   Children
The Ad Council
1233 20th Street, NW, Suite 500
Washington, DC 20036
202-986-1181; *fax* 202-331-9790

Center for Law and Social Policy
1616 P Street, NW, Suite 450
Washington, DC 20036
202-328-5140; *fax* 202-328-5195

Center for Successful Child Development
188 West Randolph Street, Suite 2200
Chicago, IL 60601
312-853-6080; *fax* 312-853-3337

Center for the Future of Children
The David and Lucile Packard
   Foundation
300 2d Street, Suite 102
Los Altos, CA 94022
415-948-3696; *fax* 415-948-6498

Child Care Action Campaign
330 7th Avenue, 17th floor
New York, NY 10001-5010
212-239-0138; *fax* 212-268-6515

Child Welfare League of America, Inc.
440 First Street, NW, Suite 310
Washington, DC 20001-2085
202-638-2952; *fax* 202-638-4004

Children Now
1212 Broadway, Suite 530
Oakland, CA 94612
510-763-2444; *fax* 510-763-1974

Children's Defense Fund
25 E Street, NW
Washington, DC 20001
202-628-8787; *fax* 202-662-3510

Coalition for America's Children
1634 Eye Street, NW, 12th floor
Washington, DC 20006
202-638-5770; *fax* 202-638-5771

Designs for Change
6 North Michigan Avenue, Suite 1616
Chicago, IL 60602
312-857-9292; *fax* 312-857-9299

Families and Work Institute, Inc.
330 7th Avenue, 14th floor
New York, NY 10001
212-465-2044; *fax* 212-465-8637

Family Focus
310 South Peoria Street, Suite 401
Chicago, IL 60607-3522
312-421-5200; *fax* 312-421-8185

Family Resource Coalition
200 South Michigan Avenue, Suite 1520
Chicago, IL 60604-2404
312-341-0900; *fax* 312-341-9361

High/Scope Educational Research
   Foundation
600 North River Street
Ypsilanti, MI 48197
313-485-2000; *fax* 313-485-0704

National Abortion Rights Action League
1156 15th Street, NW, Suite 700
Washington, DC 20005
202-973-3001; *fax* 202-973-3099

National Association of Child Advocates
1625 K Street, NW, Suite 510
Washington, DC 20006
202-828-6950; *fax* 202-828-6956

National Black Child Development
   Institute
1023 15th Street, NW, Suite 600
Washington, DC 20005
202-387-1281; *fax* 202-234-1738

The Ounce of Prevention Fund
188 West Randolph Street, Suite 2200
Chicago, IL 60601
312-853-6080; *fax* 312-853-3337

Parents as Teachers National Center, Inc.
10176 Corporate Square Drive
St. Louis, MO 63132
314-432-4330; *fax* 314-432-8963

Parents Too Soon
c/o The Ounce of Prevention Fund
188 West Randolph Street, Suite 2200
Chicago, IL 60601
312-853-6080; *fax* 312-853-3337

The Robin Hood Foundation
111 Broadway, 19th floor
New York, New York 10006
212-227-6601; *fax* 212-227-6698

Success by Six
United Way of Minnesota Area
404 South 8th Street
Minneapolis, MN 55404-1084
612-340-7628; *fax* 612-340-7675

Way to Grow
1220 7th Avenue North
Minneapolis, MN 55411
612-377-1012; *fax* 612-377-1445

Zero to Three
National Center for Clinical Infant
  Programs
2000 14th Street North, Suite 380
Arlington, VA 22201
703-528-4300; *fax* 703-528-6848

UNIVERSITY PROGRAMS AND
INSTITUTES

American Enterprise Institute for Public
  Policy Research
1150 17th Street, NW, Suite 1100
Washington, DC 20036
202-862-5800; *fax* 202-862-7177

Bush Center in Child Development and
  Social Policy
Yale University
310 Prospect Street
New Haven, CT 06511-2188
203-432-9944; *fax* 203-432-9945

Carnegie Corporation of New York
437 Madison Avenue, 26th floor
New York, NY 10022
212-371-3200; *fax* 212-754-4073

Carnegie Foundation for the
  Advancement of Teaching
5 Ivy Lane
Princeton, NJ 08540-7299
609-452-1780; *fax* 609-520-1712

Chapin Hall Center for Children
University of Chicago
1155 East 60th Street
Chicago, IL 60637
312-753-5900; *fax* 312-753-5940

Erikson Institute
420 North Wabash Avenue, 6th floor
Chicago, IL 60611
312-755-2250; *fax* 312-755-2255

Executive Service Corps
30 West Monroe, Suite 600
Chicago, IL 60603-2404
312-580-1840; *fax* 312-580-0042

Irving B. Harris Graduate School of
  Public Policy Studies
University of Chicago
1155 East 60th Street
Chicago, IL 60637
312-702-8400; *fax* 312-702-0926

National Center for Children in Poverty
Columbia University School of Public
  Health
154 Haven Avenue
New York, NY 10032
212-927-8793; *fax* 212-927-9162

THE OUNCE OF PREVENTION CENTER FOR SUCCESSFUL CHILD DEVELOPMENT HEALTH SERVICES : A MODEL

Pre- and postnatal care
Preventive pediatric care
> Well-baby and child services
> Screening, assessment, and follow-up services
> Parent health and nutrition services

Family drop-in center: parent-child activities, support groups, advocacy, and crisis intervention

Community information sharing and public education: a director works with community organizations, area residents, community leaders, and local representatives

Home visitors, linking the Center and infant's family, are trained in the recruitment of pregnant residents and child-find activities, infant screening, regular home visits (to families of infants in the target community)

Referrals for weekly neurological, physiological, and psychological assessment when developmental screening indicates follow-up services (through a child psychiatry department of a collaborating university), including medical and therapeutic services

Delivery of child development and parenting education for adolescents (as babysitters, child care workers, and as new or prospective parents). Home visitors are helped by staff from the drop-in center, formal classes, and credit courses at local high schools.

High-quality infant care center on site and an expanded system of home day care providers. The Department of Children and Family Services funds infant and toddler day care openings for the child care center. Cooperating institutions train residents of the community in providing day care services in their homes. State departments of public assistance will fund child development centers in the training of caregivers.

Head Start will collaborate with home visitors, drop-in center staff, and child care providers.

A program of collaboration between local social support/intervention networks to strengthen and expand child and family services—for example, by administering an adolescent high school–based health clinic for high-risk mothers and infants.

NOTES

ACKNOWLEDGMENTS

1. Klaus, Kennell, and Klaus (1993) explain that *doula* (as used by Dana Raphael, 1973), means a childbirth assistant, "one or more individuals, often family, who give psychological encouragement and physical assistance to the newly delivered mother." The word is "now widely accepted" for "an experienced labor companion who provides the woman and her partner both emotional and physical support throughout the entire labor and delivery, and to some extent, afterward." A doula may also be called a labor coach or monitrice (p. 4).

CHAPTER 1: RAISED IN JEOPARDY

1. Throughout my discussion I use *single parent* to mean *single woman,* as the term is used in America today.

2. The consequences of divorce by mothers of young children are not specifically gauged in these statistics. This is undoubtedly another major problem.

3. To the best of my knowledge, cities like Cleveland, Detroit, Newark, New York, and similar cities are not in the ACT universe.

4. At one point I separately asked the deans of the University of Chicago School for Business Administration and the School for Social Service Administration to make a serious study of these costs, but I never could get the deans past the point of looking bemused when I continued to ask the question.

5. The American Society for Training and Development estimates that American corporations annually spend in excess of $211 billion on retraining their employees.

CHAPTER 2: SUCCESSFUL INTERVENTION AND ITS LIMITS

1. In a few Chicago schools, however, the percentage is actually more than 80 percent.

CHAPTER 3: PRIMARY PREVENTION AND THE RIGHT TO LIFE

1. In 1983 a careful study in Illinois determined that the cost of births to teenagers for the first five years of the baby's life came to $35,000. The annual cost would be one fifth of this sum, or $7,000. Adjusting for inflation using the consumer price index, in 1992 the five-year cost would have been $49,105, or $9,821 annually. At $9,821 each, the 24,601 teenage births in Illinois in 1992 cost the state $242 million. If Illinois had more fully funded family planning services, it would have been able to reduce the number of births to teens from 24,601 to an estimated 14,355. The number of fewer teen births (10,246) would have saved the state $101 million in that one year.

2. The fact is, we have cut Title x funds in the past ten years by two thirds (after allowing for inflation). After adjustment for inflation, Title x expenditures for contraceptive services decreased by 72 percent between 1980 and 1992.

CHAPTER 5: THE ABORTION QUESTION

1. This assumes that 750,000 annual abortions would be federally funded. In 1992, 207,000 were actually paid for by state governments; this also assumes that the state would pay half and the federal government half. Eighteen percent of 4.2 million births (see table 5-3) is more than 750,000. California's rate was 18.5 percent, and the rate for New York state was 17.3 percent.

2. In 1993, the average cost for a nonhospital, first-trimester abortion was $296. Assume the federal government paid one half, and the state paid one half. This is $100 less than the average monthly AFDC benefit for a mother with two children.

3. Colorado, Idaho, Minnesota, and New Mexico recently began funding abortion as a result of successful legislative challenges.

4. Title x funding has gone back up: Although in 1985 it was $142 million, down from the 1980 figure of $162 million, it is currently $193 million. Still, the increase has not kept up with inflation, and Title x represents only a portion of the drop in public funding.

5. In addition to New York and California, eleven states fund abortions: Alaska, Connecticut, Hawaii, Maryland, Massachusetts, North Carolina, New Jersey, Oregon, Washington, West Virginia, and Vermont. Except for these thirteen states, poor women, to receive abortions, must rely on philanthropic funds.

6. All Michigan statistics concerning infant mortality, abortion, pregnancy,

and birth characteristics unless otherwise noted are from the Michigan Department of Public Health, Office of the State Registrar and Center for Health Statistics, 1987–94.

CHAPTER 6: THE CYCLE OF POVERTY AND VIOLENCE
  1. Federal law, "Education of the Handicapped Act Amendment."

CHAPTER 7: TRENDS IN EDUCATION, POVERTY, VIOLENCE, AND PUNISHMENT
  1. *Unfair Shares* (Wilkinson, 1994) was written for Barnardo's, a registered charity in the United Kingdom that was established in 1866. "Barnardo's supports families living in poverty, by providing a range of child welfare services, and by promoting self-help activity. [They] work in inner city and outlying estates where investment in local communities has practically disappeared. . . . Richard Wilkinson argues that there is a causal link between increasing economic inequality and a range of negative phenomena affecting children and young people. Barnardo's publishing this report is part of [their] contribution to this vital debate [but does] not necessarily represent the policy position of Barnardo's" (pp. v–vi).

REFERENCES

Abbey, J. M.; A.Vestivich; and I. M. Schwartz. 1991. *Michigan's Children Went Missing.* Ann Arbor: University of Michigan. A report published by the Center for the Study of Youth Policy, a division of the School of Social Work.

Alan Guttmacher Institute (AGI). 1995. "The Cost Implications of Including Abortion Coverage under Medicaid." *Issues in Brief.* March. New York.

———. 1994. *Sex and America's Teenagers.* New York: Alan Guttmacher Institute.

———. 1993. *Facts in Brief: Contraceptive Use.* New York: Alan Guttmacher Institute.

Als, Heidelise. 1994. Harvard Medical School *Journal of the American Medical Association* 272(11) (21 Sept.): 853–58. Copyright American Medical Association.

The American Millstone: An Examination of the Nation's Permanent Underclass. 1986. Chicago: Contemporary Books.

"Beethoven's Fifth." 1993. Executive Summary. Chicago: The Ounce of Prevention Fund. May.

Bell, Terrel. 1983. *A Nation at Risk: The Imperative for Educational Reform.* Washington, D.C.: National Commission on Excellence in Education/GPO.

Besharov, Douglas J. 1993. "Escaping the Dole: For Young Unwed Mothers, Welfare Reform Alone Can't Make Work Pay." *Washington Post,* 12 Dec. Sec. C3.

Boyer, D., and D. Fine. 1992. "Sexual Abuse as a Factor in Adolescent Pregnancy and Child Maltreatment." *Family Planning Perspectives* 24(1) (Jan./Feb.).

Boyer, Ernest. 1991. *Ready to Learn: A Mandate for the Nation.* Carnegie Foundation for the Advancement of Teaching. New York.

Cameron, Stephen V., and James J. Heckman. 1993. "The Non-Equivalence of High School Equivalents." *Journal of Labor Economics* 11(1) (pt. 1, Jan.).

Center for the Study of Social Policy (CSSP). 1993. *Kids Count Data Book.* Baltimore: Annie E. Casey Foundation.

Centers for Disease Control (CDC). 1995. "Trends in Sexual Risk Behavior among High School Students, United States, 1990, 1991, and 1993." *Morbidity and Mortality Weekly Report* 44(7). National Center for Health Statistics.

———. 1992. "Abortion Surveillance: Preliminary Data, United States, 1990." *Morbidity and Mortality Weekly Report* 41(50) (18 Dec.). National Center for Health Statistics.

———. 1991. "Premarital Sexual Experiences among Adolescent Women, United States, 1970–1988." *Morbidity and Mortality Weekly Report* 39(51, 52) (3 Jan.). National Center for Health Statistics.

The Chicago Metro Survey: Attitudes toward Abortion and Family Issues. 1994. Random sample telephone survey of 1,506 adults residing in the six-county metropolitan area, including Cook, DuPage, Lake, Kane, Will, and McHenry Counties. Richard Day Research. Unpublished.

Children's Defense Fund (CDF). 1992. *City Child Poverty Data from the 1990 Census.* Washington, D.C. 11 Aug.

Child Welfare League of America and the National Association of Public Hospitals. 1992. *The Youngest of the Homeless.* Vol. 2, *A Survey of Boarder Babies in Selected Hospitals in the United States.* 23 June.

Clark, Reginald M. 1983. *Family Life and School Achievement: Why Poor Black Children Succeed or Fail.* Chicago: University of Chicago Press.

Coalition for Educational Rights (CER). 1995. "Education and Criminal Justice in Illinois." Chicago: Illinois Criminal Justice Authority.

Committee for Economic Development (CED). 1987. *Children in Need.* New York.

Dagg, Paul K. B. 1991. "The Psychological Sequelae of Therapeutic Abortion: Denied and Completed." *American Journal of Psychiatry* 148(5): 578–85.

Daley, Daniel, and Rachel Benson Gold. 1993. "Public Funding for Contraceptive, Sterilization, and Abortion Services, Fiscal Year 1992." *Family Planning Perspectives* 25(60): 244–51 (Nov./Dec.).

David, H. P.; Z. Dytrych; Z. Matejcek; and V. Schuller (eds.). 1988. *Born Unwanted: Developmental Effects of Denied Abortion.* New York: Springer.

Donnison, D. 1993. "Citizenship and civic leadership." Unpublished paper presented at a Fabian Society [U.K.] seminar on social justice. December.

Donovan, Patricia. 1989. "The 1988 Abortion Referenda: Lessons for the Future." *Family Planning Perspectives* 21(5) (Sept./Oct.).

Egeland, B., and D. Brunnquell. 1979. "An At-Risk Approach to the Study of Child Abuse: Some Preliminary Findings." *Journal of the American Academy of Child Psychiatry* 18:219–35.

Forrest, Jacqueline Darroch. 1994. "Epidemiology of Unintended Pregnancy and Contraceptive Use." *American Journal of Obstetrics and Gynecology* 170:1485–9.

Forssman, H., and I. Thuwe. 1966. "One Hundred and Twenty Children Born after Application for Therapeutic Abortion Refused." *Acta Psychiatr. Scan.* Cited in Dagg, 1991.

Fraiberg, Selma; Edna Adelson; and Vivian Shapiro. 1975. "Ghosts in the Nursery: A Psychoanalytic Approach to the Problems of Impaired Infant-Mother Relationships." *Journal of the American Academy of Child Psychiatry* 14(3): 387–422.

Furstenberg, Frank Jr. 1995. "Teenage Childbearing Reconsidered." Unpublished. To appear in *Kids Having Kids: The Consequences and Costs of Teenage Childbearing in the United States.* Forthcoming report of the Robin Hood Foundation.

Greenspan, S. I. et al., eds. 1987. *Infants in Multirisk Families: Case Studies in Preventive Intervention.* Madison, CT: International Universities Press.

Gross, Ruth. 1990. "Enhancing the Outcomes of Low-Birth-Weight, Premature Infants: A Multisite, Randomized Trial." *Journal of the American Medical Association* 263(22) (13 June): 3035–42.

Henshaw, S. K., and L. S. Wallisch. 1984. "The Medicaid Cutoff and Abortion Services for the Poor." *Family Planning Perspectives* 16(4) (July/Aug.).

Hotz, V. Joseph, Susan Williams McElroy, and Seth G. Sanders. 1995. *The Costs and Consequences of Teenage Childbearing for Mothers.* Chicago: Harris School Working Paper Series 95-1. (Unpublished)

Klaus, Marshall H.; John H. Kennell; and Phyllis H. Klaus. 1993. *Mothering the Mother: How a Doula Can Help You Have a Shorter, Easier, and Healthier Birth.* Reading, MA: Addison-Wesley.

Kliman, Gilbert W., and Albert Rosenfeld. 1983. *Responsible Parenthood: The Child's Psyche.* New York: Holt, Rinehart, and Winston.

Kost, Kathryn, and Jacqueline Darroch Forrest. 1995. "Intention Status of U.S. Births in 1988: Differences by Mothers' Socioeconomic and Demographic Characteristics." *Family Planning Perspectives* 27(1) (Jan./Feb.): 11–17.

Kotulak, Ronald. 1993. "Mental Workouts Pump up Brain Power." *Chicago Tribune.* 12 April.

Lally, J. Ronald; Peter L. Mangione; and Alice S. Honig. 1987. *The Syracuse University Family Development Research Program: Long-Range Impact of an Early Intervention with Low-Income Children and Their Families.* San Francisco: Far West Laboratories.

Leroux, Charles, and Cindy Schreuder. 1994. "Racial, Class Gulf Shuts Some Kids Out." *It Begins at Birth. Chicago Tribune* investigatory series on Illinois children in poverty.

Manvel, Allen D. 1995. "Legislating Legitimacy?" *State Tax Notes.* 6 Feb.

Mauer, Marc. 1994. "Americans Behind Bars: The International Use of Incarceration, 1992–93." Washington, D.C.: The Sentencing Project. September.

Michigan Department of Public Health (MDPH). 1987–93. Office of the State Registrar and Center for Health Statistics. (All Michigan statistics concerning infant mortality, abortion, pregnancy, and birth characteristics are from these reports, unless otherwise noted.) Lansing.

———. 1990a. *Pregnancy Risk Assessment Monitoring Systems (PRAMS).* Office of State Registrar and Center for Health Statistics. Lansing.

———. 1990b. *Rising Health Care Costs for Children with Special Needs: A Budget Out of Control? Or a System Out of Balance?* Children's Special Health Care Services. Bureau of Community Services. Lansing.

————. 1992. *Michigan Task Force on Drug-exposed Infants.* Center for Substance Abuse Services. Lansing.

Milli, F.; L. D. Edmonds; M. J. Koury; and A. B. McClearn. 1991. "Prevalence of Birth Defects among Low-Birth-Weight Infants." *American Journal Diseases of Children* 145 (Nov.).

Musick, Judith. 1993. *Young, Poor, and Pregnant.* New Haven: Yale University Press.

National Abortion Rights Action League (NARAL). 1992. *Who Decides? A State-by-State Review of Abortion Rights.* Seattle.

National Center for Clinical Infant Programs (NCCIP). 1987. "Infants in Multirisk Families: Case Studies in Preventive Intervention." *Clinical Infant Reports Series* 3:345–7.

National Center for Health Statistics (NCHS). 1994. *Monthly Vital Statistics Report* 43(5) (suppl.). (U.S. Department of Health and Human Services.)

————. 1988. "Survey Estimates at Least 53 Percent of Unplanned Pregnancies Resulted from Incorrect Use of Contraceptives or Contraceptive Failure." Washington, D.C. Cited in *Wall Street Journal,* 25 May 1993.

National Commission on Children (NCC). 1991. *Beyond Rhetoric.* Final report. Washington, D.C.

Newman, Lucile, and Stephen L. Buka. 1991. *Every Child a Learner: Reducing Risks of Learning Impairment during Pregnancy and Infancy.* Denver: Education Commission of the States.

Norton, Dolores. 1995. "Early Linguistic Environment Related to Early School Achievement." Unpublished.

Ostrea, E. M.; E. Lizardo; and M. Tanafranca. 1992. "The Prevalence of Illicit Drug Exposure in Infants in the NICU as Determined by Meconium Screen." *Pediatric Res.* 31:21SA.

Pamuk, E. R., and W. D. Mosher. 1988. *Health Aspects of Pregnancy and Childbirth, United States, 1982.* National Center for Health Statistics. Series 23, no. 16. Cited in N. Eberstadt, *Infant Mortality.*

Polansky, Norman A. Summary of *Damaged Parents: An Anatomy of Child Neglect,* 1981. Chicago: University of Chicago Press.

Provence, Sally, and Audrey Naylor. 1983. *Working with Disadvantaged Parents and Their Children: Scientific and Practice Issues*. New Haven: Yale University Press.

Richardson, Gail, and Elisabeth Marx. 1989. *A Welcome for Every Child: How France Achieves Quality in Child Care, Practical Issues for the United States*. A report of the Child Care Study Panel of the French-American Foundation. New York.

Saluter, Arlene. 1994. "Marital Status and Living Arrangements: March 1993." *Current Population Reports*. Series P20-478. Washington, D.C.: GPO.
———. 1977. "Marital Status and Living Arrangements: March 1976." *Current Population Reports*. Series P20-306. Washington, D.C.: GPO.
Sameroff, A. J., and B. H. Fiese. 1990. "Transactional Regulation and Early Intervention." n.p.
Sameroff, A. J.; R. Seifer; R. Barocas; M. Zak; and S. Greenspan. 1987. "Intelligence Quotient Scores of Four-Year-Old Children: Social-Environmental Risk Factors." *Pediatrics* 79(3): 343–50.
Schwartz, I. M.; R. M. Ortega; G. Fishman; and G. Shenyang. 1994. "Infants in Non-Permanent Placement." *Social Science Review* 68(3) (Sept.): 405–16.
Seitz, V., and N. H. Apfel. 1994. "Parent-Focused Intervention: Diffusion Effects on Siblings." *Child Development* 65:677–83.
Siefert, Kristine; Ira M. Schwartz; and Robert M. Ortega. 1994. "Infant Mortality in Michigan's Child Welfare System." Social Work 39(5): 574–9.
Silberman, Charles E. 1964. *Crisis in Black and White*. Chap. 9, "The Negro and the School." New York: Random House.
Stevenson, Harold W., and James W. Stigler. 1992. *The Learning Gap: Why Our Schools Are Failing and What We Can Learn from Japanese and Chinese Education*. New York: Summit.

Torres, A., and J. D. Forrest. 1988. "Why Do Women Have Abortions?" Family Planning Perspectives 20:169. Cited in Gold, *Abortion,* 20–21.
Trussell, J.; J. Menken; B. L. Lindheim; and B. Vaughan. 1980. "The Impact of Restricting Medicaid Financing for Abortions." *Family Planning Perspectives* 12(3) (May/June).

U.S. Bureau of the Census. 1994. "Income, Poverty, and Valuation of Non-Cash Benefits, 1993." Series P60-188.

———. 1961, 1994. *Current Population Survey*. March.

U.S. Department of Education (USDE). 1994a. *Adult Literacy in America, 1992*. National Center for Education Statistics, National Adult Literacy Survey.

———. 1994b. *The Reading Report Card, 1971–88*. National Center for Education Statistics, National Assessment of Educational Progress. April.

———. 1992. *Trends in Academic Progress*. National Assessment of Educational Progress, Educational Testing Service. Table 109, Percent of students at or above selected reading proficiency levels, by sex, race/ethnicity, and age, 1971–1992.

U.S. Government Accounting Office (GAO). 1992. *Early Intervention, Federal Investments Like WIC Can Produce Savings*. GAO/HRD-92-18. Washington, D.C.: GPO. April.

———. 1990. *Drug-Exposed Infants: A Generation at Risk*. GAO/HRD-90-138. Washington, D.C.: GPO. June.

Weele, Maribeth Vander. 1994. "Fifty-Five Percent of City Schools Hit Bottom on ACT." *Chicago Sun-Times*. 28 Oct.

Weiner, J., and B. A. Bernhardt. 1990. "A Survey of State Medicaid Policies for Coverage of Abortion and Prenatal Diagnostic Procedures." *American Journal of Public Health* 80(6): 717–20.

Westinghouse Learning Corporation. 1969. *The Impact of Head Start: An Evaluation of the Effects of Head Start on Children's Cognitive and Affective Development*. Executive summary. Ohio University Report to the Office of Economic Opportunity. EDO36321. Washington, D.C.: Clearinghouse for Federal Scientific and Technical Information. June.

Wilkinson, Richard G. 1994. *Unfair Shares: The Effects of Widening Income Differences on the Welfare of the Young*. Ilford, Essex, U.K.: Barnardo's Publications.

Wilson, William Julius. 1987. *The Truly Disadvantaged: The Inner City, the Underclass, and Public Policy*. Chicago: University of Chicago Press.

Zigler, Edward, and Jeanette Valentine (eds.). 1979. *Project Head Start: A Legacy of the War on Poverty*. New York: Free Press.

INDEX